CHINA AND TAIWAN

CROSSING THE STRAIT

CHINA AND TAIWAN
CROSSING THE STRAIT

Ashok Kavi

HOW
ACADEMICS
an imprint of Highlyy Publishing LLP

ISBN: 978-93-6009-238-2
First Published : 2024

Published by : HOW ACADEMICS
an imprint of Highlyy Publishing LLP

Correspondence Address : 4/30 A II Floor, Double Storey Buildings
Vijay Nagar, Delhi-110009
Editorial: +91 9811026449
Sales : +91 9999953412
Email: info@howacademics.com
Website: www.howacademics.com

Contents

List of Figures

List of Tables

Preface

For a long time, the major countries in the Indo-Pacific region have kept each other in check, maintaining a delicate balance of "test-counterattack-dialogue" on the Taiwan issue. However, the deepening trade war between the US and China, the widening power gap between Mainland China and Taiwan, and the outbreak of the war in Ukraine have led the international community to fear that Mainland China may launch a war against Taiwan. The different perceptions of the "One China" policy are central to the dynamic relationship between the United States, China, and Taiwan. It is difficult to predict whether Chinese and US policymakers will be able to resist the strong domestic traction generated by the deterioration of US-China relations and sit down for an in-depth discussion to de-escalate the situation in Taiwan. Moreover, achieving regional stability through military conflict would be too costly for the major players in the region. It would make it difficult to secure their ultimate gains in Taiwan. Even if the mainland succeeded in recovering Taiwan, the war would attach more hidden costs to its subsequent management of the region. In the grand international arena, where power determines influence, scholars and politicians tend to be more concerned with the movements of the major powers while ignoring the choices and attitudes of the relatively weaker participants. Nevertheless, in international affairs, where the more vulnerable participants are at the heart of the contest, such participants' attitudes or rather preferences can serve as an umbrella or excuse for the other players involved. The internal situation of the region and its diplomatic approach are closely related. Compared to the tense external international environment, the internal problems of Taiwanese society may provide China with some potential opportunities. This research attempts to analyze great power dynamics in Taiwan and incorporate socio-economic studies of Taiwan, exploring alternative solutions to dialogue and military conflict.

In crafting "China and Taiwan," my aim was to illuminate the intricate tapestry of historical, political, and socio-economic threads that define the complex relationship between these two entities. This work seeks to bridge the knowledge gap by providing readers with a comprehensive understanding of the dynamic interplay between China and Taiwan, examining the nuances that shape their interactions and influence the broader geopolitical landscape of the Asia-Pacific region. The chapters within this book serve as windows into the myriad facets of this intricate relationship. From exploring Taiwan's evolving national identity to dissecting China's expansion tactics and Taiwan's resilience in Southeast Asia, each chapter unveils layers of complexity, presenting readers with a nuanced perspective on the historical and contemporary dimensions of the cross-strait dynamic. Delving into topics such as social entrepreneurship in post-developmental state Taiwan, the trajectory of Taiwanese investment in China, and the evolution of identities during different political eras, this book transcends conventional analyses. It explores the impact of Chinese youth nationalism, reconstructs Chinese national identity, and scrutinizes U.S. security relations with Taiwan. The reader will traverse through the shifting sands of identity, economic connections, and political strategies that have molded the relationship between China and Taiwan. As we navigate this intellectual journey, my hope is that "China and Taiwan" not only informs but also sparks critical conversations. This book is an invitation to dive into the complexities of a relationship that reverberates globally. Whether you are a seasoned scholar, a student eager to grasp the intricacies of international relations, or a curious mind seeking insights into contemporary geopolitics, this work endeavors to provide a comprehensive and accessible exploration of the cross-strait dynamic.

Introduction

Taiwan, whose official name is the Republic of China (ROC), is an island that is split from China by the Taiwan Strait. Since 1949, it has been run separately from mainland China and is officially called the People's Republic of China (PRC). The PRC sees Taiwan as a region that has broken away from the mainland and promises to "unify" Taiwan with the mainland in the future. There are different ideas among Taiwan's political leaders about the island's status and its relationship with the mainland. Taiwan has its own freely elected government and is home to 23 million people.

Since Taiwanese President Tsai Ing-wen took office in 2016, tensions across the Taiwan Strait have grown. Tsai has refused to accept a plan that her predecessor, Ma Ying-jeou, backed to make it easier for people from both sides of the Taiwan Strait to get along. In the meantime, Beijing has been acting more and more aggressively, such as by flying fighter jets close to the island. Concerns have been raised that an attack by China on Taiwan could lead to a war between the US and China.

Is Taiwan part of China?

People in Beijing say there is only "one China," and Taiwan is a part of it. This idea, which it calls the "One-China principle," says that the PRC is the only legal government of China. It also wants Taiwan to eventually "unify" with the mainland.

The Chinese Communist Party (CCP) and the Kuomintang (KMT) party, which ruled Taiwan at the time, came to an agreement in 1992 called the "Consensus." Beijing says that Taiwan must follow this agreement. But the two sides don't agree on what this "consensus" says, and it was never meant to answer the question of Taiwan's legal standing. President Xi Jinping of China has said that the 1992 Consensus is an understanding that "both sides of the strait belong to one China and will work together to seek national reunification." When the KMT says "one China, different interpretations," they mean that the ROC is the "one China."

China, Mongolia, Taiwan, Tibet, and the South China Sea are still considered parts of the ROC by Taiwan's KMT-written constitution. The KMT doesn't want Taiwan to be independent and has always called for closer links with China. Because the KMT lost the most recent election, party leaders have talked about whether to change the party's position on the 1992 Consensus.

A big part of the resistance to the KMT is the Democratic Progressive Party (DPP). The DPP has never agreed with the terms set out in the 1992 Consensus. Both President Tsai and the head of the DPP have said they don't agree with the deal. She has instead tried to find a different way to say it that Beijing would accept. Tsai said in her 2016 inauguration speech that she was "elected president in accordance with the Constitution of the Republic of China," which is a text that backs building a single China. It was also said that she would "protect the sovereignty and territory of the Republic of China." Tsai also said she'd "handle cross-strait matters in line with the Republic of China Constitution, the Act Governing Relations Between the People of [the] Taiwan Area and the Mainland Area, and other relevant laws." On the other hand, Beijing didn't agree with this way of putting it and quit talking to Taiwan in public.

China has always wanted Taiwan to join the mainland, with the idea of "one country, two systems." Xi said this idea again in a speech in 2019. Hong Kong was given the same plan and told it could keep its own government and economy. Along with that, it was given a "high degree of autonomy." Taiwanese people don't like how things are set up like this. One reason why Tsai and even the KMT don't agree with the idea of "one country, two systems" is that Beijing has recently limited Hong Kong's freedoms.

Is Taiwan a member of the United Nations?

No. China doesn't want Taiwan to be a member of the UN or any other foreign group that only allows states to be members. Taiwan often complains about being left out, and the US also tries to get Taiwan to really be a part of these kinds of groups. During the COVID-19 pandemic, Taipei criticized the World Health Organization (WHO) for giving in to Beijing's demands and continuing to keep Taiwan from attending the WHO's World Health Assembly as an observer. During the first two years of the pandemic, Taiwan had one of the best responses to COVID-19 in the world. Group of Seven (G7) ministers have asked for Taiwan to be included in WHO meetings.

Taiwan is a part of more than forty groups, mostly regional ones like the Asian Development Bank and the Asia-Pacific Economic Cooperation Forum. It is also a member of the World Trade Organization. It is an observer or has some other standing on a number of other bodies.

There are only thirteen states that have official bilateral ties with Taiwan. Honduras was the most recent country to cut links with Taiwan and start talking to China. This happened in March 2023. No government has ever had official diplomatic links with both China and Taiwan at the same time.

What is the United States' relationship with Taiwan?

The United States officially formed diplomatic ties with the PRC in 1979. It also cut off diplomatic links and ended its defense treaty with the ROC at the same time. The United States still sells defense weapons to the island's military and has a strong unofficial relationship with it. Beijing has asked Washington many times to stop giving Taiwan weapons and stop talking to it.

The United States' strategy is set by its "One-China" policy [PDF]. It comes from a number of sources, including three communiqués between the U.S. and China that were signed in 1972, 1978, and 1982; the Taiwan Relations Act, which was passed by the U.S. Congress in 1979; and the "Six Assurances" [PDF], which President Ronald Reagan sent to Taiwan in 1982 and was recently made public. These papers make it clear that the US:

- "acknowledges the Chinese position that there is but one China and Taiwan is part of China" and that the PRC is the "sole legal government of China" (some U.S. officials have emphasized that the use of the word "acknowledge" implies that the United States doesn't necessarily accept the Chinese position);
- rejects any use of force to settle the dispute;
- maintains cultural, commercial, and other ties with Taiwan, carried out through the American Institute in Taiwan (AIT);
- commits to selling arms to Taiwan for self-defense; and
- will maintain the ability to come to Taiwan's defense, while not actually committing to doing so—a policy known as strategic ambiguity.

The United States wants to keep the Taiwan Strait peaceful and stable, and it has asked both Beijing and Taipei to keep things the same. Washington says it doesn't want Taiwan to be independent.

For decades, the US has tried to keep a delicate balance between supporting Taiwan and avoiding a war with China through a strategy called "strategic ambiguity." But President Joe Biden has said more than once that the US would defend Taiwan if China struck, which seems to be against the policy. Officials at the White House have taken back what he said, saying that the policy has not changed. However, the president is still in charge of how to react. A number of lawmakers and experts, such as CFR President Richard Haass and Research Fellow David Sacks, have praised Biden's comments, saying that China's growing aggressiveness calls for clarity. Other experts have said that this point of view is wrong.

How have recent U.S. administrations approached Taiwan?

China didn't like how the US strengthened its relationship with Taiwan under President Donald Trump. For example, the US sold more than $18 billion worth of arms to Taiwan's military and unveiled a $250 million complex for its de facto embassy in Taipei. Trump talked to Tsai on the phone before his inauguration. This was the first time since 1979 that the two leaders had talked this much. During his last days in office, the State Department lifted long-standing limits on where and how U.S. officials can meet with their Taiwanese peers. He also sent several high-level administration officials, including a cabinet member, to Taipei.

U.S. Arms Sales to Taiwan by Recent Administrations

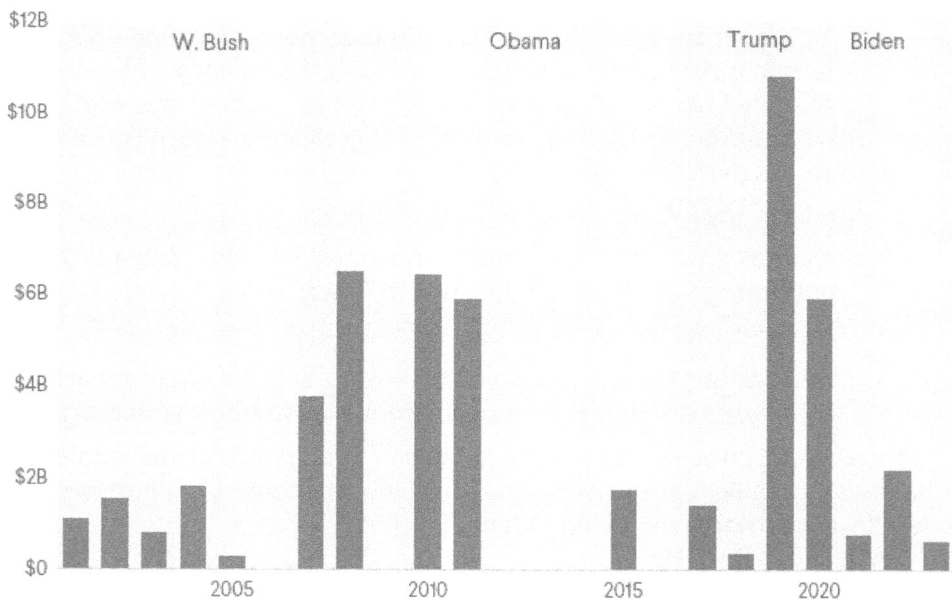

Note: Data is as of March 2023 and includes sales of defense equipment of $14 million or more, defense articles or services of $50 million or more, and design and construction services of $200 million or more.

Sources: Congressional Research Service; Defense Security Cooperation Agency.

In the same way, the Biden administration has kept up arms sales and supported the Trump administration's move to make it easier for U.S. and Taiwanese officials to meet. Biden was the first president of the United States to ask people from Taiwan to the inauguration. The US has military training and talks with Taiwan, and it often sends ships through the Taiwan Strait to show that it has a military footprint in the area. The US has also asked Taiwan to spend more on defense.

Also, lawmakers from both parties have supported Taiwan over the years, proposing and passing laws to improve relations between the U.S. and Taiwan, strengthen the island's defenses, and urge it to join international groups. The most recent bill proposal, the Taiwan Policy Act of 2022 [PDF], calls for Taiwan to be named a major non-North Atlantic Treaty Organization (NATO) partner. Nancy Pelosi (D-CA), who was House Speaker at the time, went to Taipei in August 2022 and met with Tsai. She was the first speaker to do so since Newt Gingrich (R-GA) in 1997. Beijing strongly opposed the visit and, as a reaction, planned military drills that would surround the island and made it illegal to bring some fruits and fish into China. Not long after that, in March 2023, Tsai talked with Kevin McCarthy (R-CA), who was then Speaker of the House. McCarthy was the most important person in the U.S. in almost thirty years to meet a Taiwanese president in person. Even though the visit was only short, China responded just as strongly, with condemnation, new penalties, and a show of force in the Taiwan Strait.

Could war erupt over Taiwan?

U.S. experts are very worried that China's growing military power and assertiveness, along with the worsening of relations between the two sides of the Taiwan Strait, could lead to a war. A disagreement like this could lead to a fight between the U.S. and China. Taiwan's "reunification" could be achieved through force, and the US hasn't said it won't support Taiwan if China attacks. This is what the U.S. Department of Defense said in a report from 2021: "China's military, the People's Liberation Army (PLA), is "likely preparing for a contingency to unify Taiwan with the PRC by force, while simultaneously deterring, delaying, or denying any third-party intervention, such as the United States."

But experts have different ideas about how likely and when a Chinese attack is likely to happen. The top U.S. military leader in the Indo-Pacific said in 2021 that China might try to invade Taiwan in the next ten years [PDF]. However, some experts think that this will happen much later. Others think that 2049 is a very important year. Xi has said that unifying with Taiwan is important for achieving what he calls the "Chinese Dream," which is for China to become a big power again by 2049.

Russia's invasion of Ukraine in early 2022 sparked a new discussion. Some analysts said that Moscow's actions could give Beijing the confidence to invade Taiwan in the same way, while others said that Beijing might be more careful after seeing Russia's challenges. China will still be ready to use force, according to Sacks of CFR. However, "Chinese leaders will examine Russia's failures and adapt their operational plans to avoid making similar mistakes."

No matter what, one of the PLA's top goals is getting ready for a Taiwan scenario, and Taiwan has been a big part of China's military modernization. The PLA said in a 2019 defense white paper that it would "resolutely defeat anyone attempting to separate Taiwan from China."

Analysts say Taiwan probably doesn't have the tools to defend itself against a Chinese attack without help from other countries. China's defense spending is still about twelve times Taiwan's, even though Tsai and the DPP have made it a priority to raise defense spending. For example, the record budget for 2023 is over $19 billion. It was agreed by politicians in Taiwan in 2022 that the Tsai government could spend an extra $8.6 billion on defense over the next five years. To protect Taiwan's coasts, some of this increased military spending will be used to buy cruise missiles, naval mines, and high-tech surveillance systems.

How has China tried to intimidate Taiwan?

China has used many forms of pressure other than war to get what it wants, and it has stepped up these actions since Tsai's election in 2016. Its goal is to weaken Taiwan so that the people who live on the island will decide that joining the mainland is their best choice. China wants to do this by increasing the number and size of patrols by PLA bombers, fighter jets, and observation planes over and around Taiwan. It has also been sending more and more troops and aircraft carriers through the Taiwan Strait to show strength.

Taiwan says that every day, thousands of cyberattacks from China are aimed at its government offices. Recently, there have been a lot more of these strikes. In 2020, Taipei said that four Chinese groups had hacked into at least ten Taiwanese government offices and 6,000 official email accounts since 2018 to get to personal and government data.

Beijing has also put pressure on Taiwan in ways other than armed ones. In 2016, China shut down a way for people on both sides of the Taiwan Strait to talk to each other. It put limits on travel to Taiwan. From 2015 to 2019, the number of mainland tourists who went to Taiwan dropped from over 4 million to 2.7 million. China has also put pressure on international companies, like hotel and airline groups, to list Taiwan as a Chinese province. China has also threatened countries that have ties with Taiwan. For example, in 2021, China cut off trade with Lithuania because the country opened an office for Taiwanese officials in its city.

Has Beijing undermined Taiwan's democracy?

Besides the above methods, China has also become more involved in Taiwan's polls. Some of the things it does are spread false information on social media and get more power over Taiwanese media outlets. For example, during the 2020 election, China shared false information to hurt Tsai and help the KMT's presidential candidate. These actions are part of China's bigger plan to use force to make people not trust Taiwan's government and to split up Taiwanese society. But experts see the DPP's recent wins in polls, like Tsai's reelection in 2020, as a message to Beijing.

Taiwan's democracy is still pretty new. From 1949 to 1987, the KMT ruled under martial law. At that time, political dissidents were harshly crushed, and Taiwanese who had lived on the island before 1945 were treated badly. Taiwan's first free races for the legislature were in 1992, and its first free races for president were in 1996. It has quietly changed hands between parties several times since then.

Even though China has made threats, Taiwan seems to have so far avoided the trend of regressive moves that affects governments around the world. Taiwan was called a "full democracy" for the first time by the Economist's Democracy Index in 2020. The index said that Taiwan [PDF] was the tenth most democratic country in the world in 2022. It ranked better than both of its Asian neighbors (Japan was ranked sixteenth and South Korea was ranked twenty-fourth) and the US, which was ranked thirty-first. A lot of people have voted in recent elections.

Do Taiwanese people support independence?

In Taiwan, most people want to keep things the same. Opinion polls from National Chengchi University show that only a small number of people want freedom right away. Even fewer say they want Taiwan to become one country with China. A huge majority of people are against a "one country, two systems" approach. This view has grown stronger as Beijing limits Hong Kong's freedoms.

More and more Taiwanese feel like they belong to Taiwan more than to the mainland. A survey by National Chengchi University in 2022 found that almost 61% of the island's people thought of themselves as only Taiwanese. 33% said they were both Taiwanese and Chinese, which is less than the 40% who said they were both a decade ago. A view that has become less common since 1994, when 26% said they were only Chinese, only about 3% of people now say that. One person who sees themselves as Chinese is former Taiwanese President Ma Ying-jeou. He said "we are all Chinese" during his first trip to China as president of Taiwan since the KMT took over the island in 1949.

What is Taiwan's economic situation?

China, which is Taiwan's biggest business partner, is still very important to the island's economy. But their economic relationship has been rocky lately, in part because Beijing is putting pressure on the island and Taiwanese leaders are becoming more worried that the country depends too much on trade with China.

From 2008 to 2016, President Ma was in charge of Taiwan. During that time, the two countries made more than twenty agreements with the PRC. One of these was the Cross-Straits Economic Cooperation Framework Agreement [PDF], which let them trade more freely. Direct sea, air, and mail lines between China and Taiwan were shut down for decades but were now open again. Also, banks, insurance companies, and other financial service providers decided to be able to work in both markets.

China Makes Up the Largest Share of Taiwan's Trade

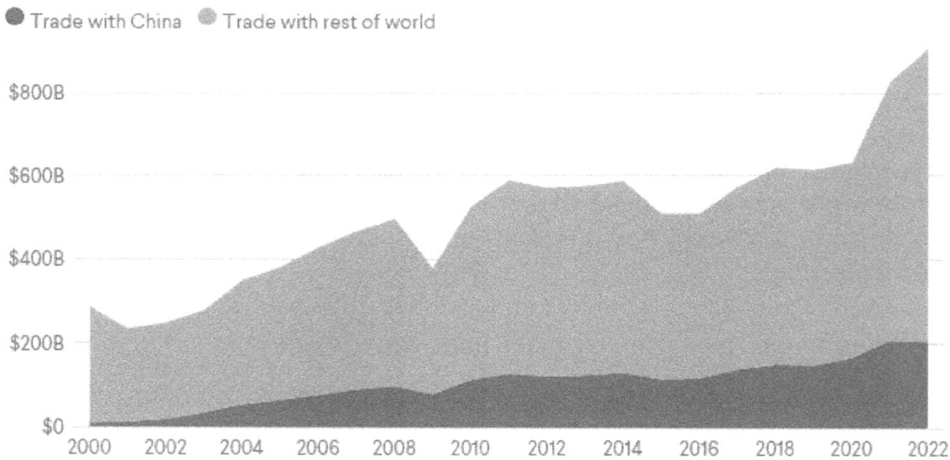

Source: Taiwan Ministry of Finance.

On the other hand, Tsai and the DPP have tried to expand Taiwan's trade partnerships, but the results have been mixed. As part of her signature plan, the New Southbound Policy, Tsai has been able to increase trade and business with Southeast Asian and Indo-Pacific countries. Between 2016 (when the plan was first announced) and 2022, trade between Taiwan and the 18 countries it was aimed at almost doubled. Taiwan has also slowly put more money into those countries. There is a three-year plan by Tsai to encourage Taiwanese makers to move back to Taiwan from the mainland. It was announced in 2019.

Still, Taiwan's trade with China reached a new high in 2021. Countries have been told not to sign free trade deals with Taiwan by Beijing. Some countries, like New Zealand and Singapore, have made free trade deals with the island. These are the only developed economies that have done so. Taiwan should not be a part of any multilateral trade blocs, such as the Comprehensive and Progressive Agreement for Trans-Pacific Partnership (CPTPP) or the Regional Comprehensive Economic Partnership (RCEP). (China is part of the RCEP but not the CPTPP.) Taiwan is also not a part of the Indo-Pacific Economic Framework put forward by the Biden government.

Have cross-strait tensions hurt Taiwan's vital semiconductor chip manufacturers?

Even though there are problems across the Taiwan Strait, Taiwan is the world's largest contract manufacturer of semiconductor chips, and its business is growing. With artificial intelligence, these chips are in almost all technology, like computers, smartphones, cars, and even weapons systems. In 2022, more than 60% of the money that the world's semiconductor contract makers made came from businesses in Taiwan.

A lot of that is due to Taiwan Semiconductor Manufacturing Company (TSMC), which makes more chips than any other company in the world and is Apple and other U.S. companies' main source. Samsung, based in South Korea, is the only other company in the world with the technology know-how to make the smallest and most advanced chips. It makes more than 90% of those chips.

Some experts say that the US's need for Taiwanese chip companies makes it more important for the US to protect Taiwan from a Chinese attack. Biden has worked to strengthen the U.S. chip business because he knows how much the U.S. depends on TSMC for important chips. In August 2022, Congress passed a $280 billion bill to encourage chip manufacturing in the U.S. After that law was passed, the Biden government put in place strict export controls that make it harder for China to get advanced chips, even from TSMC. Experts say that these restrictions could hurt China's tech industry. Before the restrictions, China bought about 70% of its chips from TSMC. Beijing is now trying to grow its own chip industry. One way it is doing this is by getting Huawei, a Chinese telecoms giant that Washington says Beijing could use for spying, to make more chips.

Chapter 1
Taiwan
Navigating the Ebbing Aspirations for Reunification

China and Taiwan are one of the four countries that were split apart by the Cold War. This split was meant to be temporary at first, but as the Cold War heated up in the late 1940s, each "half" became deeply involved in the front lines of its side, making reunion impossible. This divide has been especially hard to fix because of how civil wars, like China's revolutionary civil war, were made worse by ideological differences between countries. Still, reunion has been a part of China's and, to some extent, Taiwan's original plans for national self-realization from the start.

This last part looks at why the dream seems to be fading, even though it was brought back to life when the KMT (Nationalist Party) won in 2008. In the first part of the chapter, the reasons why unity was a good idea as a national goal are explained. The second part takes a critical look at how the story of reunion has changed since 1949. The third tries to explain why things are now going against unity.

Need for Reunification

The attraction of national unification comes from the desire to find shared roots, which are, in a way, basic. The Chinese claim to Taiwan has roots in both history and language. Some mainland historians say that Taiwan has been a part of China since the start of the Sui dynasty (598-618), but official dynastic histories as late as the Ming (1368-1644) make no mention of Taiwan in the section on administrative geography (the dilizhi, which lists all provinces, prefectures, subprefectures, and counties of the Ming state), so we can assume that it was then just a frontier area. By the 1300s, however, there were a lot of Chinese settlements on the island. The island's fertile land and mild temperature attracted people looking for work. Early imperialists were also interested in the island. In 1622, the Dutch forced the Spanish to leave and set up a settlement. In the name of the recently defeated Ming, a rebel named Cheng Chenggong (known in the West as Koxinga) set up a "pirate" garrison near Tainan. However, the Qing sent their navy under Admiral Shi Lang to destroy the Zheng fleet in the Battle of Penghu (1683), and the island was then added to Fujian Province as a prefecture. Taiwan finally became a region of China in 1887, but Japan took it over just eight years later after China lost the Sino-Japanese War. From 1895 to 1945, it was a colony. After taking back control of China by force in 1945 and 1947, the Nationalists fled to the island when they lost the civil war on the mainland in 1949. They said they would try to change the result as soon as they could.

The People's Republic of China (PRC) fully expected to "liberate" the island as soon as they took control of southern China. This would finish their revolution and end "one hundred years of humiliation" (bainian guochi) by overthrowing the "unequal treaty" of Shimonoseki, which gave Taiwan to Japan. But when China helped the Democratic People's Republic of Korea in the Korean War in November 1950, the US stepped in to help the Nationalists. This put plans to end the civil war on hold for good. All but about 2% of the people, both natives and people who moved there from the mainland, are Han Chinese. They speak a local version of Mandarin and follow Chinese customs.

Since the Second Civil War didn't end, the goal of unity has been a big part of how people on both sides of the Strait see themselves. The Chiangs both died believing in "one China," and it is well-known that they turned down the chance for Taiwan to keep its diplomatic status and membership in the UN General Assembly as an independent country if that meant giving up its claim to be part of China. This claim is in the constitutions of both the People's Republic of China (PRC) and the Republic of China (ROC). It is also on the flags, coins, stamps, and history books of both countries. During Chiang's rule, Taiwan continued to represent all mainland provinces in the (mostly symbolic) National Assembly, just as Taiwan was represented by delegates in both the Chinese People's Political Consultative Congress and the National People's Congress. Taiwanese, whether they are native benshengren or waishengren, are called "compatriots" (tongbao) and are different from outsiders (waiguoren) on the mainland. Even though the dream of reunion has lost some of its appeal in recent years, there is a legacy that keeps bringing up the question. In fact, neither side can bring up nationalism without bringing up this question again. The desire to make the country stronger is also important. A free and united China would be even more powerful and respected on the world stage than it is now.

From a global point of view, the Taiwan question is a strange political problem that hurts. During the Cold War, it was an unstable point in the structure of global bipolarity, as shown by refugee flows, inflammatory language, unilateral threats, and crossing red lines. Since the end of the Cold War, it has stayed a constant international flashpoint that could still start a war between two nuclear powers and pull in other states. So, the world community, such as it is, would in general be happy with a peaceful, orderly end to the conflict. Since 172 independent states, including the U.S., have officially agreed with China's claim that there is only one China and that Taiwan is a part of China, they would be contradicting themselves if they opposed reunification. Some American friends, like Australia, have even said they would like to leave the alliance if it got involved in the China-Taiwan conflict. And, as Ping-Kuei Chen, Scott Kastner, and William Reed say above, some analysts want the US to give up on Taiwan to make reunification easier and improve ties with the PRC, which is more important from a strategic point of view. In 2014, the Chicago Council on Global Affairs did a survey that showed only 26% of Americans agree with the idea of sending troops to help Taiwan. In contrast, 47% of Americans back the idea of sending troops to South Korea. Since 1982, many different studies have come to the same conclusion. Even though no one agrees with China's threats to use force as a last option to bring about reunification, few are ready to fight if it does.

Even though both sides of the Strait are very interested in unification, that doesn't mean they agree on how to get there, who should run the reunified state, or how it should be set up. It also doesn't mean that everyone has the same amount of interest. In the past, the more powerful side has been the most interested in reunification and ready to use more forceful methods to get it, assuming that it will still be in charge of the united state. Using the same idea, the weaker side, on the other hand, tends to hesitate or put things off and try to stop the use of force to bring people together.

Quest for Unification

If history and the balance of power in the world are so strongly in favor of reunion, then what is stopping it? There have been two replies from Taiwan. The first argument, which is mostly supported by the Democratic Progressive Party (DPP), is that Taiwan has not been a part of China for well over a century, that Taiwan's democratic government meets all the requirements for statehood, and that Taiwan's independence should be recognized by changing its name and changing its constitution. The second argument, made mostly by the Nationalist Party or KMT, is that the ROC was established and internationally recognized after the Xinhai rebellion in 1911, and that it has never been defeated (there has never been an armistice or peace treaty), but was forced to flee to Taiwan, where it continues to claim sovereignty over the Chinese mainland. Since the late 1990s, the first argument has won more votes on the island, but it is called "splittism" on the mainland. The second argument, which was reaffirmed by the Ma Ying-jeou regime in 2008, is accepted by Beijing through the "1992 Consensus," which says that each side can define "one China" in its own way.

But that would be jumping ahead in our story. During the Cold War, both "Chinas" said they were committed to unity, and they used force to try to make it happen. While the two leaders of the civil war stayed in power for the first 30 years of Taiwan's existence, war-like conditions remained. The Nationalists imposed martial law, used anticommunism to justify their authoritarian rule and the prosecution of political dissent, and promised to "recover the mainland" (huifu dalu) by force, with the help of a popular anticommunist uprising (like in the Bay of Pigs). In 1954–55 and 1958, Beijing caused two cross-Strait crises by threatening to invade the islands still held by Taiwan in the sea. It also bombarded the islands with deadly artillery and kept doing so, mostly with propaganda leaflets, until January 1979. But neither the Chinese nor the Nationalists ever invaded Taiwan or the mainland. After the Sino-American security alliance was formed in 1954, the balance of forces was too strong for the People's Liberation Army (PLA), and the US refused to "unleash" a Nationalist invasion of the mainland in the disastrous aftermath of the Great Leap or during the Cultural Revolution. But each side's plans for unity involved getting rid of the other government. The ROC government represented "China" in the United Nations (including the Security Council) and in most foreign embassies. It enforced a "one-China policy" by breaking diplomatic ties with any country that accepted the PRC. Since 1971, when the PRC replaced Taiwan in the UN, it has turned the tables and now refuses to recognize any country that accepts Taiwan.

Because Nixon started the Sino-American detente, the end of the Cold War happened in Asia about two decades before it did in Europe. This gave people the chance to try new things without being limited by the ideological frameworks and internal alliance networks that had kept the issue tied to bloc solidarity in the past. Starting with "reform and opening" in China and Taiwan's transition to democracy a decade later, both sides looked for new ways to break the stalemate. Soon after getting diplomatic recognition from the US (which led to Taiwan's de-recognition and the end of the Sino-American Alliance), Beijing made plans for "three direct links" (travel, trade, and mail) across the Strait and used the slogan "One country, two systems" to describe a form of reunification that would give Taiwan a "high degree of autonomy" for fifty years. This was Beijing's most generous offer so far, and it was the first time they gave a calm unification plan that seemed pretty good. Chiang Ching-kuo's first reaction was "three nos," which meant "no contact, no compromise, and no negotiation." However, the mainland did not give up, and before Chiang Ching-kuo died, he allowed retired soldiers to visit their home villages on the mainland. The next government, led by Lee Teng-hui, set up a National Unification Council at the cabinet level. In 1991, the council released "National Unification Guidelines," which stated that the ultimate goal of national unification was to preserve Chinese culture and achieve political democracy, economic liberalization, and social pluralism in the PRC.

These offers were incompatible with each other. The Chinese offer gave Taiwan no reason to think that a totalitarian government would give full power to a former enemy, and the Taiwanese offer made changes to the mainland government but none to Taiwan. But both offers envisioned a peaceful reunion and a positive-sum system of government after the reunification, which opened the door to more talks. First, Taipei and then Beijing set up organizations that were kind of like diplomatic bodies. These were the Straits Exchange Foundation (SEF) and the Association for Relations Across the Taiwan Straits (ARATS). After secret talks in Hong Kong, where the 1992 Consensus was reached, the two sides held a series of meetings in Singapore to talk about what else could be done to make it easier for trade, mail, and other exchanges to happen. Even though the "three direct links" didn't happen, trade, indirect investment, and travel through Hong Kong rose steadily.

While this was going on, politics, which was supposed to be a dependent variable of socioeconomic unity, moved in a random way and didn't follow neofunctionalist or Marxist logic. Both sides tried to protect themselves, which showed how much they still didn't trust each other. Taiwan tried to make peace with China, but it also tried to make peace with the West through "flexible diplomacy" (such as dollar diplomacy, vacation diplomacy, and other quick fixes that didn't last). Beijing tried to protect itself by promising a peaceful reunification but refusing to give up the use of force and continuing to build up its military on the Fujian coast. Roughly speaking, there was a "thaw" in politics from 1988 to 1995. This was followed by the 1995-96 missile crisis, which caused a "freeze" from 1995 to 2005. From 2005 to 2015, there was another, warmer "thaw." The PRC started this pattern when it put national reunification at the top of its list of goals for the 20th century and set up a small group of politburo members in 1979 to organize the effort.

Investments followed, which brought in even more trade. Some industries were drawn by the promise of access to the China market, while others used China's cheap labor pool to make goods for export, taking advantage of the price advantage that China's cheap currency gave them. The Taiwan Strait crisis of 1995-1996 temporarily slowed down trade (some money left the country, and between July 1995 and March 1996, Taiwan's stock market lost nearly 30% of its value), but trade kept growing, which Lee's government tried to stop with his "go south" and "go slow" policies. But economic problems in other places, like the Asian financial crisis of 1997–1999 and the global high-tech recession of 2000, drove Taiwanese investors back to the mainland. Even the election of former "Taiwan independence" (taidu) activist Chen Shui-bian of the DPP in 2000 didn't have a big negative effect on ties across the Strait. The mainland did not try to stop trade or investment, but it did try to get political concessions by demanding an end to "splittist" attitudes. This happened most forcefully in 1995–96, but it also happened in 2000 and 2004. China also tried to force well-known Taiwanese investors who supported Taiwan's freedom, like Hsu Wen-long, to stop supporting the DPP. But for the most part, China didn't let politics get in the way of a business relationship that helped both of them.

So, business kept growing, whether the government was good or bad. By 2014, more than 40% of Taiwan's trade was with the mainland, and about 80% of its foreign direct investment (FDI) went there. More than 100,000 Taiwanese businesses were running on the mainland. Taiwan has always made more money from trade than it loses. After a decade of Taiwanese political leaders who were against China, the gap between economic and political paths grew. Without official contacts with the mainland, the DPP worked to "de-Sinify" official political culture and build Taiwanese nationalism. They did this by using Chinese threats and "soft power" like reorienting educational curricula, renaming holidays, and building museums and monuments. In 2012, the number of Taiwanese who wanted reunification either right away or in the future reached a historical low of about 10%. But in the meantime, Beijing showed that it had the power to cut off the island's economic and diplomatic lifelines and stop other countries from sending troops to help. Even though the DPP didn't like it, economic dependency kept growing.

Beijing learned from what it went through. After Chen was narrowly re-elected in March 2004, Beijing changed its no-contact policy by using a mix of "harder sticks and sweeter carrots." On May 17, 2004, Hu Jintao made an offer to Taipei to resume negotiations for the "three links," clear up misunderstandings, and talk more. In March 2005, the National People's Congress unanimously passed the Anti-Secession Law (ASL). This law gave the government permission to use "nonpeaceful means" in reaction to Taiwan's formal declaration of independence. But the ASL forbade "secession" instead of requiring reunification, and it did not set a date for talks. It also made it official for the first time that Beijing would negotiate on the basis of equal status between the two sides. It also changed its demand for "one China" as a condition for talks, quietly letting the other side know that the 1992 Consensus would be a good way to understand "one China." The Chinese Communist Party (CCP) also started talking to the opposition on a party-to-party level. In 2005, it invited "pan-Blue" (KMT and People First Party) leaders to the mainland and held the CCP-KMT Forum, which was a clear revival of the United Front, which had worked in the past to bring people together despite their different ideas. And when Chen Shui-bian resumed his push for independence by "freezing" the National Unification Council and National Unification Guidelines in early 2006, Beijing said it didn't agree but didn't threaten to use force. This caused the US to reprimand Chen for breaking the "five nos" that he had promised after his election in 2000 and again in 2004 (no declaration of independence; no change in the ROC's name; no "state-to-state description in the constitution"; no reun Beijing helped the KMT win both the legislative and presidential elections in 2008 by making cross-Strait ties less tense and removing a threat from the mainland that the DPP could use to attack the KMT.

Ma Ying-jeou's reaction to Beijing's new Taiwan policy was good from a diplomatic point of view, but he kept things low-key at home because he knew that public opinion in Taiwan has been moving away from reunification since the early 1990s. Ma tried to stop the fight over who was who and get people to focus on how well the government was doing economically. His plan was to avoid "future nation preference" problems, court the middle-of-the-road voter who cared less about the name of the country than how well it did, and count on the pan-Blues as captive voters. So, Ma tried to change Taiwan's politics by making the economy the major issue instead of national identity. The corruption case against Chen Shui-bian came as a surprise to the KMT, which used it to back up its claims that the DPP had bad management.

After the KMT won a landslide victory in both the legislative and executive elections in 2008, the new Ma administration wasted no time in pursuing reconciliation with the mainland along the same lines as the 2005 pan-Blue visits to the mainland. Ma defended this change from his campaign rhetoric by saying that better cross-Strait relations would greatly improve the island's economy. In his first speech as president, Ma said "three nos"—no unification, no independence, and no war (butong, budu, buwu)—to reassure the people. He kept quiet about where cross-Strait rapprochement would lead after a peaceful and successful working relationship. He would go from easy to hard, from economic to political problems, in preparation for a (repeatedly delayed) discussion of a peace treaty across the Taiwan Strait. Taiwanese trade and investment with the mainland were no longer limited, and Chinese investment on Taiwan was now allowed for the first time. The SEF-ARATS negotiating group was brought back together, with visits alternating between Beijing and Taipei. By December 15, 2008, the two sides had officially set up "three direct links," which made it easier for almost two million Chinese tourists to visit in the first two years. The SEF and ARATS met again and held many sessions, which led to about 23 cross-Strait agreements and, in the summer of 2010, an Economic

Cooperation Framework Agreement (ECFA) that lowered trade barriers between the two sides and made it possible for Taiwan to negotiate preferential trade agreements with several Southeast Asian countries.

After winning a second term in 2012 with a comfortable but less impressive margin, Ma's government started a "re-Sinification" effort to bring back support for the ROC and the Nationalist symbols it stands for in the country. Cross-Strait relations remained a top priority in foreign policy. Ma arranged the next step in economic integration, the Cross-Strait Service Trade Agreement (CSTA), while moving away from earlier talk of a peace treaty or political talks. The CSTA was stopped by procedural problems and what seemed to be resistance to Ma from within his own party in Taiwan's legislature. The Sunflower Movement, which was led by students and occupied the legislature in March 2014, was the final obstacle. Ma said that political talks would only happen if China took steps to build trust, which it did not do. By the end of 2014, the PLA had over 1,500 ballistic and cruise missiles aimed at Taiwan. This was ten times more than in 2000, and the missiles were more accurate and dangerous than those fired during the Strait crisis. Ma has asked the PRC to get rid of this weaponry many times, most recently at the summit in Singapore in December 2015. However, this has not happened. While this was going on, Taiwan's spending on arms was low, and Ma's promise to increase it to 3 percent of GDP was not kept—Taiwan's budget for defense has continued to go down. The US was still the only country with a strategic commitment to defend Taiwan, but China's weapons acquisition program, which focused on advanced A2AD (Anti-Access Area Denial) weapons meant to stop US troops from coming close to the Strait, made the US's commitment more "ambiguous." Beijing also didn't like it when other countries sold Taiwan weapons to close the defense gap. They saw this as a meddling in China's internal affairs. And the number of US weapons sold to Taiwan has gone down over time. Ma tried to change the subject at home from cross-Strait relations to economic growth, but he was wrong to think that improving cross-Strait relations would boost economic growth. After a huge jump in growth in 2010, Taiwan's economy stopped growing.

In 2016, the KMT lost both the election for president and the election for the legislature. President Tsai Ing-wen got 56 percent of the vote, and her DPP won 68 of the 113 seats in the legislature, giving it its first-ever majority. The CSTA and the Trade in Goods Agreement that came after it sat around for a long time, with only a small chance of passing in the government, which was now controlled by the DPP. President Tsai Ing-wen has said she wants to keep good ties with the mainland, but she won't sign the 1992 Consensus, which Beijing says is a requirement for talks. Beijing is very wary of Tsai because she is thought to be the one who came up with the "two states" plan.

Lee Teng-hui defined PRC-ROC relations as "state-to-state relations" in 1999, and he was chair of the Mainland Affairs Commission (MAC) when Chen came up with the idea of "one country on each side" of the Taiwan Strait in 2001. This means that Taiwan and mainland China are two separate countries, not two political parts of the same country, China. Since Tsai took office in May 2016, official ties have been cut and the number of tourists has dropped by a lot. But the Chinese government hasn't made any violent threats, and economic integration is going on without any meddling from the government.

Progress and Repercussions

Beijing has always wanted reunification on its own terms, either by continuing a civil war until it was won militarily (before Korea) or by making a deal with Taiwan's KMT leaders, who are likely homesick after leaving the mainland. When Taiwan's first-generation leaders died, these chances went away, so Beijing came up with a plan to peacefully bring the island under its control. Beijing would cut off Taiwan's lifelines to the rest of the world by denying the island's legal existence unless it was part of "China." Trade relations are harder to control than diplomatic ones, but by joining the growing "noodle bowl" of Asian free trade agreements and making its own trade depend on denying Taiwan's legal existence, Beijing would be able to cut Taiwan off from the rest of the world. The three most important parts of the plan were (1) the possible use of force, (2) the convergence of socioeconomic factors, and (3) the difference in political power. Why has this plan not worked?

First of all, the split between China and Taiwan was caused by war, and force has always been a possible solution to the problem. For many years, the mainland has threatened "armed liberation" of the island, and it has never given up that option. Meanwhile, the Nationalist regime has used U-2 surveillance flights and occasional raids to try to "recover the mainland." In the early 1990s, Taiwan gave up the idea of using force to "recover the mainland," saying that it did not actively challenge Chinese sovereignty over the mainland, but only over Taiwan and the nearby offshore islands. The mainland never acknowledged this, instead insisting on sovereignty over Taiwan based on the "one-China principle" and the "right" to use force to defend it. Ironically, Beijing even convinced Taipei to rescind its own denial of mainland sovereignty in 2008 to comply with China's "one-China principle." Beijing has focused its contingency planning for force on a quick and decisive fait accompli that prevents escalation or outside intervention. To do this, you would need superiority on land and sea to win a local offensive war and enough naval and air power in the area to keep big powers from getting involved. China thinks it has made progress on the first, making

US intervention much more expensive than it was in 1996. It also has a credible deterrent against US nuclear blackmail with its mobile intercontinental ballistic missiles (ICBMs), MIRV (multiple independently retargeted vehicle) capability, and submarine-launched ballistic missiles (SLBMs). Beijing hasn't been involved in military operations since 1979, but it knows how expensive war is and would like to avoid it with the US. However, Beijing is more committed to unification than the US is to stopping it, so it could use this to stop the US from getting involved. If there is another missile crisis, will the US send aircraft carriers to the Strait if Chinese antiship ballistic missiles can destroy them? If the US decides that Taiwan's independence is not worth the cost, and if Taiwan's armed forces are clearly weaker than those against them, China can take control of the island without firing a shot.

But this scenario, which is based on the idea that locals are always better, has risks that China is not yet ready to take. Until then, Beijing's use of force through forceful diplomacy is likely to backfire because the use of too little force can hurt democracy. If the force is strong enough, like it was in 1975 when Vietnam was reunified, it can be a good way to bring people together. If force doesn't work, like in the Korean War or the Taiwan Strait situation of 1995-1996, it just makes the other side angry and loses credibility. But Beijing still thinks that threats of force are necessary to stop official moves toward independence and show that it is still committed to reunification. Other than that, Beijing seems to have taken force out of its public actions and started using carrots instead. But Taiwan knows that just because threats are played down in public, which could hurt Beijing's charm offensive, it doesn't mean that the weapons are no longer there. Beijing is in a tough spot because force can't be used, but it can't stop threatening to use it.

Reuniting a country always requires more than just putting the two parts back together. Even after the Cold War ended, "great powers" have tended to feel that any change to the status quo threatens their interests and to step in. Since 1950, the United States' involvement as a great power has always been a problem for reunion. In a "strategic triangular" move against the USSR at the beginning of the 1970s, the US gave up Taiwan and became friends with China. Since the latter broke up in 1991, Washington has tried to change its role from supporter to neutral judge in order to keep its influence with both sides. It has said that the two sides can decide the issue either way as long as they don't use force. As the United States sees the rules of the game after the Cold War, hegemonic action has two contradictory goals. One has been to keep the peace, and the other has been to stop changes to the territory that would hurt the military interests of the hegemon. In an age of globalization, keeping the peace is important because fights are unpredictable and, at best, stop people from doing business. Both sides can agree on this goal. But unification led by Beijing, even if it is peaceful, could change the balance of power in the area in a way that hurts American strategic interests. American strategy toward China has tried to solve this problem. After signing three communiques with the PRC in which it said it was committed to neutrality, the US only gets involved in the reunification issue when the two sides are on the verge of war. This is because if war breaks out, the US is informally obligated to fight China, which it would rather not do. So, during the early Strait crises, it only did defensive things, like blocking China's moves against the outlying islands and not letting Chiang's plan to attack the mainland after the Leap disaster happen.

Even though Taiwan is no longer recognized by the U.S., the U.S. continues to act as a counterweight by selling arms to Taiwan. This has angered the PRC, which believes that reunification on terms good for the mainland would happen quickly if the U.S. didn't do this. Beijing would rather talk about the problem in "domestic" (bilateral) terms, leaving the United States out of the picture. Formally, the US "one-China" policy forces the US to accept peaceful reunification, even if that goes against US national interests. However, Beijing has a good reason to think that US backing encourages "China threat theory" supporters in Taiwan to fight reunification. Chen, Kastner, and Reed all say in this book that this could be wrong, and it would be risky to act on such beliefs anyway. Still, if both Beijing and Taiwan think that US arms sales have this hardening effect, they will probably try to stop reunification by force until the balance of power changes.

So, when it comes to force, China is strong but unhappy for the time being. After a long time, the PLA is finally getting a local military advantage over Taiwan. But if it tries to take Taiwan by force or threatens to do so, it could cause the US to step in. Unless China can stop this, a conflict would lead to either an asymmetric war or an embarrassing retreat, which would make Chinese threats less credible, as it did in 1996. So, the United States is very important. China must have local superiority over US troops that try to step in, and it must also have a strong enough deterrent to stop it from using its local power to blackmail the US with nuclear weapons (for example, by sinking an American aircraft carrier). So, China's concerns about US arms sales aren't really in the right place. What China really needs from the US is a promise that it won't get involved if it uses force across the Strait. However, if China asked for this, it would hurt its peaceful unity plans and make Taiwan angry.

Second, China under Mao was a radical rejection of both traditional Chinese culture and Western bourgeois ideals. This was very different from Taiwan, which saw itself as the last bastion of Confucian civilization. After "reform and opening," the CCP leadership under Deng Xiaoping pushed for "emancipation of the mind." This was a more pragmatic approach to the capitalist world that involved trying to bring in better economic, technological, scientific, and cultural practices from more advanced countries. These innovations helped speed up the growth of the economy, but they also caused problems in society and the environment. China had a lot of protests in the 1980s, but Tiananmen Square was the biggest and most well-known one. After the Tiananmen Square event and the fall of the communist bloc, China had a hard time believing in its own ideas. For the next two years, the leaders were in a tough spot. Some defended the ideas of the time before the reforms by blaming "peaceful evolution" on the Western capitalists, while the reformers who were still alive were blamed for letting the protests happen.

The impasse wasn't broken until Deng's "voyage to the south" in 1992 in support of continuing economic reform. China would quietly stop trying out new political ideas and adopt the Singapore compact of political authoritarianism and economic eclecticism. They would also bring Zhu Rongji up from Shanghai (at first as vice-premier) to stop inflation, get China ready to join the World Trade Organization, and restructure banks and state-owned companies in line with international standards.

Taiwan, meanwhile, came out of the Cold War to get rid of the Nationalist martial law system and set up a democracy capitalism system. The economy continued to grow by focusing on exports while industry moved up the value chain into computer peripherals and IT with help from Silicon Valley. When Taiwanese entrepreneurs crossed the Strait in the early 1990s, they were welcomed by local elites who were focused on growth, a cheap and skilled labor force that spoke the same language (and even the same dialect), and an open domestic market and/or export possibilities. Taiwan did not join the sanctions that the Organization for Economic Cooperation and Development countries put in place after Tiananmen. In fact, Taiwan asked the U.S. to stop the sanctions. As the economies on both sides of the Strait grew, it became clear that economic and cultural similarities were good for both sides. As a result, Taiwan's economic elites started to set up companies and move to the mainland. China became Taiwan's biggest trading partner and investor. Over two million Taiwanese have moved to the mainland, where they have jobs, families, schools, business connections, and a good way of life. A recent poll found that about one-third of Taiwanese under the age of 40 wanted to find work in China because they could make more money and move up in their careers there. Under ECFA, the island is now home to millions of Chinese tourists, thousands of Chinese permanent residents (most of whom are the wives of Taiwanese), and some Chinese businesses. With the return of traditional ideals ("harmonious society") to the mainland, cultures have also started to come together.

Shu Keng and Emmy Ruihua Lin report that social assimilation hasn't had much of an effect on politics. "Blue" votes have gone up and "Green" votes have gone down, and business practices have become more compatible, but Taiwanese national identity hasn't changed much on either side of the Taiwan Strait. Voting is one thing, but the island's ruling leaders haven't shown any signs of supporting reunification by Taishang yet. And Xi Jinping has made it clear that the ideological unity that happened under the pragmatic Deng Xiaoping has slowed down.

Why is politics still different? The economy has been the main force behind convergence. Twenty years of double-digit growth in China made it hard for businesses in Taiwan to stay away. When the global financial crisis hit in 2008, it cut demand for Taiwan's exports everywhere but China. This seemed like a good thing at the time, as China's huge stimulus package in 2009 also helped Taiwan get back on its feet. But after a big jump in Taiwan's GDP to 10.8% in 2010, growth slowed down. Even though many people in Taiwan think that inequality has also gotten worse, a close look at the numbers shows that this claim is not true. Over 60% of Taiwan's economy depends on exports, and Taiwan's biggest trade partners are China and Hong Kong. However, Taiwan's exports have been very choppy since they fell sharply in 2009, and they went back into negative territory in 2015. Part of this is because China's GDP growth has been going down every year since 2010. But why is the drop in Taiwan so much steeper? At least one reason is that since 2009, people have been trying to move Chinese industry into a niche with more technology and better added value. This has hurt Taiwanese industries, whether they are on Taiwan or the mainland, in favor of a "red supply chain" of Chinese manufacturers.

In Taiwan, on the other hand, the overall effect of outsourcing has been a drop in job prospects. The overall job numbers show a rise, from 5.2% unemployment in 2010 to 3.79 percent unemployment in 2015. But the jobless rate for young people has been stuck between 12 and 13 percent, with a peak of 14.02 percent in August 2014. So, Taiwan's young people backed the Sunflower Movement in 2014 and voted for the DPP by a large margin in 2016. Taiwan has only seen a small portion of Hong Kong's mainland tourists (3.4 million in 2015 compared to 47 million in Hong Kong), but the quick influx has been felt: they have high incomes per person and put about US$200 billion into the economy each year. But they make the same old complaints: people say they are loud, rude, and wasteful, which drives up prices. Even though the KMT's attempt in the CSTA to open Taiwan's economy to investment from the mainland could have led to an economic boom, people were afraid of a "Trojan Horse" in the form of Chinese purchases of media and high-tech companies.

In conclusion, economic convergence has brought the two sides closer together, but it has also raised expectations faster than they could be actually met and led to unintended side effects. In the meantime, the most important economic factor is not convergence but growth, which has slowed on both sides of the Taiwan Strait for the first time since detente began in the early 1990s. It turns out that reunion can't be based solely on a constant economic boom.

Third, the balance of power on both sides of the Strait has changed over time, which has changed how the reunion process works. Assuming that the better side will be in charge of the reunified state, it has more reason (and resources) to take the lead in the reunification process. One big problem is that the weaker side has lost interest in political unity as a result of having less power than the stronger side. So, Ma Ying-jeou gave up on his early idea for a peace treaty across the Taiwan Strait and kept putting off starting political negotiations. The reasoning of asymmetry says that the stronger state must be very kind if it wants to gain the trust of a weaker state that has to deal with more risks. But this goes against the way people usually act, which is for the strong to use their power to hurt the weak. Given that people tend to be suspicious of what Mao called "sugar-coated bullets" even when terms seem better, the best time for plausible reunification plans has been during times of relative symmetry. The best of these times was in the early 1990s, which KMT leaders now look back on as a golden age (dianfeng shiqi). On both sides, there was a desire to be free: Taiwan from the authoritarianism of the Chiang family, and China from Mao's erratic rule and the Cultural Revolution. The institutions of the Cold War had broken down, and it was a new world. Both sides were more willing to try new things with an open mind. "China fever" (dalu re) brought back human contact and the informal realization of Beijing's "three links." At the time, despite Taiwan's small size and population, its economy was almost half as big as China's and more technologically advanced. From a security point of view, the island still had a quality edge that was enough to stop any threat of invasion without US help.

Today, there has been a huge shift in the balance of power. In 1990, China's GDP was only 2.4 times as big as Taiwan's. By 2010, however, it was 13.7 times as big. Interdependence in trade has become unequal, meaning that Taiwan has more to lose than the mainland. China is Taiwan's largest trading partner, but China's fifth-largest trading partner is Taiwan. While 80% of Taiwan's FDI goes to the mainland, which is up from 50% in 2003, only a small amount of China's FDI goes to Taiwan because China has doubts about doing business there.

When it comes to military power, the difference is even more obvious. This is because even a small part of the world's second-largest economy is a very large budget for arms, and because the PRC has been able to stop many other countries from giving arms to Taiwan. According to the Stockholm International Peace Research Institute, Beijing's military budget has grown eight times in the last twenty years. In 2012, it made up 10 percent of all military spending around the world. Beijing is more sure than ever that it can beat Taiwan quickly in a war between the two countries. Diplomatically, Beijing gave Taipei equal standing in 2005, but this is only true between the two countries. Internationally, Beijing works with others to make Taiwan look bad unless it is called "Taipei, China" or "Chinese Taipei."

Even though the PRC is becoming more powerful, it has tried to keep bilateral noblesse oblige by giving a high degree of autonomy in future reunification plans, as well as generous trade packages and a lot of exchanges. During the time of getting closer, Beijing was kind enough to offer a real, if very limited, diplomatic cease-fire. But none of these are more than temporary solutions, as Taiwan's shrinking political space during the Tsai administration has shown. And the difference between the country's generous bilateral policy and the fact that it is still being shunned by the rest of the world, as well as the fact that internal restrictions on civic freedom are getting tighter as the government cracks down on dissent, tends to make people skeptical about purpose-rational bilateral concessions. China's economic wonder has put it far ahead of Taiwan in terms of money and promises to put it ahead of Taiwan in terms of technology and, eventually, living standards as well. This has made China a proud giant that doesn't want to change the "one country, two systems" plan that Deng offered in the early 1980s. Since then, the only concession has been the addition of "differing interpretations" to "one China" in 1992, which Xi Jinping now wants to get rid of. The recent events in Hong Kong have made it harder to believe that Taiwan will be a part of China in the future.

Conclusion

The relationship between China and Taiwan has always been very unstable. It has changed a lot since freedom came to Taiwan and reform and opening happened in China, but it is still very unstable. At one point, it seemed like shared interests might be able to fix a tense relationship that has been hard to fix through both military and diplomatic means. But now even that bubble of hope has burst. Even if they could have, it's unlikely that economic interests could have kept bringing the two sides of the Strait together. Now, though, the economic engine is slowing down. Even though it didn't lead to a reunion, there isn't much that can be done in the other way. Beijing still wants the dream to come true. Even if Beijing were to ignore a formal statement of independence, which is very unlikely, geographical, social, and economic ties are now too strong for the island to move away from Beijing.

What are the main things that have caused the dream to fade? Of course, the threat to use force is still one of them. This is now mostly controlled by Beijing, though military drills and an arms race are still going on. China says it has the right to use force and may feel strong and brave enough to do so in the future. Still, there has been some progress. Both sides agree that a peaceful reunification that starts with economic cooperation is better than using force. Beijing has learned that using force is bad for politics unless it is used in a clear way. This makes the use of force less likely and more dangerous. Since there aren't as many problems now, there aren't as many big-power interventions. The military buildup on the Fujian coast has not stopped, nor have arms sales to Taiwan. However, since the Strait Crisis, there seems to have been an unspoken agreement that as Chinese threats and crises decrease, American arms sales will not upset the balance. This is why there are no submarines or fifth-generation stealth fighters. It would be better if there was no fear of force at all, but that would take a lot more trust than there is right now. Even if people don't trust each other, if they don't use force for a long time (i.e., there aren't any problems), the likelihood of them doing so may decrease over time.

Socioeconomic unity has been one of the most important changes. Even though Taiwanese "self-ghettoization" in homogeneous neighborhoods and discrimination against mainlanders can slow things down, there is no language barrier, and people on both sides of the Strait have mixed a lot. Mutual understanding doesn't always mean that people like each other or agree on politics, and financial convergence hasn't yet led to changes in national identity that can be seen. If Taiwanese and Chinese people keep marrying each other, this may have to wait until the next generation. It may be the last thing to change. Before that, there might be changes in how people vote, the growth of vested interests, and finally some political agreements from both sides. For views to really change, it would also help to talk about politics honestly, which is hard to do now, especially on the mainland. This will take a long time.

There's also the issue of how much each person is getting. Even though reunion would be good for both sides and good for the world as a whole, it might be better for one side than the other. In particular, it is better for the stronger power than for the lesser power. A rational stronger power, like Germany, tends to make few concessions and push for simple annexation while making few changes to the status quo at home. This makes the process more popular at home, but it makes the smaller power want to fight back. The relationship between Taiwan and China has become very unequal, and if current growth rates continue, this is likely to get worse, making Taiwan less likely to move toward unity. For the stronger side to feel better, the stronger side will have to be very sensitive. So, China gives Taiwan "early harvest" and other favors as "loss leaders" to get the economy to work better together. The taishang answer as "free riders," meaning they are happy to take whatever is given to them. This makes economic integration stronger, but it's not clear if the Taiwanese become more publicly committed to the PRC. This is frustrating for the person who made the concession, but he or she can't blame the person who got the concession of bad faith because the political trade-off was never made clear. Making it clear would add political "quid pro quos" to Beijing's "no-strings-attached" and "win-win" model for building trust. So, we have weak blending of different cultures and not much political gain, at least in the short term.

Growing differences between the two sides has become one of the biggest surprises in the way of reunion. The Chinese economic miracle is a great feat in and of itself. One of its goals was to get ahead of Taiwan. It thought that once China was in an undisputedly better situation, all resistance would end. Cross-Strait "win-win" business integration was also helped by economic growth. Yet the same economic miracle that pushed China's economy (as a whole) past Taiwan's and made the PLA possible also caused Taiwan's economy to fall. Asia's biggest army has also built a powerful party-state that is a threat to anyone who gets in its way. To be fair, Beijing has made many concessions since 2005 to try to win Taiwan over. But none of this is enough. The world's second-largest economy wants to become a "pole" that controls its own strategic periphery and connects Eurasia with ports and high-speed rail, but it doesn't think it needs to change its party-state to give Taiwan a real say in how China is run if Taiwan is reincorporated. To make fun of Yang Jiechi, Taiwan is small and China is big. Taiwanese people have been able to tell the difference between economic convergence and political assimilation, and they have been able to accept economic convergence while avoiding political assimilation. The Xi Jinping government doesn't like this and doesn't want it to keep going. What they can do to stop it without hurting their own business and reputation around the world too much is still unknown.

So, in light of recent events, it may still be hard and take a long time to come up with a plan for shared authority that works for everyone. Beijing's geoeconomic "boxing in" plan may make it impossible for Taiwan to ever be free of it. But Beijing might not be able to bring the long-separate island country peacefully into its vision of "one China" with the same ideas.

Chapter 2
Taiwan's National Identity and Cross-Strait Relations

Since the Second World War, the Taiwan Strait has been one of the most dangerous places on the planet. Even though the Soviet group fell apart, there is still a chance that communist China and the United States will go to war with each other. After former president Lee Teng-hui went to the U.S., there was a crisis with missile tests in 1995 and 1996. This showed how fragile cross-Strait ties were and how quickly the political situation could get out of hand.

Compared to what they were like when Chen Shui-bian was president from 2000 to 2008, cross-Strait ties have been pretty calm in the last eight years, from 2008 to 2016. This peaceful coexistence is mostly due to President Ma Ying-jeou's policy toward mainland China. He replaced "confrontation" with "engagement," set up "three direct links" (postal, transportation, and trade) between mainland China and Taiwan, and got the Economic Cooperation Framework Agreement (ECFA) and another twenty bilateral agreements with mainland China. These agreements covered everything from trade promotion to crime prevention, food safety, enforcing human rights, and environmental protection.

But Ma's policy on the mainland was harshly slammed by the Democratic Progressive Party (DPP) and was often called a betrayal of Taiwan's real interests. Critics said that Ma's government and the Nationalist Party (also called the Kuomintang or KMT) "sold Taiwan to China" because the KMT was a pro-unification party and Ma never saw himself as being from Taiwan. Even though the accusation was emotional and exaggerated, it had a political effect on those who did not benefit from his policy on the mainland. The general discontent with that policy, along with the poor performance of the government and nasty intraparty cleavages (first between Ma and Wang Jin-pyng, then between Eric Chu and Hung Shiu-chu), led to the KMT's historic loss in the 2014 local elections and the 2016 presidential election.

The DPP's big win in the 2016 election could be a turning point in how things go between Taiwan and China in the long run. The DPP has always supported a policy of de jure independence for Taiwan, and the newly chosen president, Ms. Tsai Ing-wen, is seen as a careful but firm supporter of Taiwan's independence. She came up with the "two states" (liang guo lun) idea of former Republic of China (ROC) president Lee Teng-hui and was a strong supporter of Chen Shui-bian's "one country on each side [of the Taiwan Strait]" (yi bianyi guo) idea. Both of these ideas say that Taiwan and China are two separate countries and go against the idea that there is only one China. During the presidential race, Tsai said that most Taiwanese do not identify with China and that "most youths are naturally inclined to Taiwan independence." We should look closely at how Tsai's policy toward mainland China will affect Ma's legacy and how it will affect cross-Strait ties and East Asian security.

In Taiwanese politics and ties across the Taiwan Strait, issues of national identity and unification/independence are always seen as important. This chapter starts by explaining what "national identity" means in the context of Taiwanese politics. It then looks at the different ways to measure "national identity" in Taiwan and shows that, no matter how it is measured, Taiwanese identification has risen sharply over the past 20 years. Then I talk about the "one-China principle," which I think is more important and deserves more attention than national identity or the choice between unification and independence. Lastly, I look at what could happen to cross-Strait relations after the 2016 election. I do this while keeping in mind that cross-Strait relations are not just two-way, but involve Taiwan, mainland China, and the U.S. in a strategic triangle. I end with suggestions for how to improve cross-Strait relations.

Evolution of National Identity in Taiwan

In Taiwan, people have talked a lot about theories of nationalism and national identity in the last few decades. About the meaning of a country, there are two main schools of thought: the modernist and the primordial. The modernist school says that the country is a new political idea that came about as states were built. Since the global system of nation-states didn't come into being until the 17th century, modernists say that the ideas of country, nationalism, and national identity are all very new ways that society has made sense of the world. On the other hand, the primordial school says that even though the nation-state system is a modern thing, the nation has an objective existence that calls people's loyalty and identity, mostly based on shared history, myth, genealogical ties, or religious belief, long before the modern state learns how to mobilize its citizens in the name of a fatherland.

Most Taiwanese scholars tend to agree with the modernist argument and see the "Taiwanese people" as a modern social creation that grew out of the process of decolonization and democratization. Most of the time, they agree on the following: (1) A nation is a group of people who feel connected to each other because they share a shared ancestry, language, religion, or history, even if that sense of connection is more imagined than real. (2) National identity is the way a person feels about his or her imagined group, which is made up of a homeland, a people, a shared history, and a shared public culture. (3) Taiwanese nationalism and the Taiwanese nationalist movement, whose political goal is Taiwanese freedom, come from Taiwanese identity. As building a nation-state is usually seen as the highest achievement of nationalism, Taiwanese nationalist scholars have little trouble accepting nationalism as a doctrine that says "the political and the national unit should be congruent," as Ernest Gellner puts it.

Taiwan has come up with and uses three different ways to measure Taiwanese national identity. The first one tries to make people realize that being Taiwanese is different from being Chinese. The second is about how Taiwanese people feel about merging with mainland China or making the island state de jure independent. The third one looks at how much people think they are Taiwanese nationalists or Chinese nationalists. I'll look at all three methods in order and argue that none is a perfect way to measure the collective awareness of Taiwanese people, even though each has its own purpose.

Let's start with the most common way to understand Taiwan's national identity: deciding whether or not you are Taiwanese or Chinese. People who say they are only Taiwanese are thought to belong to a political group called Taiwan. People who say they are only Chinese are thought to have a Chinese national identity. People who say they are both Taiwanese and Chinese have a dual national identity.

According to a survey done by the Election Study Center at National Chengchi University, Taiwanese people's sense of self has changed dramatically from being mostly Chinese in the early years of democracy to being mostly Taiwanese during Ma's second term as president. Figure 2.1 shows that in the early 1990s, almost 25.5 percent of the people asked in this study said that they only thought of themselves as Chinese. In 2001, when Chen Shui-bian took office, the number dropped to 10.6 percent. In 2016, it was only 3 percent. On the other hand, the number of people who thought they were only Taiwanese went from 17.6% in 1992 to 41.6 % in 2001 and then to 59.3% in 2016. That is, almost two-thirds of Taiwan's people now say that they are only Taiwanese, and a lot of this growth happened while Ma Ying-jeou was in charge. During the same time period, the number of people who thought of themselves as both Taiwanese and Chinese went from 46.4% to 33.6%.

Figure 2.1. Changes in the Taiwanese/Chinese Identity of Taiwanese as tracked in surveys by the Election Study Center, National Chengchi University (1992-2016)

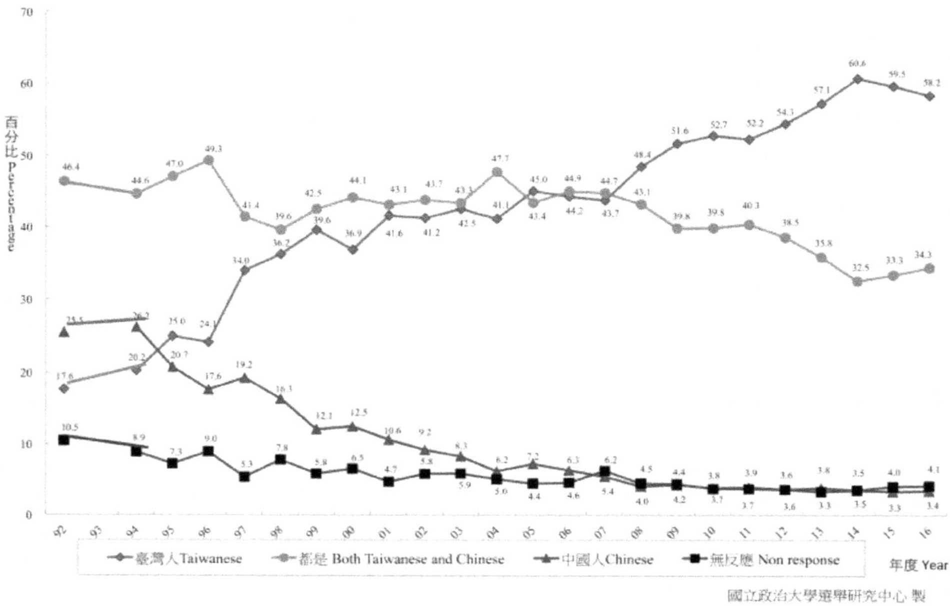

source: Hui-ling Chen, "Taiwanese/Chinese Identification Trend Distribution in Taiwan (1992/06-2016/12)," Election Study Center, National Chengchi University, August 24, 2016, http://esc.nccu.edu.tw/course/news.php?Sn= 166.

I've said before that the classification of Taiwanese, Chinese, or both is not a good way to measure Taiwan's national identity, but it does show important things about how Taiwanese group self-awareness is changing. One big reason is that the word "Chinese" can mean more than one thing in Mandarin. It can be used to refer to someone who identifies with Chinese culture but not with a specific political body. It can also be used to refer to someone who aligns with either the ROC or the PRC. When someone says "I'm a Chinese" in response to the question "Are you Chinese or Taiwanese?" there is no way to know if they are talking about their cultural identity or their political identity. People who live in mainland China, Taiwan, Hong Kong, or even Chinese groups outside of China won't have any trouble thinking of themselves as "Chinese" if they're thinking in terms of culture or ethnicity. If we think of Chinese identity in cultural terms, as many scholars did when they cited the poll, then the category of "being Chinese" cannot be thought of as people who identify with the PRC, and the category of "being both Chinese and Taiwanese" cannot be thought of as dual national identity or confusion of national identity. This may have nothing to do with a person's political personality and more to do with how they feel about different cultures.

The second way to figure out who Taiwanese people are is to find out how they feel about unification and freedom. If a person wants Taiwan to be united with mainland China instead of being independent, he or she is thought to have Chinese national identity. A person with a Taiwanese national identity would be the exact opposite of this. The Election Study Center's study team took the two choices of unification or independence and made them into six groups. Figure 2.2 shows how things turned out.

If we combine "independence as soon as possible" and "maintain status quo, move toward independence," "unificat on as soon as possible" and "maintain status quo, move toward unification," and "maintain status quo indefinitely" and "maintain status quo, decide at a later date," we find that the number of people who want independence went from over 11 percent in 1994 to almost 23 percent in 2016. From 20% in 1994 to just over 10% in 2016, there was a steady drop in the number of people who supported union. Also, the number of people who like the way things are went from about 48% in 1994 to almost 60% in 2016, which is still the most people in the last 20 years.

Figure 2.2. Changes in the unification-independence stances of Taiwanese as tracked in surveys by the Election Study Center, National Chengchi University (1994-2016).

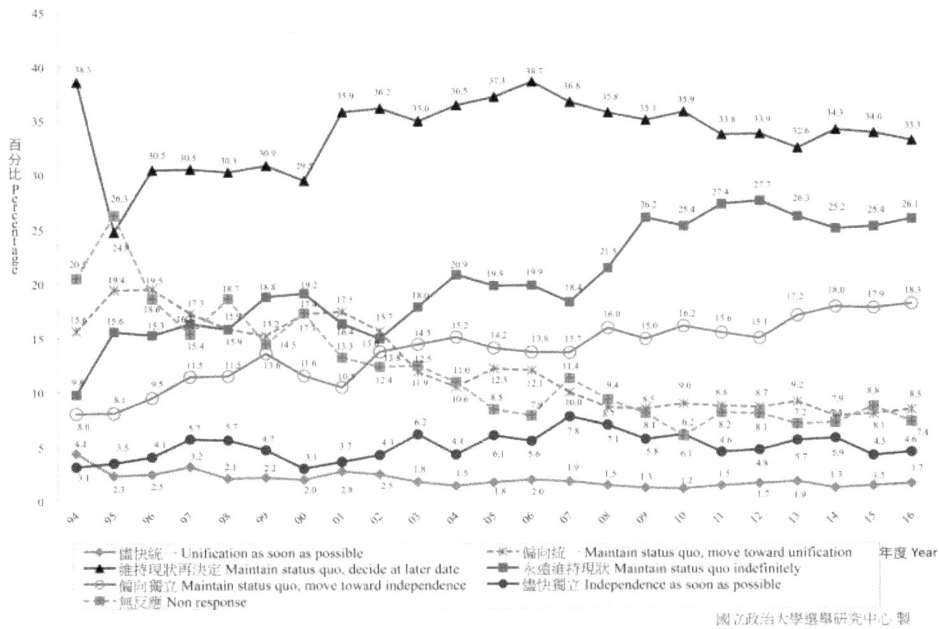

Source: Hui-ling Chen, "Taiwan Independence vs. Unification with the Mainland Trend Distribution in Taiwan (1992/06~2016/12),'> Election Study Center, National Chengchi University, http://esc.nccu. edu.tw/co urse/news.php?Sn= 167.

The poll is important for understanding how Taiwanese feel about "unification/independence," but it is more about Taiwanese people's choices for the future than about their national identity. These two questions are similar but not the same. It's hard to say what kind of national identity "the status quo" means, especially when more than 60% of people say they like the way things are now. I'll talk more about the different ways people understand "the status quo" later.

Scholars have pointed out that there is a problem with the first two ways. Wu Naiteh says that a country's national character, as it is thought of in the unification/independence choice, can be changed by unfavorable political circumstances from the outside, and that people will change their views to be more practical in the short term. He made a questionnaire with two key questions to find out about the secret, long-term view of national identity: (1) If Taiwan's independence wouldn't cause a war, would you think that Taiwan should become an independent country? (2) Would you agree that the two sides of the Taiwan Strait should become one country if Taiwan and China reached the same level of economic, social, and political development?

Wu calls people who say "yes" to the first question but "no" to the second "Taiwanese nationalists." These are people who want independence if the conditions are right and who don't want to join China even if China gets as rich as Taiwan. People who say "no" to the first question but "yes" to the second are called "Chinese nationalists." These are people who want unification in a good situation but don't want Taiwan to be independent even if there's no war. Wu calls people who answer "yes" to both questions "pragmatists," and people who answer "no" to both questions "conservatives" (Table 2.1).

From their poll, Shen and Wu found that the number of Taiwanese nationalists went from 9.3 percent in 1992 to 27.7 percent in 2005, which is a big jump. However, the number of nationalists seemed to stop short of 30 percent. On the other hand, the number of Chinese patriots went from 38% in 1992 to 13% in 2005 in a steady way. The trend of Taiwanese identity getting stronger and Chinese identity getting weaker is the same as what the other two methods found. But what bothered Shen and Wu was that there has always been a large group of pragmatic people who "are willing to accept an independent Taiwan if their security is not threatened, and they are also willing to accept unification with China if there are no negative economic or political consequences." Their share was 25% in 1992, 30% in 2005, and peaked at almost 40% in 1996, when ties across the Strait were at their most dangerous point since the 1950s. Shen and Wu couldn't tell if these pragmatists had two national identities or none at all, so they chose to leave this mystery for future researchers to figure out.

I think Wu's questionnaire is a good way to try to find people who want to follow their nationalist cause, whether it's independence or unification. But Wu's argument would be stronger if he added two more questions: (3) If Taiwan's freedom would lead to a war, do you still think Taiwan should be its own country? (4) Would you agree that the two sides of the Taiwan Strait should become one country if Taiwan and China never reached the same level of economic, social, and political development? Only if (1) and (4) are true, can we tell who the real Chinese nationalists are (those who don't want independence even if there's no war and want to join China even if the political, social, and economic conditions on both sides of the Strait can't be the same), and only if (2) and (3) are true, can we tell who the real Taiwanese nationalists are (those who don't want unification even if conditions on both sides of the Strait

Table 2.1 Variations in Taiwanese National Identities (Simplified from Wu and Shen's 1992-2005 Classification)

	Accept unification if no disparity between Taiwan and China	**Reject unification even if no disparity between Taiwan and China**
Accept Taiwanese independence if no war happens	Pragmatists	Taiwanese Nationalists
Reject Taiwanese independence even if no war happens	Chinese Nationalists	Conservatives

Sources: Shiau-chi Shen and Nai-teh Wu, "Ethnic and Civic Nationalisms: Two Roads to the Formation of a Taiwanese Nation," in The "One China" Dilemma, ed. Peter C. Y. Chow (New York: Palgrave Macmillan, 2008), 122.

The real problem, though, is that Shen and Wu's poll still can't explain why there are so many "pragmatic" respondents. Instead, it skirts the issue by looking for principled "nationalists." If so-called "pragmatists" have been the majority of the people for decades, isn't that a clear sign that the questionnaire may be misleading when it comes to asking about national identity? It's a good way to find out how determined someone is to seek freedom or unification, but it's not a good way to measure someone's national identity. For example, a person could be sure of their political identity with the ROC but refuse to fight for Taiwanese freedom or refuse to unite with mainland China under bad conditions. We couldn't say that this person didn't have a political identity in this case. After all, "having an identity" and "having a strong identity" are not the same thing.

Because of this, I have come up with another way to look into Taiwan's national identity. Liu I-chou said many years ago that we should try to figure out what a person's national identity is based on how they see the land of their country and who else lives there. Based on this line of thought, the questions would be: (1) Do you think your country's area includes mainland China or just Taiwan? (2) Do you think your countrymen are only those who live in Taiwan or also those who live in mainland China? People with a Taiwanese (or ROC) national identity only claim Taiwanese land and people as their own. People with a Greater Chinese national identity, on the other hand, include mainland China in their region and consider people from mainland China to be their own people.

In 1998, when Liu gave this survey to people living in Taiwan, about 77% of the people who filled it out had a Taiwanese identity and about 9% had a Greater Chinese identity. The rest had different names or didn't answer. In the years that followed, the questionnaire was not given again. My guess is that after more than a decade of growing Taiwanese consciousness, the number of people with a Taiwanese national identity has grown even more and now probably makes up more than 85% of the population, while the number of people with a Greater Chinese national identity may now be less than 5%. Liu's measure is the best way to explain what makes Taiwanese people who they are. The large majority of Taiwanese who identify with the country on the island may have different ideas about their cultural and ethnic identities (whether they feel Taiwanese, Chinese, or both) or about whether Taiwan should be de jure independent or join with mainland China in the future, or about how patriotic they are about the ROC (or Taiwan), but they all identify with the ROC (or Taiwan) in a political sense. As long as they follow the ROC's constitution and rules, the few people who identify with mainland China (or a larger China) should be respected.

In other words, if we understand the idea right, national identity in Taiwan is not as divisive as many experts think or say it is. Taiwanese may have different feelings of cultural belonging, different ethnic backgrounds, different political views, or different levels of commitment to their ideas. They may also have different tastes in food and clothes, different ways of having fun, different ways of thinking about life, and so on. But a well-known Taiwanese writer once said, "Taiwan is definitely a country. "If that's not a country, what is?" Most disagreements aren't about whether Taiwan is a country or not. Instead, they are about whether it should be called "the Republic of China" or just "Taiwan." In other words, the problem of Taiwan's national identity is complicated not because of its size, population, or sovereignty, but because of a disagreement over the "one-China" principle, which is what we'll talk about next.

The Challenge of 'One-China'

As was said in the last part, some ways that Taiwan tries to measure national identity don't exactly show what they are supposed to measure. The

"Taiwanese/Chinese/both" classification helps us understand how two different cultures that overlap affect how Taiwanese see themselves, but it can't be turned into a political identity that corresponds to a specific region and sovereignty. The categories of "unification," "independence," and "status quo" tell us what kind of political future Taiwanese want, but this only makes sense if Taiwan is a political body that can choose. The poll combines "independence if there is no war" and "unification if China is well developed" to find out what factors Taiwanese might think about when they have to choose between independence and joining China. It might help us tell the difference between moderate and hard-line nationalism, but it is not a measure of national identity in and of itself.

If we focus on what national identity is really about, which is a sense of belonging to a sovereign region and a group of people who have lived similar lives, it's clear that Taiwanese do know where their country is and who their fellow citizens are. A small number of people don't agree with the vast majority on this question, but that's not a big deal. People in Taiwan may have different opinions about freedom or unification, but they all know who they are as a country. In other words, Taiwan's national character is not a big deal. It is, sadly, the way that many politicians like to get people to vote during elections.

Unification or freedom is also not a big deal. People often say that the KMT wants unification and the DPP wants freedom. That is true if we believe that they are true to their party platforms and that their candidates are only fighting against each other for the sake of unification or independence. Still, all studies show that more than 60 percent of Taiwanese want to keep things the same. Only about 24 percent of Taiwanese want to move toward independence, and only 9 percent want to move toward unification. Both the KMT and the DPP are aware of what the public thinks, so neither has said that it will follow a clear policy of unity or independence. On the other hand, both sides are busy trying to convince people that they will keep things the same better than the other. Politicians who don't stick to the status quo and instead push for independence or union are either trying to target a certain group of voters or are committing political suicide.

If national identity isn't a big deal and unification or freedom isn't a must-decide issue, then why is Taiwanese politics so tumultuous and full of conflict? The answer has to do with the Chinese Communist Party's (CCP) challenge to the "one-China policy" in mainland China.

Since 1949, when the CCP won the civil war and forced the Nationalist government to flee to Taiwan, the communist government has said that the People's Republic of China (PRC) is the only legal representation of China in the world. At the same time, the defeated Nationalist government has said that it is the only legal representation of China. In the decades that followed, Beijing has always stuck to the "one-China principle," which says that there is only one China in the world, Taiwan is part of China, and the PRC is the only government with the right to speak for China. From this idea comes the policy that all countries that want to have diplomatic relations with the PRC must end their official ties with the ROC. These countries must accept the PRC as the only legitimate representative of mainland China and Taiwan, or at least acknowledge its claim on the matter.

The PRC and the ROC both lose when they play the "one-China policy" game. When a country accepts the PRC's legal status, the ROC cuts diplomatic ties with that country right away, and vice versa. Because Taiwan can't afford to compete with China politically or economically, this strategy also forces Taiwan to take a more defensive stance in the international arena.

China's plan of isolating Taiwan from the rest of the world is well known to Taiwan. After the ban on tours across the Taiwan Strait was lifted in the late 1980s, the ROC realized it couldn't avoid talking to the PRC about administrative matters. But when the Tiananmen Square event led to harsh international sanctions against the PRC and pro-independence forces in Taiwan grew stronger, the PRC felt it had to change its policy toward Taiwan. That was the setting for the "1992 Consensus" between the Straits Exchange Foundation (representing Taiwan) and the Association for Relations Across the Taiwan Straits (representing mainland China).

The most important part of the 1992 Consensus is that the ROC and the PRC agree that there is only one China. They also agree that each side can have its own idea of what "one China" means, so that they can continue to do useful work without being distracted by arguments about sovereignty. On November 3, 1992, the SEF made the following statement: "During the Hong Kong talks, the ARATS insisted that both sides make "public statements" on the subject of "one China." With permission from the Mainland Affairs Council, the SEF is willing to talk about how they each see the situation. As for the content of this oral statement, we will stick to the Guidelines for National Unification and the National Unification Council's decision on the meaning of "one China," which was passed on August 1, 1992. This is the famous "one China, different interpretations" (yizong gebiao) way to deal with Beijing's "one-China principle": the ROC is willing to accept the principle that there is only one China in order to handle cross-Strait issues, but it reserves the right to interpret what "one China" means and, not surprisingly, sees itself rather than the PRC as "one China."

Soon after the SEF made its announcement, the ARATS said, "The SEF has officially told the ARATS that it has received permission from the relevant authorities in Taiwan for 'an oral statement of their respective interpretations.'" The ARATS takes the SEF's idea very seriously and agrees with it. . . . Now, the ARATS wants to share the most important parts of its public statement with the SEF: Both sides of the Taiwan Strait stick to the "one China" idea and work toward national unification. However, the meaning of "one China" shouldn't come up in functional talks across the strait. From 1993 to 2008, the 1992 Consensus was not followed, but we can't say why here. When Chen Shui-bian took power in 2000, he went so far as to say that such an agreement did not exist. But when he became president in 2008, Ma Ying-jeou chose to get the talks between the SEF and the ARATS back on track based on the 1992 Consensus. From then on, the new idea of "one China, different interpretations" was a very important part of stabilizing ties across the Taiwan Strait and made it possible for the two sides to sign twenty-one agreements.

The 1992 Consensus was a big deal for the KMT because it was a big step toward better ties between China and Taiwan. It was also mentioned in statements given by Assistant Secretary of State James Kelly to the US Congress and in a phone call between Chairman Hu Jintao and President George W. Bush. But DPP leaders have either refused to agree that the agreement exists, refused to agree that it is valid, or refused to agree that it is good for Taiwan.

People who say there is no 1992 Consensus say that the idea was made up by Su Qi, who used to be the deputy minister of mainland affairs. And if they do recognize something like a compromise between the two sides, they say it's not real because it talks about the "one-China principle," which can only mean that Taiwan is part of China. They know that the Nationalist government says that the ROC is "one China," but they don't think that "one China" can be interpreted differently by Taiwan because of the consensus. They think that mainland China will control the interpretation because it is much stronger and has more resources in the international world than Taiwan.

Tsai Ing-wen's official statement in 2000, when she was minister of the Mainland Affairs Council under Chen Shui-bian, was a good example of the DPP's view on this issue: "The so-called "one China, different interpretations" is just a phrase we use to describe how the meeting went. It's a way to talk about things that the new government can agree with, but that doesn't mean we agree with Beijing's "one-China principle." In 2003, she reaffirmed her position on the matter by making it clear that the ROC and the PRC were not the same thing. "One side, one country," she said, "is a statement of fact."

In 2012, when Tsai ran for president, she tried to get rid of the Chinese identity of Taiwanese people by pushing Taiwanese identity as a replacement. She maintained: "The Republic of China is an exile (alien) government, which rules Taiwan at the moment. The ROC's Chineseness must move from being a matter of opinion to being a matter of fact, and it must give way to Taiwaneseness. She also tried to get people to think about the relationship across the Taiwan Strait in a new way by saying, "There is no 1992 Consensus. What I propose is to create a Taiwan consensus to replace the 1992 Consensus, which would be ratified by legislation and a referendum. This new agreement should then be used as a starting point for talks with the PRC."

Tsai lost the 2012 presidential election. Many political experts think that the fact that she couldn't show that the Taiwanese Consensus could work was a big reason, if not the most important one. It explains why she chose not to use the language again during her 2016 campaign for president. Still, she has not changed her mind at all about the 1992 Consensus. With the prospect that the DPP might win both the 2014 local elections and the 2016 general election, she was confident enough to believe that even the PRC would yield to her view about the 1992 Consensus afterwards. In an interview, she said, "Whoever is in charge, different parties will change their ways to help them." The DPP's biggest challenge is to do well in this year's local elections. If we do a good job, even China will move toward the DPP. If they feel that the DPP has the best chance of winning in 2016, they will automatically create the conditions for that."

With this self-assurance, Tsai was ready to speak to the majority of people who liked the way things were, even though she didn't agree with the 1992 Consensus. Her successful strategy in the 2016 presidential election was to replace the unwelcome "Taiwan Consensus" with the popular "maintaining the status quo" but not to discuss what "the status quo" actually meant. In her speech at the Center for Strategic and International Studies on June 3, 2016, she repeated that maintaining the status quo "serves the best interest of all parties concerned," and she vowed to be "committed to a consistent, predictable, and sustainable relationship with China." She also emphasized that, if elected, she would "push for the peaceful and stable development of cross-Strait relations in accordance with the will of the Taiwanese people and the existing ROC constitutional order" (my italics). Nevertheless, when asked by the audience to elaborate her views on the issue and explain how her thesis could be reconciled with the DPP's independence platform, she refused to explain further and only asked them to carefully read her speech again.

Maintaining the status quo, as we point out in the previous section, has remained the favorite option of the majority in Taiwan. However, "the status quo" can mean different things to different people. Some think the status quo is a country called the Republic of China, which agrees with mainland China that both sides can interpret their concept of China respectively. Some think the status quo is a separate country called Taiwan, which has never agreed with

China regarding the idea that there is only "one China" under which they should be subsumed. As Ma Ying-jeou reiterated several times, the status quo for most Taiwanese is a peaceful cross-Strait relationship created by his policy of three nos—"no unification, no independence, and no use of military force" under the framework of the ROC constitution. It is also a result of cross-Strait dialogues based on the 1992 Consensus (namely, "one China, differing interpretations"). If Tsai Ing-wen's "status quo" was similar to the status quo that Ma created, he would be very glad to have the leader of the opposition party follow his own mainland policy. Unfortunately, Tsai is clear that she will not accept the 1992 Consensus or agree that Taiwan and the mainland belong to the same China, even though that is the frame of the ROC constitution. She is going to change the status quo and pretend that she does not.

Table 2.2 Diverse Perspectives on the 'One-China Principle' among Various Stakeholders

	China	KMT	USA	DPP
There is only one China in the world.	X	X	X	X
Taiwan is part of China.	X	X	X	
"China" can be interpreted differently.	?	X		
China is represented by the PRC.	X		X	X
China is represented by the ROC.		X		
Taiwan is not part of China.				X
China and Taiwan are two countries.				X

Now, Tsai agrees that there were talks between the two sides of the Taiwan Straits in 1992, but she still doesn't agree that the two sides came to an agreement. This small change to her original stance on the 1992 Consensus came out just before the election and came up again in her inauguration speech on May 20, 2016. She said, "As a matter of history, there was a bilateral summit in 1992, and both sides agreed to "seek common ground while putting disagreements aside."" Still, she wouldn't agree that the "common ground" was the 1992 Consensus or "one China, different interpretations," let alone the idea that Taiwan is or will be a part of China, no matter what "China" means. Beijing said right away that this wasn't the right answer "to the exam," but it looks like the CCP is ready to wait until Tsai changes her mind in the near future.

Before we end this part, it might be helpful to show where different players stand on the "one-China" question (Table 2.2). From this table, we can see that China, the USA, the KMT, and the DPP can all agree that "there is only one China in the world," even though they have very different ideas about other parts of the "one-China" question. It also explains why the simple statement "There is only one China in the world" can't be easily turned into a "one-China policy," a "one-China principle," a "one-China framework," or any other term that includes "one China." In Taiwan, the most divisive problem isn't national identity or whether to join China or stay independent. Instead, it's the meaning of "one China" and what it means."

Outlook for Cross-Strait Relations

Cross-Strait ties are never just a problem between Taiwan and the rest of China. It includes the PRC, the ROC, and the US, and it's a point of disagreement between the KMT and the DPP in the ROC. So, it can be thought of as a triangle-shaped relationship between four key people. To understand this complicated problem, you have to think about what each player is doing and how they interact with each other.

In international relations theory, the relationship between the PRC, the Soviet Union (later Russia), and the US is called a "great strategic triangle," while the relationship between Beijing, Taipei, and Washington is called a "small strategic triangle." It's a triangular relationship because the ROC needs the US to stand up to the PRC's political and military pressure, the PRC needs the US's tacit support to stop the ROC from trying to get legal independence, and the US wants the PRC and the ROC to stop being so hostile to each other. Also, the small strategic triangle is not balanced because the PRC and the US are much stronger and have more impact than the ROC. Yu-shan Wu says that when the power difference between two characters is different, the way their moves are interpreted and predicted should also be changed. Power imbalance also affects other things, such as the reasons for economic integration, the likelihood of armed conflict, changes in national identity, the strategy of election campaigns, and so on.

With this framework in mind, we can now start to look at what the four players want from cross-Strait interactions and what they try to avoid. The PRC wants to finish unifying China in the 21st century, especially with Chairman Xi Jinping's "Chinese Dream" of wealth, power, and development for the whole country as a guide. The PRC knows that more and more Taiwanese have a Taiwanese identity and want freedom, even though the majority still wants to keep things as they are for now. The PRC wants to reach a political agreement with Taiwan that officially recognizes that there is only one China in the world and that both the mainland and Taiwan are parts of China. This would stop Taiwan from moving toward de jure independence. But when Ma's government was politically challenged by the conflict with Speaker Wang in 2013 and the chaos of the Sunflower Movement in 2014, it almost lost the drive to negotiate any kind of political agreement with mainland China, whether it was a "framework of peace agreement" or a "mechanism for military mutual trust." With the DPP's huge win in the 2016 election, the best that the PRC can hope for is that other countries will agree to the 1992 Consensus and "one China" in a vague way. If this minimum goal can't be met, Xi Jinping might have to think about other choices. When China has so many more important goals to reach, it is not in the PRC's best interest to fight with the US, but the Taiwan independence problem is too important to be ignored. Xi does not want to be the first Chinese leader in history to lose Taiwan. This would be a huge blow to his political career and to the CCP's credibility. So, the task is to get the US to help stop the DPP from making the 1992 Consensus useless.

Former President Ma and his political allies in the KMT think that the 1992 Consensus (in the sense of "one China, different interpretations") is the best way to deal with ties across the Taiwan Strait. But the present chair, Ms. Hung Hsiu-chu, has a very different view of relations across the Strait. Hung says that the DPP is working for Taiwanese independence in the name of democracy. He says that this will "bring threats to national security, make Taiwan even more isolated, cause economic stagnation, and fuel hatred in society." Still, she was not happy with the current strategy of "one China, different interpretations." She said that "one China, same interpretation" (yizhong tongbiao) was the best policy for cross-Strait relations and that Taiwan should sign a peace agreement with mainland China as long as the ROC constitution was kept and the will of the people was respected. Most people think that Hung's comment is in favor of unification, which makes the KMT politicians, who prefer Ma's "three nos," suspicious and critical right away. Hung says that her policy doesn't "replace" the 1992 Consensus, but rather "enhances" it. This is so that people in her own party won't be so against it. Still, it's becoming clearer and clearer that she won't continue Ma's program. Her move toward unity will make the DPP look more like it wants to keep things the same. We don't yet know how Beijing will respond to Hung's idea.

For the DPP, Tsai Ing-wen's biggest task is to convince the people of Taiwan, the PRC, and the US that she won't try to make Taiwan de jure independent while she is president. She needs to find a delicate balance between the DPP's "Taiwanese Independence Platform," which calls for a new constitution and the creation of a Republic of Taiwan, and the public's worries about the risk of war if the DPP pushes for Taiwanese independence or changes some important parts of the current constitution. By saying "maintaining the status quo" over and over again, Tsai is trying to reassure the people that she won't go for full independence or try to change the ROC law to support independence. Still, her DPP supporters, especially the "fundamentalists," or hard-liners on the issue of independence, will say that her stance and Ma's are the same. Since she took office, she has been careful not to directly challenge mainland China. However, her consistent denial of the 1992 Consensus, her changing position on the South China Sea dispute, her indifference to the Chinese people who died in a mysterious bus accident in Taiwan, her appointment of several pro-independence grand justices to the Supreme Court, and her tacit support of the Hong Kong independence movement all make the CCP doubt her sincerity about mai. Many experts on cross-Strait relations say that Tsai is trying to get Taiwan to be independent under the (brief) cover of the ROC. This may make the US happy, but it won't win the trust of China.

Lastly, the United States' part is always important. The United States seems more like a pivot than a partner in the small strategic trio of Beijing, Taipei, and Washington. The US has a stake in this problem because it wants to keep relations across the Taiwan Strait calm and stable, without any sudden political or military moves made by one side. In 1996, when there was a problem with missile tests, the United States sent battle groups from its aircraft carriers to this area. The US government spoke out against Chen Shui-bian's "one country on each side" debate and independence vote. From the way Washington has stepped in and handled different situations in the past, it is clear that the U.S. would rather keep things as they are, with few surprises and few risks. So far, the US seems to want Taiwan and the mainland to keep talking. This is based on Beijing's claim that there is only one China and that only one government has the right to speak for it. The US also seems to want a peaceful end to the conflict between Taiwan and the mainland. It doesn't support Taiwanese independence by itself, and it doesn't support the 1992 Consensus or the "one China, different interpretations" strategy either. But as China's rise to power becomes more and more dangerous, many people are starting to wonder if the US will change its mind and try to get Taiwan to stay farther away from China. Some DPP leaders think that even if Taiwan moves toward independence, the US reaction might be different from what it was in 2002–2004. This is because the US and the PRC have so many different interests in the East China Sea and the South China Sea. Still, the PRC may ask the US to clarify its stance on "one China" in the future for the same reason. Huang Jing says that Xi Jinping has always said that Taiwan is one of China's most important concerns, and he won't let Taiwan be used as a trading chip in talks with the US about the PRC's new relationship with the US. After so many years of talking to the US, Beijing is more and more sure that the US is serious about "not supporting Taiwanese independence." What remains to be seen is how much the PRC will let the US take advantage of Taiwanese anti-China feelings and implicitly support the DPP's claim that Taiwan is not part of China. From Washington's point of view, continuing to back cross-Strait dialogue based on the 1992 Consensus means stability in East Asia, but Taiwan may become more connected to mainland China. On the other hand, pushing for a new cross-Strait strategy without the 1992 Consensus opens up some new strategic options for the US and its East Asian allies, but it also puts Beijing at risk of retaliation. How Washington decides on this problem will have a big impact on how things will go in this area in the future.

Relations across the Strait are very difficult and hard to predict. When Ma Ying-jeou was chosen president of Taiwan, he was determined to make things better with mainland China. He was able to do this by reaching dozens of agreements with China. During his first time as president, things looked so good that some scholars thought it might be possible to write a peace treaty between the PRC and the ROC. But just a few years later, Taiwanese people spoke out about how worried and suspicious they were about how quickly things were getting better with China.

Compared to the years 2000–2008, the last eight years have been relatively peaceful and stable because the two sides have been able to talk to each other and work together in a positive way. But now that the DPP is back in charge of politics, people are talking about the unpleasant chance of a military conflict. Scott L. Kastner says, "It is possible to imagine a number of future events, such as a return of the DPP to power in Taiwan, a continued rise in Taiwan-centric identity despite deeper economic integration across the Strait, or a period of economic malaise in the PRC, that could cause Beijing to be less optimistic about long-term trends in the Taiwan Strait." If any of these things happen, you can't rule out a "preventive war fought to change unfavorable long-term trends." Kastner thinks that there are reasons to be hopeful about the short- to medium-term future of cross-Strait ties, but he also says that the current detente needs to be carefully managed all the time.

What will happen if the Tsai government keeps rejecting the 1992 Consensus? It's hard to answer this question. The PRC has many tools, including diplomatic, economic, political, and armed ones, to get the DPP back on the "one-China" track. The PRC can sneak up on Taiwan diplomatically by asking several countries to cut off official ties with Taiwan right away or by stopping its backing for Taiwan's membership in international groups. In terms of the economy, the PRC can make it harder for Taiwanese companies to get money to do business with China, stop Taiwanese goods and services from entering China, or limit the number of Chinese tourists who can visit Taiwan. Politically, it can stop all talks, meetings, academic cooperation, sports events, and culture exchanges across the Taiwan Strait. Military-wise, it can fire missiles again over the island, do military operations around Taiwan's harbors, break into the Air Defense Identification Zone, or send aircraft carriers and naval ships to police the Taiwan Strait. The people of Taiwan may feel more anger and contempt than fear because of these actions, but it might be hard for the PRC to do anything else.

Some of the steps will only hurt Taiwan, while others could make the US nervous and force it to take measures of its own. There may not be a full-scale war between China and the US (and its East Asian friends), but there could be a political stalemate or a military showdown. Since Tsai took office, China seems to be putting pressure on Taiwan in a way that gradually gets worse instead of using all the tools it has. As long as Tsai doesn't openly support Taiwan's independence, it's unlikely that China will use its military power against Taiwan. However, there are also no signs that China will give in to Tsai's rejection of the 1992 Consensus. Relations across the Taiwan Strait may be best described by the term "new detente" in the years to come.

Conclusion

Taiwan's national identity and how it affects ties with China might seem like a "domestic" issue or, at most, a problem between Taiwan and China. But as I've shown, this problem affects a lot more people than you might think at first look. It not only shows where different groups in Taiwan stand on the issue of unification vs. independence, but it also has to do with Xi Jinping's "Chinese Dream." It's not just about the US forming a maritime alliance against China; it's also about how countries are changing in the 21st century. If we don't pay enough attention to the political effects of a small island country's "domestic" problem, we won't be able to deal with one of the hardest problems East Asia is facing right now.

In political theory, national identity is a vague idea. Sometimes it means a person's sense of belonging to a certain ethnic or national group. Other times, it means a person's sense of being a citizen of a certain state. Nationalist scholarship tries to combine the two to show or predict how a nation-state will form, but this is not a good idea because the identity of a cultural group isn't always the same as the identity of a political community. When studying national identity, starting with the idea that the government unit and the cultural unit should be the same is a bad place to start.

All three of the most common ways to measure national identity in Taiwan—the Chinese/Taiwanese/both identity measure, the unification/independence measure, and the "Chinese Nationalist versus Taiwanese Nationalist" measure—tell us important things about the Taiwanese as a whole, but none of them tell us enough about their political identity. So, I'd like to suggest a fourth way that is often left out of Taiwan studies: looking at how people define their countrymen and homeland. When we look at it this way, Taiwan's national character is not as divisive as many scholars and politicians say it is. People in Taiwan may have different ideas about whether they are Chinese or Taiwanese, and they may also have different ideas about their political future (to unify with China or seek independence), but most of them like the status quo (neither unification nor independence), and maybe more than 85 percent of them know which country they are from.

But the question of how to deal with the one-China principle in the 1992 Consensus is a real problem in Taiwan, even though national identity is not a real or pressing issue in and of itself. During Mas's time in office, the government made twenty-one agreements with mainland China based on the 1992 Consensus. The DPP agrees with the signed agreements, but it won't discuss with the PRC until the 1992 Consensus is met. The new mainland policy of the DPP and how the CCP responds to it will affect the security of East Asia and make the already tense relationship between the PRC and the US even worse.

There are many ways that conflicts could be reduced across the Taiwan Strait. One would be to convince Tsai Ing-wen and the DPP that it would be good for Taiwan to keep cross-Strait relations based on the 1992 Consensus. However, Xi Jinping or the PRC would have to agree with the "different interpretations" part of the consensus as well as the "one-China" part, which is their favorite part of the consensus. In this situation, Tsai might be able to keep things the same if she sticks to the name ROC. Another option is for the U.S. and the PRC to finally agree that the 1992 Consensus is not the only way to keep peace and security in the Taiwan Strait, and for Tsai to come up with a new policy that is creative, realistic, and convincing. This would mean the end of the era of the 1992 Consensus and the start of a new era whose direction no one can predict right now. The third option would be to get everyone involved to talk about how the meaning of "one China" is changing and see if there is a better way to define or explain it that would work for everyone. It is hard to say which option would lead to the best result. But everyone involved should do their best to keep political tensions from getting worse and to keep people living in peace.

Chapter 3
China's Expansion Tactics and Taiwan's Resilience in Southeast Asia

In October 1949, the People's Republic of China (PRC) was founded, and China was formally split into two parts. Because of the civil war, the government of the Republic of China (ROC) fled to Taiwan in December 1949. Relations between the two sides of the Taiwan Strait have changed a lot in the last 60 years. There are four steps to these changes, which have had a big effect on how China and Taiwan get along in Southeast Asia.

From December 1949 to October 1971, the first stage was when the PRC was not yet a member of the United Nations (UN). Over the Taiwan Strait, there was a military standoff and a political fight between the PRC and the ROC, who both told the rest of the world that they were the real Chinese leaders. Because of its relationship with the United States, the ROC was able to keep formal diplomatic ties with Thailand, the Philippines, and the former Republic of Vietnam. On the other hand, the PRC was more or less alone in the region because it supported communist movements in Southeast Asia so much.

During the second stage, from October 1971 to July 1987, the PRC joined the United Nations and Taiwan's political isolation started. But the economy of the island kept growing, and it became known as one of the four Asian dragons. Under the "one-China" policy, countries could accept either the PRC or the ROC as the official government of China, but not both. This meant that the PRC could stop Taiwan from making more diplomatic connections. Because of this, the ROC lost all of its official ties to Southeast Asia in 1975. Even though there were only 23 official diplomatic partners for the ROC around the world by the middle of the 1980s, the number of Taiwan's regional offices in other countries kept growing. Because of something called "pragmatic diplomacy," there were 85 foreign representative offices in 1987.

From 1987 to 1997, the third stage took place. In July 1987, martial law was ended in the ROC. This was a big step forward for ties between the two sides of the Taiwan Strait. In May 1991, the time of mobilization to put down communist rebellion ended. This meant that the civil war with communists on the Chinese mainland was officially over. Slowly, more interactions between Taiwan and China began to happen. For example, the Straits Exchange Foundation (SEF) was set up in Taipei in March 1991, and the Association for Relations Across the Taiwan Straits (ARATS) was set up in Beijing in December 1991. But when it came to negotiation, neither side changed its mind. Taiwan's business ties with Southeast Asia kept getting stronger, while China's political power in the area kept growing.

The fourth phase of cross-Strait ties began in 1997 with the Asian financial crisis. China's economic power grew, while Taiwan's stayed pretty much the same. China was now an economic giant because it not only made its own money but also helped other economies in the area. This trend is still going on, and it has given China more power in the area. China keeps growing its political and economic power in Southeast Asia. It wants to replace the U.S. as the region's powerhouse. Because of this, Taiwan can no longer compete with China. Instead, it has to fight to stay alive, not just in Southeast Asia but all over the world.

China has set its expansion goals in order to build up its political economy in Southeast Asia. As a result, it has put in place a complete plan for building political and economic ties with countries all over the area. In the meantime, Taiwan's plan for staying alive is to keep growing economically and try to set up conditions that will let it connect politically and economically with Southeast Asian countries.

This chapter compares China's strategy for growth and Taiwan's strategy for staying alive in Southeast Asia, both of which have been going on since the turn of the century. It says that China's plan to grow has made it easier for it to get along with most Southeast Asian countries. But it faces problems that could stop it from growing more in the area. Even though Taiwan still faces the problems of political isolation and economic marginalization, its political resilience may help it stay alive in the international community. With the recent shift toward democracy in Southeast Asia, Taiwan has won more support and friendship in the region than China has been able to keep up with.

China's Southeast Asia Expansion : Forging a Dominant Economic and Political Landscape

During the Cold War, China didn't have much of an impact in Southeast Asia, even though it had official ties with all of the countries there by 1991. With the start of the Good Neighbor Policy in 1990, China started to change the way it dealt with other countries in the area. After the bloody massacre in Tiananmen

Square on June 4, 1989, the country tried to change its image. In August of 1990, China's leader at the time, Li Peng, went to Indonesia, Singapore, and Thailand. He went to Malaysia and the Philippines in December 1990. It was the first time a Chinese leader had been to five big Southeast Asian countries in just four months. The Asian giant had been on its own until 1991, when it was asked to the annual meeting of the Association of Southeast Asian Nations (ASEAN). In July 1996, it was accepted as a full dialogue partner. This was a good start for China's political relationships with other countries in Southeast Asia.

Because China had a strong currency in 1997, the Asian financial crisis gave China more chances to work with Southeast Asia. After the financial crisis, most currencies in Southeast Asia lost value. However, China's currency, the yuan (RMB), kept its value. This kept other currencies in Southeast Asia from falling even more. Southeast Asian countries had a hard time getting help from the United States and international financial organizations like the World Bank and the International Monetary Fund (IMF) that were controlled by the West. China, on the other hand, was quick to help by giving big loans and economic aid to countries in the region that were hurting.

Since the turn of the century, China has grown its political and economic ties with Southeast Asia and tried to replace the U.S. as the most powerful country in the area by creating a political economy there that is controlled by China. So, China's plan for Southeast Asia over the next 100 years is to fully dominate the area and bring it under its control. The plan has three parts. The first is to get more involved in regional politics. The second is to solve security problems with Southeast Asian countries. The third is to set up a new way to handle regional issues.

Getting more involved in political issues in the area. Even though China had good relationships with Burma and Laos during the Cold War, it didn't do much in the area before 1990. But things changed for the Asian giant in 1991, when it was invited to the Twenty-Fourth ASEAN Ministerial Meeting in Kuala Lumpur. Then, in July 1996, it was invited to the Twenty-Ninth ASEAN Ministerial Meeting in Jakarta and given the full position of a dialogue partner.

Since the turn of the century, China has kept improving its formal ties with the other countries in the area. This is clear from the many deals and talks that China and the ASEAN countries have made and attended. One of the most important was signed at the Seventh ASEAN-China Summit in Bali, Indonesia, in October 2003. It was a joint declaration on strategic partnership for peace and development. Around the same time, China signed the Treaty of Amity and Cooperation in Southeast Asia (TAC), making it the first ASEAN dialogue partner to join the deal. When China joined TAC, it became closer to its countries to the south.

At the Thirteenth ASEAN-China Summit in Ho Noi, China, in October 2010, ASEAN approved a four-year partnership plan for 2011–2015. This raised the level of political and strategic cooperation between the group and ASEAN. In November 2011, China opened the ASEAN-China Center (ACC) in Beijing. It is the first and only organization between China and ASEAN that is run by both governments. The ACC is a one-stop information center meant to encourage cooperation in a number of areas, such as trade, business, tourism, education, and culture. In September 2012, the PRC sent its first resident ASEAN ambassador to Jakarta and made an official purpose statement for its role in ASEAN. This again made its ties with the other countries in the area stronger.

In October 2013, at the 16th ASEAN-China Summit and the 10th anniversary of the ASEAN-China strategic partnership, China and ASEAN issued a joint statement about expanding bilateral cooperation in eleven priority areas: agriculture, information technology, human resources development, Mekong Basin development, investment, energy, transport, culture, public health, tourism, and the environment. The comment was a great example of how China works with Southeast Asia as a whole.

Southeast Asian countries have security problems that need to be solved. China has a long history of territorial conflicts with its Southeast Asian neighbors. One of the biggest is with Vietnam and the Philippines over a number of islands and reefs in the South China Seas. Before, China demanded that these territorial and security disputes be handled bilaterally with each Southeast Asian country. But China now seems ready to work with other countries on territorial and security issues through multilateral platforms. In November 2002, China and the ASEAN countries signed a Declaration on the Conduct of Parties in the South China Sea (DOC) after a number of talks and meetings. At the Fourteenth ASEAN-China Summit in Bali, Indonesia, in July 2011, rules for putting the DOC into action were agreed upon. At the summit, China's then-prime minister, Wen Jiabao, said that China would give RMB 3 billion to start the China-ASEAN Maritime Cooperation Fund. This fund would help ASEAN members with things like maritime scientific study, connectivity, and navigation safety.

In October 2013, at the Sixteenth ASEAN-China Summit, China and ASEAN talked about writing a Code of Conduct (COC). In 2014, there were two meetings to talk about how to adopt the DOC and talk more about how to build the COC. The Tenth ASEAN-China Joint Working Groups on the DOC took place in March in Singapore, and the Seventh ASEAN-China Senior Officials' Meeting on the DOC took place in April in Thailand. At the Conference on Interaction and Confidence Building Measures in Asia in May 2014, Chinese leader Xi Jinping said, "Things in Asia must be taken care of by Asians in the end, Asia's problems must be solved by Asians in the end, and Asia's security must be protected by Asians in the end." This showed that China was trying to get closer to Asian countries on security problems in the area and make things harder for the US and its Southeast Asian partners.

Even though the DOC and the COC have been faulted for being ineffective and moving slowly, a multilateral platform has been set up for China and ASEAN to talk about and deal with their long-standing disputes in the South China Seas. The people who signed the DOC have to follow ten points, such as respecting each other's views and working to make the South China Seas a peaceful, friendly, and harmonious place. But now it's not clear if the DOC and the COC are official documents or if all the people who signed up for conflict resolution have to follow them. Since January 1974, China and Vietnam have been going to war over a group of islands and rocks called the Paracel Islands. In January 1995, Chinese troops also stopped a Filipino fishing boat on Mischief Reef in the East Vietnam Seas. Even though things have calmed down a bit in the South China Seas since the DOC was signed in 2002, there were fights between China and the Philippines in late March 2014 and between China and Vietnam in May 2014.

Along with the DOC and the COC, China and ASEAN have made success on nontraditional security issues that have become more common since the turn of the century. The Joint Declaration of ASEAN and China on Cooperation in the Field of Non-Traditional Security Issues was signed by China and ASEAN leaders at the Sixth ASEAN-China Summit in November 2002. Since then, Chinese leaders have said again and again that China wants to work with Southeast Asia on security problems that are not typical. This was shown on October 30, 2006, when China's premier at the time, Wen Jiabao, said at the Tenth ASEAN-China Summit that China and ASEAN should expand their already successful economic networks and work together more on cross-border issues like counterterrorism, transnational crime, maritime security, rescue operations, and disaster relief.

In 2009, China and ASEAN signed a new Memorandum of Understanding on Cooperation in the Field of Non-Traditional Security Issues for the next five years, from 2010 to 2014. Since then, China has held a series of training workshops for ASEAN members to help them carry out a plan of action on these problems. The scope of these workshops has grown to include illegal drug and narcotics trafficking.

Setting up a new way to handle regional issues. For many years, the United States has been the most powerful country in the world. China has become the economic and political powerhouse of Asia since the turn of the century. It has been working on new ways to deal with international issues, especially in the Asia-Pacific area. The official start of the Boao Forum for Asia (BFA) was in February 2001. This showed that China wanted to set up a place to handle issues in the Asia-Pacific area. The forum is made up of 26 Asian and Australasian countries, and the PRC is not only one of the founding members but also a driving force in the international, non-governmental, nonprofit group.

Boao, Hainan, in the southern part of China, is where the permanent offices are. Article 3 of the BFA Charter says that the BFA was made to encourage and improve economic exchanges, interactions, and cooperation within the region and between the region and other parts of the world. Article 3 also says that the BFA should "provide high-level venues for dialogues between government leaders, private enterprises, academic institutions, and regional associations, so that they can talk about, trade, and develop ideas about economic, social, environmental, and related issues." At its annual general meetings, the most important issues are talked about. The BFA also sponsors other meetings and forums that talk about other concerns and issues related to Asia, such as the Youth Forum in 2010, the International Capital Conference in 2011, the Asia Financial Cooperation Conference in 2012, the SME Conference (for small and medium-sized businesses) in 2013, and the Energy, Resources, and Sustainable Development Conference in 2014. Clearly, the BFA has become an important place for Asian leaders, important businesses, and academics to talk about a wide range of problems in depth.

Annual BFA meetings are often attended by Chinese leaders and government officials. Many other political leaders, business tycoons, and well-known academics are also called. In 2008, when the BFA was also celebrating the 30th anniversary of China's open-door policy, the 20th anniversary of Hainan Province's Special Economic Area, and the opening of the 2008 Olympics in Beijing, the ROC's vice-president at the time, Vincent Siew, was asked to attend. This led to an important meeting between the vice-president of the ROC and Hu Jintao, who was president of the PRC at the time. China did have a very important year. At the same time, the number of people who went to BFA kept going up. There were 1,000 guests at BFA 2003, 1,700 at BFA 2008, and 2,800 at BFA 2015. Business tycoons from other countries have taken part in BFA, such as Bill Gates in 2013 and 2015 and Ratan Tata in 2014. Tata was the first Indian person to be chosen to serve on the BFA board. Given how bad things were between China and India at the time, this was a very unusual choice.

Since the BFA was started in 2001, it has become clear that China wants to use it to increase its power in Asian matters and make the US feel even worse about itself by preventing it from taking part. Indonesian political analyst Bambang Suryono says, "The Boao Forum will strongly push for the integration of Asia and the development of a common destiny for a closer-knit Asian community."

Chinese-Led Economic Growth

During the 20th century, China was not as important to Asia's economy as Japan, the US, or even the four "Dragons" (Hong Kong, Singapore, South Korea, and Taiwan). But in 2002, China started its "go global" program, which has changed the way it does business in the area. The goals of China's economic expansion are to create an economy in Southeast Asia that is dominated by China. This will be done by: 1) increasing trade with Southeast Asia, 2) increasing investment in the Southeast Asian region, 3) becoming a major source of tourism revenue in the Southeast Asian region, and 4) making a plan for more economic growth in the region.

Getting more business with Southeast Asia. The amount of trade a country does with other countries shows how strong its economy is. The economy of a country is stronger the more it trades with other countries. Most of the time, China and the United States can trade more with other countries because they are bigger and stronger. Before the Asian financial crisis, China didn't have much of an economic impact on Southeast Asia because it didn't deal much with other countries in the area. In 1997, China was ASEAN's eighth largest trade partner, after Japan, the United States, Hong Kong, Taiwan, South Korea, the United Kingdom, and Germany.

But because the Chinese economy kept growing during the Asian financial crisis, in 2000 China became ASEAN's sixth-largest export market, taking 3.5% of the market, and its fourth-largest importer, buying 5.2% of ASEAN's goods. In 2010, China was ASEAN's biggest export market (12.1% of the market) and import market (15.9% of the market) (see tables 10 and 11). In 2011, Japan was ASEAN's largest export market, overtaking China. However, China remained ASEAN's biggest importer and was also ASEAN's largest export market that year. In 2012, China did even more business with Southeast Asia. It bought 12.2% of all of ASEAN's goods and 16.2% of all of its imports. Most of these trends stayed the same in 2015, and they are likely to keep going in the years to come. China's foreign trade volume is growing faster with Southeast Asia than with any of its other top trading partners. This is because China's trade with Southeast Asia is growing quickly. As the PRC's exports to Southeast Asia have grown, these countries' trade deficits have grown and they have become more economically dependent on the Asian powerhouse. The PRC is now Southeast Asia's biggest trade partner, with more exports and imports than Japan, the EU, and the US combined. China will continue to be the trade leader in the area as economic integration and regionalization grow.

Table 3.1 ASEAN'S Leading Export Markets

	2010	**2011**	**2012**	**2013**	**2014**	**2015**
ASEAN	25.0	26.4	25.8	26.0	25.5	25.9
China	12.1	11.4	12.2	11.8	9.2	11.3
Japan	9.8	11.7	10	9.7	9.3	9.6
USA	9.5	8.6	8.6	9.0	9.5	10.9
EU	10.9	10.2	10	9.8	10.3	-

Sources: Figures for 2010 and 2011 come from ASEAN, ASEAN Statistical Yearbook. 2012 (Jakarta: ASEAN Secretariat, 2013), 78; figures for 2012 from the ASEAN Economic Community Chart Book 2013 (Jakarta, ASEAN Secretariat, 2013), 22; and figures for 2013 to 2015 from ASEAN Statistics, http://asean.org/storage/2016/06/table21_as-of-30- Aug-2016-2.pdf, accessed October 10, 2016.

Table 3.2 Leading ASEAN importers (% of market share)

	2010	**2011**	**2012**	**2013**	**2014**	**2015**
ASEAN	25.9	23.6	22.8	22.4	22.5	21.9
China	15.9	15.5	16.2	17.4.0	17.5	19.4
Japan	10.8	11.2	11.2	9.5	8.8	11.4
USA	9.0	8.1	7.5	7.4	7.3	7.6
EU	9.8	9.4	9.6	9.8	9.4	-

Sources: Figures for 2010 and 2011 come from ASEAN, ASEAN Statistical Yearbook 2012 (Jakarta: ASEAN Secretariat, 2012), 78; figures for 2012 from ASEAN, ASEAN Economic Community Chart Book 2013 (Jakarta: ASEAN Secretariat, 2013), 22; and figures for 2013 to 2015 from ASEAN Statistics, http://asean.org/storage/2016/06/table21_as- of-30-Aug-2016-2.pdf, accessed October 10, 2016.

Getting more money to Southeast Asia. Foreign direct investment (FDI) is another sign that a country's economy is doing well. The more foreign funding a country can get, the stronger its economy needs to be. This is shown by places like Japan, the United States, and China.

Because China's economy was weak throughout the 20th century, it only put a small amount of money into Southeast Asia. ASEAN's numbers show that China's share of FDI in Southeast Asia was less than 1% before the year 2000 (Table 3.3). From 1995 to 2003, it was an average of 0.29 percent per year, while the United States had an average of 16.47 percent and Japan was second with 12.90 percent of Southeast Asia's FDI.

Table 3.3 China's FDI share in ASEAN (%)

	1995	2000	2005	2011	2012	2013	2014	2015
China	0.49	0.19	1.4	8.1	4.7	5.1	5.4	6.8
Japan	20.12	4.03	15.5	10.0	20.8	19.8	12.1	14.5
USA	15.38	22.79	7.7	9.4	9.7	5.7	11.3	10.2
EU	17.98	35.83	27.5	30.4	15.8	19.6	19.2	16.4

Sources: Figures for 1995 and 2000 come from ASEAN, ASEAN Statistical Yearbook 2004 (Jakarta: ASEAN Secretariat, 2004), 146; figures for 2005 from ASEAN Statistical Yearbook 2012 (Jakarta: ASEAN Secretariat, 2012); figures for 2011, 2012, and 2013 from ASEAN Statistics table 27, "Top ten sources of foreign direct investment inflows in ASEAN," www.asean.org/wp-content/uploads/images/2015/January/foreign_direct_investment_statistic/Table%20 27.pdf, accessed February 10, 2015; and figures for 2013-15 from ASEAN Statistics, http://asean.org/storage/2015/09/ Table-272.pdf, accessed October 10, 2016.

China has been putting more money into ASEAN since 2010. Because of this, its total FDI grew gradually from 1.4% in 2005 to 8.1% in 2011. It did go down in 2012, to 4.7%, but then it went up to 5.4% in 2014, and then it went up again in 2015, to 6.8% (Table 3.3). Since 2011, China has become the third-largest foreign investor in Southeast Asia. This is a big change from the late 20th century, when it was the fifth-largest foreign investor in the region. Since China's economy is growing, it is certain that China will continue to spend more in Southeast Asia and become more important in the region's economy.

Southeast Asia's tourism is becoming a major source of income. Tourism is another thing that can show how strong a country's economy is. The stronger a country's economy, the more people from both inside and outside the country will visit. When a country pushes tourism in another country, that country becomes more important to the country that is hosting the tourists. During the 20th century, Europeans, Americans, Japanese, and people from the four Asian Dragon countries spent the most money on tourism in Southeast Asia. At that time, China wasn't a big deal when it came to tourists in ASEAN. In 1995, Chinese tourists to Southeast Asian countries made up only 2.8% of the market share in the area, compared to 11.1% from Japan, 7.2% from Taiwan, and 4.9% from the United States.

Since the turn of the century, there have been a lot more Chinese tourists all over Southeast Asia. China's market share was 5.9% in 2000, but it went up to 6.3% in 2007, 10.4% in 2012, and 12.4% in 2014 (see Table 3.4). But it should be mentioned that even in 2000, China was the second largest source of tourists to Southeast Asia, after Japan, with a 5.9% share. Since 2007, it has grown its share to 6.3% and become the country that brings in the most international tourists to Southeast Asia (ASEAN tourist business). Since 2007, the number of Chinese tourists in Southeast Asia has grown a lot and is still going up, while the number of Japanese and American tourists has been going down. This trend, which is likely to keep going for a long time, is another way that China is showing its power in the area.

Table 3.4 Distribution of Visitor Arrivals to ASEAN Nations by Country of Origin Percentage

	1995	2000	2005	2007	2011	2012	2013	2014
China	2.8	5.9	5.9	6.3	9.0	10.4	12.4	12.4
Japan	11.1	9.9	5.9	5.9	4.5	4.8	4.8	4.8
USA	4.9	5.0	4.4	4.1	3.5	3.3	3.1	3.1
EU	14.5	13.6	11.3	12.5	12.1	9.1	8.5	8.8

Sources: Figures for 1995 and 2000 are from ASEAN, ASEAN Statistical Yearbook, 2004 (Jakarta: ASEAN Secretariat, 2004), 228-29; figures for 2005 and 2007 from ASEAN, ASEAN Statistical Yearbook, 2012 (Jakarta: ASEAN Secretariat, 2012), 168; figures for 2011 and 2012 from ASEAN Statistics, table 30, "Top Ten Country/Regional Sources of Visitors to ASEAN," www.asean.org/wp-content/uploads/images/resources/2014/Jan/StatisticUpdate28jan/Tourism%20Update/ Table%2030.pdf, accessed February 10, 2015; and figures for 2012 to 2014 from ASEAN Statistics, www.asean.org/storage/2015/n/tourism/Table_30.pdf, accessed October 10, 2016.

Putting together a plan for geoeconomic development. Asia-Pacific Economic Cooperation (APEC) was started in 1989. At first, the United States took the lead in this group. But from 2000 to 2008, American leaders rarely attended APEC meetings because President Bush was busy with anti-terrorism policy. Not until July 2009, when former US Secretary of State Hillary Clinton announced the "Returning to Asia Policy" at the yearly ASEAN Regional Forum, did the US start to care again about what was going on in Asia and the Pacific. Since then, high-ranking US officials have said the same thing at different foreign events. In January 2012, US President Barack Obama said that the US would change its global military strategy by putting 60% of its troops in the Asia-Pacific region by 2020.

During the Bush era, when the US was getting less involved in Asia, China was growing its economic ties and political power in Southeast Asia. At the Fourth ASEAN-China Summit in November 2000, the Chinese president, Zhu Rongji, suggested a free trade zone with ASEAN. It was made public in November 2001, and on November 4, 2002, at the Sixth ASEAN-China Summit, it became law. In 2010, ASEAN set up the groundwork for its older members to join the ASEAN-China Free Trade Area (AFTA). In 2015, younger members joined. Even though AFTA is mostly about business, it has also had an effect on politics in the area.

China was able to get closer to ASEAN countries because of the geo-economic base.

Xi Jinping became the secretary general of the Chinese Communist Party (CCP) in November 2012, and in March 2013 he became the president of the PRC. As president, he kept China's strategy of expanding into Southeast Asia. During a trip to Kazakhstan in September 2013, he suggested the New Silk Road Economic Belt. This is the land-based part of his "One Belt, One Road" plan to connect China to Europe through central and western Asia. In a speech to the Indonesian parliament in October 2013, he suggested the Twenty-First Century Maritime Silk Road as the maritime part of this strategy. He also said that he planned to use the China-ASEAN Maritime Cooperation Fund to help China's grand development plan come to life.

Xi talked about this aggressive geo-economic plan again at the APEC Summit in November 2014 and again at the BFA in 2015. He said that China would put US$50 billion into the Asian Infrastructure Investment Bank (AIIB) and US$40 billion into the Silk Road Fund. This showed that Xi wanted to make a growing China the "center of a new Asian order." Even though the United States was against the AIIB, Southeast Asian countries and important European countries like the United Kingdom, Germany, France, and Italy were very supportive of it. On April 15, 2015, China said that 57 countries had joined the AIIB from the start.

Around the same time, China's premier Li Keqiang was also growing China's financial diplomacy in Southeast Asia. When Li went to Myanmar for the 25th ASEAN Summit in November 2014, he announced that China would lend US$20 billion to ten ASEAN countries for building projects. In December 2014, Li went to Bangkok for the fifth summit of the Greater Mekong Subregion (GMS). There, he promised another huge amount, US$11.5 billion, to the five GMS neighboring countries. This included US$1 billion for interconnected infrastructure, US$490 million to help fight poverty, and US$10 billion in special loans. Li also said that China would help Thailand build its first standard-gauge train line, which would be 800 kilometers long and cost about US$10.6 billion to build. In addition to working together on the rails, the Chinese president promised to help stop flooding in the area by spending $16.4 million to dredge waterways along the Mekong River.

In addition to the "One Belt, One Road" geoeconomic strategy and giving Southeast Asian countries more money, there are rumors that China is planning to build a massive transportation system that will connect China and Southeast Asia. This will help Southeast Asian countries improve their infrastructure and economies, and it will also increase China's economic and political power in the area.

Obstacles Facing China's Expansion Efforts in Southeast Asia

Even though China is expanding strongly in Southeast Asia, it still has to deal with four big problems.

How people in Southeast Asia see China as a "threat." China's strategy of expanding into Southeast Asia has made friends all over the region, but the growing hegemonic power doesn't seem to be getting much respect from its southern neighbors. This is mostly because China's land issues with Southeast Asian countries in the South China Sea are getting worse. China is often seen as a threat to the countries in Southeast Asia, while the United States is usually seen as a power that helps to keep things stable. This is the first thing China has to deal with.

Even though China and ASEAN signed the DOC and the COC, they are still at odds with Vietnam and the Philippines over who owns islands and rocks in the South China Seas. China put an HD-981 oil rig in Block 143 of Vietnam's Exclusive Economic Zone all on its own on May 2, 2014. China then moved in almost 80 ships, including warships from the People's Liberation Army military, to protect itself. The situation got worse when Vietnam sent out its Coast Guard to protect its territory and the Chinese captain told his ships to use water cannons to hurt the Vietnamese ships on purpose. In this case, the Chinese attack also hurt a few of the Vietnamese team members.

After the event, China and Vietnam met several times. But at a press conference in June 2014, Hong Lei, a spokesman for China's foreign minister, stuck to China's stance that the oil rig was put in China's traditional territory. ASEAN foreign ministers also said in public comments that they were very worried about what China was doing in the South China Seas. They asked everyone to follow international laws and rules, such as the DOC, the COC, and the UN Convention on the Law of the Sea. Even though China wasn't mentioned by name, the message still showed support for Vietnam. Japan and the US showed their support for Vietnam by saying that China's moves were too much.

The Vietnamese started a nationwide effort against China to protest what they saw as a Chinese "invasion" of their waters. In the south of Vietnam, protesters were so violent that they took over some foreign companies and shops and destroyed their doors, windows, and equipment inside. Most of the damage was done to workplaces and shops owned by Taiwanese people because protesters thought they were owned by Chinese people. In an interview, a Taiwanese manager who works in Vietnam said that the Vietnamese protests were really against Chinese workers in Taiwanese-owned companies. This made the Taiwanese and their properties the scapegoats in the incidents. Vietnam had campaigns against China in 2012 and 2013 because of a similar disagreement over who owned the South China Seas. But the May 2014 protest was the biggest one ever held in Vietnam, which is usually very Buddhist. It also happened at the same time that anti-Chinese feelings were getting a lot worse.

China has put both Vietnam and the Philippines in danger. During their annual security talks in 2015, Evan Garcia of the Philippines and Daniel Russel, the top US diplomat for East Asia, said that China's land reclamation in the disputed South China Seas was "massive" and "a clear violation" of the 2002 accord. They said this at a press conference. They did, however, agree that people should be able to sail on seas that don't belong to any country. When the Permanent Court of Arbitration in The Hague ruled in favor of the Philippines and against China's South China Sea claims in early July 2016, Filipino activists held a protest rally in front of the Chinese Consulate in Manila, calling for a "Chexit" and demanding that China leave Philippine territorial waters.

When President Rodrigo Duterte took office in July 2016, things changed for the Philippines. At the end of September 2016, he told people in Hanoi that he wanted to stop joint military drills with the United States, which has been a longtime friend of the Philippines, in the disputed South China Seas. From the time he took office, he was very hostile to then-President Barak Obama and to US policies in Asia. Because of these attacks, Obama stopped meeting with Duterte in September 2016 while he was at the ASEAN Summit in Vientiane. This move could affect how the Philippines and the US and the Philippines and China get along politically. In any case, it seems like a lot of Southeast Asian countries are very worried about a new, hostile Chinese Empire.

Coming into conflict with the major powers in the area. The second problem for China is that other big countries, like Japan and the United States, are getting more involved in Southeast Asia. Japan and China have also been having territorial conflicts over the Diaoyu Islands, also called the Senkaku Islands, in the East China Seas. When Shinzo Abe became prime minister of Japan in December 2012, he started a policy that was against China. This quickly made things worse between Japan and China. In the last three years, Mr. Abe has been to most of the Southeast Asian countries and has offered to help them more. Japan's military links with the US got stronger after the prime minister's successful trip to the US at the end of April 2015. At the beginning of February 2015, Japan's defense minister, General Nakatani, said that Japan was "deepening its cooperation with the US" and that the situation in the South China Seas had affected their national security. General Na-katani also said that Japan was committed to improving the surveillance powers of Vietnam and the Philippines.

Since July 2009, when Secretary of State Hillary Clinton announced the Asia rebalancing strategy, the United States has become even stronger in Southeast

Asia. At the Forty-Third ASEAN Foreign Ministers' Meeting in July 2010, Secretary Clinton said that the US would stay in Asia because of its "national interest in freedom of navigation, the maintenance of peace and stability, and respect for international law in the South China Sea.... The US shares these interests not only with ASEAN members but also with other maritime nations and the rest of the world."

At the Sixth East Asia Summit (EAS) in November 2011, where most Southeast Asian leaders were also present, US President Barack Obama talked to Chinese Premier Wen Jiabao directly about China's recent growth in the South China Seas. The first US president to go to the EAS was Barack Obama. In January 2012, President Obama also said that by 2020, 60 percent of the U.S. troops would be stationed in the Asia-Pacific area. This was a direct response to more Chinese aggression in the area. In April 2014, while on a trip to Asia, President Obama talked about the Philippines' problems with the resource-rich Spratly Islands. He said, "Our commitment to defend the Philippines is ironclad, and the United States will keep its commitment, because allies never stand alone. International law must be upheld." Freedom of navigation must be kept. Disputes must be settled calmly, not through threats or violence." Early in April 2015, President Obama also said, "We worry about China when it doesn't always follow international rules and norms and when it uses its size and power to push other countries into subordinate positions."

Members of the US Congress have also spoken out against China's recent land-grabbing and growth in the Spratly Islands. In mid-March 2015, four top US senators (John McCain, Bob Corker, Jack Reed, and Bob Menendez) sent letters to US secretary of state John Kerry and US secretary of defense Ash Carter saying that China's recent actions in the South China Sea were "a direct challenge, not only to the interests of the United States and the region, but to the entire international community" They also said that the United States should take "specific actions" to slow down or stop China from reclaiming land.

Due to the recent actions of Japan and the United States, there are more rumors that the two countries are working together to create a policy of "containment" toward China. This would make it more likely that China and the major powers in Southeast Asia will have to fight. This is a real problem that China needs to work hard to solve.

The economic difference between China and Southeast Asia is getting bigger. China's business ties with Southeast Asian countries have gotten better since the turn of the century. Its economic growth has also been faster than that of its neighbors to the south. This has made the gap between China's economy and those of most Southeast Asian countries bigger. Table 3.5 shows that China's

GDP per person in 2000 was US$949. This was just a little bit more than the GDP per person of Cambodia, Laos, Myanmar, and Vietnam, the four least developed countries in Southeast Asia. But China's GDP per person has gone up as its economy has grown. In 2015, China's GDP per person hit $7,925, which was only less than Singapore, Brunei, and Malaysia, the three most modern countries in Southeast Asia. China has a huge population of 1.3 billion people, so it's clear that its economic power and potential are much higher than those of Southeast Asia as a whole, where the population is only 600 million. The table shows that in 2013, China had the second-highest economic growth rate among all the Southeast Asian countries. As the economic gap between China and Southeast Asia keeps getting bigger, its economy is likely to grow in the near future.

Table 3.5 also shows that the gap between China and the countries with the weakest economies is getting bigger, while the gap between China and Malaysia, Brunei, and Singapore is getting smaller. These three countries are still ahead of the dominant power. In 2015, China's GDP per person was $7,925, which was just a little less than Malaysia's ($9,657). This is very different from China, whose GDP was only $949 in 2000, while Malaysia's was $3,844 that same year. In 1996, China had a GDP per person of $703, which was a lot less than Thailand's $3,134. But in 2011, China's GDP per person (US$5,447) was more than Thailand's (US$5,116) for the first time. Since then, the difference in GDP per person between the two countries has only grown. In 2015, China had a GDP per person of $7,925, while Thailand had a GDP per person of $5,737. When China's huge economy and growth rate are compared to those of its southern neighbors, there has been a rising sense that something isn't fair.

Tensions are rising between new Chinese immigrants and people who already live there. Lastly, there are more and more problems between new Chinese immigrants and local people in Southeast Asian countries. This is a problem that the Chinese have to deal with. When China started doing more business and investing in Southeast Asia around the turn of the century, Chinese residents moved into most of the countries and brought Chinese goods, shops, restaurants, hotels, and casinos with them. Some of these Chinese investments have been very controversial because building projects like dams and highways have caused a lot of damage to the environment. People in the area have also lost their land and jobs because of these projects.

China's growing interests in Laos are a good example of this. One investor from the Lao People's Democratic Republic said he was worried that his people were slowly losing their independence because China was taking over more and more of their land and wealth. One news source in Hong Kong called China's recent economic growth in Laos and the resulting tensions between Chinese immigrants and Laotians "reckless nationalism."

Table 3.5 Economic Disparities between China and Southeast Asian Nations (GDP per capita in US$ and GDP growth rates)

	China	Brunei	Cam-bodia	Indo-nesia	Laos	Malay-sia	Myan-mar	Philip-pines	Singa-pore	Thai-land	Viet-nam
1996	703	17,096	312	1,167	393	4,766	109	1,184	25,127	3,134	337
1998	821	11,961	268	488	244	3,257	144	896	20,892	1,900	361
2000	949	18,469	288	807	375	3,844	192	978	23,007	1,976	403
2002	1,135	17,158	309	932	369	3,884	136	956	21,098	2,001	440
2004	1,490	21,863	392	1,105	487	4,877	191	1,039	25,791	2,501	555
2006	2,069	29,922	515	1,636	645	5,902	233	1,351	30,053	3,164	725
2009	3,744	28,454	735	2,362	913	7,215	538	1,828	37,960	3,946	1,128
2011	5,447	42,431	881	3,497	1,262	9,962	868	2,339	51,247	5,116	1,404
	6,808	39,678	1,046	3,466	1,505	10,420	916	2,706	55,183	5,678	1,908
2013	(7.7%)	(-1.8%)	(7.0%)	(5.8%)	(8.2%)	(4.7%)	(7.5%)	7.2%)	(3.9%)	(2.9%)	(5.4%)
2014	7,587	41,505	1,105	3,526	1,741	11,153	1,277	2,854	55,904	5,892	2,053
	7,925	30,942	1,198	3,357	1,831	9,657	1,246	2,850	52,744	5,737	2,109
2015	(5.9)	(-0.6)	(7.1)	(4.8)	(7.6)	(5.0)	(7.1)	(5.8)	(2.0)	(2.8)	(6.7)

Sources: China's figures are from World Bank, "GDP per Capita (Current $US)," http://data.worldbank.org/indicator/NY.GDP.PCAP.CD, and "GDP Growth (Annual %)," accessed March 12,2015, http://data.worldbank.org/indicator/NY.GDP.MKTP.KD.ZG. Figures for the 1996 to 2006 ASEAN countries statistics come from ASEAN, ASEAN Statistical Yearbook 2003 (Jakarta: ASEAN Secretariat, 2003) and ASEAN Statistical Yearbook 2008 (Jakarta: ASEAN Secretariat, 2008); figures for 2009 to 2013 ASEAN GDP per capita figures are from ASEAN, table 7, "Gross Domestic Product per Capita in ASEAN, at Current Prices (Nominal), in US Dollars as of December 2014," www.asean.org/storage/2o15/o1/macroeconomics/T7-dec14.pdf; ASEAN's 2013 economic growth rates are from ASEAN, table 2, "Selected Key ASEAN Macroeconomic Indicators as of December 2014," www.asean.org/storage/images/2o15/January/ selected_key_indicators/table2_as%2oof%2oDecember%2O2oi4_R2.pdf; 2015 growth rates are from World Bank, "GDP Growth, Annual Percent," http://data.worldbank.org/indicator/ NY.GDP.MKTP.KD.ZG, accessed February 12, 2015.

Different ways of life and cultures have also brought new Chinese newcomers and local people into conflict. For example, since the turn of the century, about a million Chinese people have moved to Singapore, making it the place where the most Chinese people have moved. But there is a big difference between them and the people who live there. This is mostly because they don't know much about the local culture or the strict laws. In the general election in May 2011, one of the representative districts for the People's Action Party (PAP), which was in power, was lost. This was mostly because many Singaporeans didn't like how the PAP government always handled immigrants. When asked about the new Chinese immigrants, one Singaporean said, "Singaporeans look down on mainlanders as country bumpkins, and they look down on us because we don't speak proper Chinese."

Two decades of field research in Singapore, Thailand, Malaysia, Indonesia, the Philippines, and all of Southeast Asia except East Timor show that tensions are rising between new Chinese newcomers and people who were born there. Anti-immigration feelings have also been growing in Thailand as of late. At the moment, though, this seems to be more about cheap foreign workers from Myanmar, Laos, and Cambodia than it is about the Chinese.

Preserving Taiwan's Political Economy in Southeast Asia: Strategies for Survival

In contrast to China, which has an aggressive plan for expanding into Southeast Asia, Taiwan, which is smaller and less powerful diplomatically, has had to come up with a way to stay alive in the region and build relationships with its Southeast Asian neighbors. Taiwan's goal in politics is to keep the strong ties it already has with the most important countries in Southeast Asia. This means: 1) not using an aggressive "scorched-earth diplomacy" like the one used by former president Chiu Shui-bian, and instead using President Ma Ying-jeou's "diplomatic truce" approach; and 2) increasing Taiwan's political interactions with major Southeast Asian countries.

Changing "Scorched-Earth Diplomacy" into a "Diplomatic Truce" Taiwan's government has changed hands several times since the turn of the century. From 2000 to 2008, the Democratic Progressive Party (DPP) was elected for two terms, and from 2008 to 2016, the Chinese Nationalist Party (Kuomintang) was elected for two terms. Chen Shui-bian of the DPP and Ma Ying-jeou of the KMT had very different ideas about how to deal with China. The DPP government took a more hostile attitude to politics, which hurt Taiwan's relationships with other countries in Southeast Asia.

During his time in office, President Chen started his "scorched-earth diplomacy," which was a zero-sum game in which Taiwan went to great lengths to get China's diplomatic partners to leave in order to increase Taiwan's number of diplomatic partners at China's cost. Taiwan's goal in making this strategy was to win more political and economic ground. Some experts, like Yasuhiro Matsuda, say that Chen's diplomacy was mostly caused by a change in the DPP's internal politics. On the other hand, others, like Elizabeth Larus, say that Taiwan was using "soft power" to get more international respect. In any case, it backfired and made things worse between Taiwan and Southeast Asia. It also made the US government so angry that when Chen was on an official trip to Latin America in May 2006, it wouldn't let his plane stop in San Francisco to refuel. China already didn't trust President Chen because he supported "Taiwanization" policies, which China saw as controversial and possibly a step toward Taiwanese claims of independence. So, China stepped up its own competitive moves by blocking Taiwan in many international arenas and making aggressive diplomatic moves, causing Taiwan to lose nine of its diplomatic partnerships and reducing the number of countries with which it had official diplomatic ties.

Even though Chen kept up Taiwan's "southward policy" of building relationships with Southeast Asia, his fights with China in 2002 made things worse for Taiwan's relationships with its Southeast Asian allies. During the 1990s, Taiwan and its Southeast Asian neighbors had a lot of conversations and visits from high-level government leaders. For example, in February 1994, former president Lee Teng-hui went to three Southeast Asian countries. From 1991 to 1996, Mr. Habibie, who used to be Indonesia's state minister for science and technology, went to Taiwan three times. During Chen's rule, these kinds of conversations happened much less. When vice-president Annett Lu made an unplanned trip to Indonesia in mid-August 2002, China put pressure on the Indonesian government to say that Taiwan was an important part of the PRC.

When President Ma Ying-jeou took office in May 2008, he tried to make peace with China. This made things better not only across the Taiwan Straits but also with the United States, which has been one of Taiwan's most important political and economic friends for a long time. He thought that since China's power was growing around the world, it would be better to be friendly with the mainland because this would make things more safe and peaceful for Taiwan. Ma's plan made it much harder for China to stop Taiwan and gave Taiwan more freedom to act in foreign settings. From 2008 to 2016, he was in charge of Taiwan's government. During his time in office, Taiwan kept all but one of its diplomatic relationships and made great political progress in Southeast Asia.

President Tsai Ing-wen was sworn in on May 20, 2016. She started a "new southward policy" right away. This policy was meant to improve Taiwan's overall relationships in Southeast Asia even more than what her predecessors had done. This might help Taiwan's relationships with other countries, but since the president won't accept the 1992 Consensus, the success of this strategy is very uncertain. Relations across the Taiwan Strait have gotten worse since she took office. In the coming years, China may make it hard for Taiwan to do business and politics in Southeast Asia.

Getting more involved in Southeast Asia's political life. During President Ma's time in office, relations across the Taiwan Strait were calmer, so Taiwan could have more formal talks with Southeast Asian countries. Southeast Asia's most important countries sent high-level government officials to Taiwan, where they met and talked with high-level officials from both countries. Most of the time, though, these weren't talked about in the news.

In 2010, for example, Taiwan and Singapore started talking about making a deal to work together economically. The Agreement between Singapore and the Separate Customs Territory of Taiwan, Penghu, Kinmen, and Matsu on Economic Partnership (ASTEP) was signed on November 7, 2013. Then, on March 25, 2015, when President Ma Ying-jeou heard that Singapore's former prime minister Lee Kuan Yew had died, he went on a secret trip to pay his last respects to the leader of Singapore and the city-state's founder. Singapore was the site of an important meeting between President Ma Ying-jeou of Taiwan and President Xi Jinping of China in early November 2015. But the meeting didn't lead to any deals between the two leaders. So far, Singapore is the only country that has won the trust of both of these governments, which shows just how unique their relationship is.

Taiwan has put the most money into Vietnam out of all the Southeast Asian countries. Taiwan's ties with Vietnam also got a lot better after President Ma took office. In January 2009, Taiwan and Vietnam signed an agreement to work together on science and technology. In September 2011, Taiwan's Minister of Finance Lee Sush-der went to Vietnam and saw the signing of the Memorandum of Understanding on Financial Cooperation between Taiwan and Vietnam. In May 2012, Taiwan and Vietnam signed the Memorandum of Understanding on Tourism Cooperation. In November 2012, Taipei was the site of the first Taiwan-Vietnam Conference on Tourism Cooperation. Vietnam's statistics show that 409,385 Taiwanese people visited Vietnam in 2013. This was a 13.39 percent increase from the year before, making Taiwan Vietnam's fifth-largest source of foreign tourists. More than 90,000 Vietnamese went to Taiwan in 2013, which is a 40% rise from 2012. In 2014, there were about 150,000 Vietnamese foreign workers in Taiwan. There were also about 90,000 Vietnamese wives and 5,000 Vietnamese students. In the coming years, the two countries are likely to keep getting closer to each other.

The political link between Taiwan and Indonesia is also important. From 2009 to 2013, there were a number of high-level meetings between the two countries. In 2010, Indonesia's ministers of education and economics came to visit, and the minister of economics went back to Indonesia in 2011. In 2013, the ministers of finance, the Economic Development Council, and education all came to visit. In 2009 and 2012, the head of the Overseas Chinese Affairs Council went there, and in 2009 and 2013, the head of the Mainland Affairs Council did the same. In the same time period, high-ranking Indonesian officials who went to Taiwan included the minister of fisheries, Fadel Muhammad, in 2010 and

2011, the minister of labor, Muhaimin Iskandar, in 2011, the deputy minister for coordinating economic affairs, Rizal Lukman, in 2013, and the deputy minister of agriculture, Rusman Heriawan, in 2013. In 2010, Indonesia and Taiwan signed the "One Village, One Product, and Agri-Business Cooperation Plan." In 2012, they signed a memorandum of understanding on cooperation in immigration, human trafficking, and stopping smuggling, as well as an agreement on agricultural and technical cooperation.

Because President Ma improved political ties, most Southeast Asian countries gave Taiwanese citizens either visa-free privileges, like in Singapore and Malaysia, or arrival visas, like in Thailand, Indonesia, Cambodia, Laos, Brunei, and Timor-Leste. Malaysia was the last big Southeast Asian country to let Taiwanese people visit without a visa in 2011. Because of these special rights, Taiwanese people now have easy access not only to trade and invest in Southeast Asia, but also to socialize and learn about other cultures in the area.

Since May 2016, President Tsai Ing-wen has been trying to get Taiwan and its Southeast Asian friends to get along much better. Even though China might try to stop it, Taiwan plans to have more formal talks with its southern neighbors.

Enhancing Taiwan's Economic Ties with Southeast Asia

In Southeast Asia, Taiwan had already built a strong economy by the 1990s. If Taiwan wants to keep doing well economically in the area, it will need to build better economic ties with its southern neighbors and keep signing agreements and memorandums that focus on business. In September 2011, Taiwan and Vietnam signed an agreement on customs administration cooperation. In October 2014, Taiwan and the Philippines signed a memorandum of understanding on the promotion of trade and business. With the signing of these official documents, politically isolated Taiwan might be able to do three things to improve its economic ties with Southeast Asian countries: 1) improve its economic ties with Southeast Asian countries; 2) build a platform for economic interactions between countries in the region; and 3) keep trying to join economic blocs in the region.

Getting Taiwan's economic ties with Southeast Asia stronger. As was already said, foreign investment and the amount of trade with other countries are two important signs of a country's economic health and its ties with other countries. The closer a country's economic ties are to another country, the more trade and business that country does with that country.

Before 1980, Taiwan's economy was not as developed as it is now, so it did not trade or spend much in Southeast Asia. But starting in the middle of the 1980s, Taiwan started to improve its economic ties with Southeast Asia. This was partly because Taiwan's currency gained value against the U.S. dollar and partly because Taiwan's economy started to grow quickly in the early 1980s.

In 1990, Taiwan's trade with the ten ASEAN countries in Southeast Asia was worth only US$11.02 billion. In 1995, it was worth US$25.54 billion, and in 2000, it was worth US$38.71 billion. Taiwan's trade in Southeast Asia has continued to grow since it started its "southward policy." In 2005, it did a total of US$48.53 billion worth of business. It went up to US$70.84 billion in 2010 and US$93.64 billion in 2014. But in 2015, it went down to US$79.3 billion, which is a big change (Table 3.6). Table 3.6 shows that Taiwan's share of trade with Southeast Asia went from 9 percent in 1990 to 13.4 percent in 2000 and then to 15.6 percent in 2015. Another important fact is that since 2010, Southeast Asia has become Taiwan's second-biggest trade partner, after China.

At the opening ceremony of the 2014 Asian MICE (Meetings, Incentives, Conferences, and Events) Forum in September 2014, W. S. Chiang, Taiwan's deputy director of the Bureau of International Trade, said that Southeast Asia was becoming a great place for global businesses and manufacturing industries to show off their products and that the Taiwanese government would keep working to improve the economy in this part of the world. This sentence shows how Taiwan has kept up its attempts to improve its business relationships with Southeast Asian countries.

The island is improving its economic ties with Southeast Asia by putting most of its foreign investments there. At the beginning of the 1990s, Taiwan didn't have much foreign investment in Southeast Asia. Since then, it has put a lot more money into the area. Taiwan's investments in Southeast Asia reached a high point of US$5.1 billion in 1994. However, after the Asian financial crisis in 1998, Taiwan's investments in Southeast Asia went down. In fact, the 1990s were Taiwan's best time to invest in Southeast Asia. At the time, Taiwan was one of the top foreign investors in the area, especially in Vietnam, where it was either the largest or second-biggest source of foreign investment for more than 20 years.

Taiwan's investments in Southeast Asia have gone up and down a lot since the turn of the century, as shown in Table 3.7. It reached its peak in 2008, when Taiwan spent a total of US$12.4 billion in the area. After the 2008 financial crisis, Taiwan's investments in Southeast Asia went down for three years, but in 2012, they went back up to US$5.8 billion. But the total amount invested changed from 2013 to 2015 (Table 3.7). Even though the numbers have gone up and down over the last 20 years, the table shows that Taiwan is still interested in spending in Southeast Asia.

Table 3.6 Trade Figures and Market Share of Taiwan in Southeast Asia (in US$ billion)

Year	1990	1995	2000	2005	2008	2010	2012	2013	2014	2015
Trade volume	11.02	25.54	38.71	48.53	64.60	70.84	88.07	91.37	93.64	79.3
Share of total trade	9.0	11.8	13.4	12.7	12.9	13.4	15.3	15.8	15.9	15.6

Source: Taiwan's trade share and totals with Southeast Asia calculated at Bureau of Foreign Trade, Ministry of Economics, Republic of China, http://cus93.trade.gov.tw/FSCI/, accessed October 10, 2016.

Creating a bridge between Taiwan and Southeast Asia. In the last 30 years, Taiwan has put in place a number of policies to boost economic growth and improve business ti ,kes with other countries in the Asia-Pacific area. During the 1990s, Taiwan's then-ruling KMT party suggested setting up an Asia-Pacific Regional Operations Center (APROC) to make Taiwan a center for economic activities in the area. This plan did not work, though, because in May 2000, when President Chen Shui-bian took office, power was democratically given to the DPP. The new government then came up with a plan called "Green Silicon Island" for Taiwan's future economic growth. When Ma Ying-jeou became president of the KMT in May 2008, the plan had to be scrapped.

At first, President Ma tried to bring back the APROC, but in 2012, he came up with the idea of the Free Economic Pilot Zones (FEPZs). Its main goal was to make Taiwan a free economic zone so that it could improve economic ties with countries all over the Asia-Pacific region. The main goals of the FEPZ were to allow free movement of money, people, and things through deregulation, open markets, internationalization, institutional reform, and international alignment. Ma said that FEPZs would bring Taiwan's open market in line with other regional economies, give tax breaks for buying land, encourage industrial cooperation across borders, and make a good place to do business. The first step of the FEPZs started in August 2013, and it included six of Taiwan's harbors. Several laws had to be passed for the second stage, but disagreements between the KMT and its opponents, the DPP, stopped the plan from going any further.

Table 3.7 Investment by Taiwan in Southeast Asia (1990-2015, in US$ billion)

1959-89	1990	1994	1997	2000	2004	2008	2010	2012	2013	2014	2015
5.1	4.1	5.1	4.8	1.6	1.9	12.4	2.3	5.8	1.3	2.7	2.1

Source: "Woguo zai dong xie geguo touzi tongji biao" [China's investment statistics in the ASEAN countries], http:// twbusiness.nat.gov.tw/old/pdf/inv_3.pdf.

Now, President Tsai Ing-wen's government is putting the new southward strategy into action and trying even harder to improve Taiwan's relations with the rest of Southeast Asia. Even though Taiwan's political problems sometimes get in the way of its economic growth plans, the country has no choice but to move forward.

Trying to join regional economic blocs is still going on. The ten countries that make up ASEAN are all in Southeast Asia. This organization has made a number of free trade agreements with major neighboring countries, such as its 10 Plus 1, 10 Plus 3, and 10 Plus 6 deals, and they have all been successful. This organization is also continuing to grow its economic integration and cooperation.

Recently, the formation of two more regional economic blocs has drawn a lot of attention from around the world. The Regional Comprehensive Economic Partnership (RCEP) and the Trans-Pacific Partnership (TPP) are the names of these two agreements. The RCEP was first talked about at the 19th ASEAN Summit in November 2011. It was made up of members from the 10+6. At the Twenty-First ASEAN Summit, which was held in November 2012 in Cambodia, all sixteen of the leaders of its member countries agreed with it. Its goal is to make trade and investment easier, which will help the economy grow, make it easier for businesses to work together, and make the region's economy more integrated. In June 2016, the sixteen countries that took part finished the thirteenth round of talks about topics like goods and services, investment, intellectual property, and how to settle disagreements. Even though the talks are behind schedule, they are going well and a final draft should be ready soon.

The TPP is basically an expansion of the Pacific Three Closer Economic Partnership (P3 CEP), which is made up of Chile, Singapore, and New Zealand. So that Brunei could join, it was changed to the Trans-Pacific Strategic Economic Partnership (TPSEP, or P4) in 2005. In January 2008, the U.S. showed interest in talking with the P4 countries, and when President Barack Obama took office in January 2009, he also reaffirmed America's pledge to the TPP. Since the end of 2014, participating countries have had nineteen formal rounds of negotiations about TPP-related issues, such as cooperation and capacity building, cross-border services, e-commerce, financial services, government procurement, intellectual property, and getting rid of tariffs and other trade and investment barriers.

Even though Taiwan is in the Asia-Pacific region, it is politically separated, which makes it hard for it to join the economic blocs in that area. A country can join ASEAN in at least four ways: as a full member, as an observer, as a candidate member, or as a conversation member. Taiwan has worked very hard over the past 30 years to make a link with ASEAN. China's ongoing political and economic blockage, which continues to hurt Taiwan's economic growth, has stopped these plans from going forward.

In September 2013, Taiwan's government said that it wanted to join both the RECP and the TPP. At an international meeting in Taipei on February 17, 2014, President Ma Ying-jeou said that Taiwan had made it a "unshakable goal" to join the RCEP and TPP, and that it would work "simultaneously" to join the two trade blocs as soon as possible. Ma also said that Taiwan already had a 34.4 percent share of trade with the 12 countries that were negotiating the TPP and a 56.6 percent share of trade with the 16 states that were negotiating the RCEP in 2013. At the Boao Forum 2015 on March 29, 2015, Vice President Vincent Siew of Taiwan talked with President Xi Jinping of China. The vice-president of the ROC at the time said that Taiwan was also ready to join the AIIB. Two days later, on March 31, Taiwan's government sent a formal application to join the AIIB. They wanted to be a founding member of the PRC-led financial body.

Taiwan has had a hard time getting into regional economic blocs, but it has managed to reach deals with China, Singapore, and New Zealand that are similar to free trade. These include the Cross-Straits Economic Cooperation Framework Agreement (ECFA), which went into effect in August 2010; the Agreement between New Zealand and the Separate Customs Territory of Taiwan, Penghu, Kinmen, and Matsu on Economic Cooperation (AN-ZTEC), which went into effect on December 1, 2013; and ASTEP, which went into effect on March 19, 2014. In March 2013, talks between Taiwan and the US about a Trade and Investment Framework Agreement got back on track.

One study says that between 23% and 27% of foreign companies would put more money into Taiwan if the island could join these new business groups in East Asia. Taiwan must continue to work hard to join business groups in the region.

Challenges for Taiwan's Survival

Isolation on the political stage and an uncertain future. As we've seen, Taiwan has been able to build strong, stable relationships with the most important Southeast Asian countries. But a close friendship is not the same as an official diplomatic bond. Even though Taiwan has been in this awkward position for more than 30 years, there isn't much chance that it will change in the near future.

In the past, Taiwan's foreign survival was mostly due to US support and China's political and economic weaknesses. But as China builds a stronger political economy, its strong influence on international politics, its strategic relationship with the US, and the possibility of a US-China alliance in international affairs make it hard for Taiwan to stay diplomatically isolated.

Since the ROC government ended martial law in July 1987, there has been a lot of talk about whether Taiwan should join China, stay the same, or try to be independent. China has said for decades that if it needs to, it will use armed force to "liberate" Taiwan. In 1992, only 17.6% of the people said that they were only Taiwanese. But this number has been slowly going up, from 36.9% in 2000 to 52.79% in 2010 and 60.66% in 2014. In June 2016, the number went down a little, to 59.3 percent. The number of Taiwanese people who say they are only Chinese has also been going down, from 25.5% in 1992 to 3.5% in 2014 and 3.0% in June 2016. The number of people who say they are both Taiwanese and Chinese has also been going down, from 46.4 percent in 1992 to 32.5 percent in 2014, with a slight rise to 33.6 percent in June 2016.

Chengchi University's Election Study Center says that the number of Taiwanese who want to keep things as they are but eventually move toward independence has steadily gone up, from 8% in 1994 to 18% in 2014 and then to 19% in June 2016. On the other hand, the number of Taiwanese who want to keep things as they are but move toward unification has gone down, from 15% in 1994 to 7.9% in 2014 and then to 8% in June 2016. So, even though China's political and economic power is rising and it is making diplomatic and economic progress, the island still feels separate from the mainland because more people are claiming Taiwanese identity.

China is now Taiwan's biggest economic partner, making up about half of its world trade and seventy percent of its foreign direct investment (FDI). Based on the Economic Cooperation Framework Agreement (ECFA), which Taiwan and China signed in June 2010, Taiwan is likely to become more economically dependent on China in the coming years. China plans to use economic means to reach its political goal of unifying with Taiwan, but politically isolated Taiwan continues to focus on achieving economic growth without giving up its political autonomy.

Because of how the political economy between Taiwan and China is changing, Taiwan's leaders and people will always have to deal with tough problems about Taiwan's future.

Economic Exclusion and Development in the Future. During the Cold War, Taiwan was called one of the four Asian Dragons because it had done well economically and opened up to the rest of the world early on. This chapter has shown many ways in which the island's growing business ties with Southeast Asia go beyond diplomacy. During a speech at the annual dinner of the Asia Society in mid-June 2002, former US Secretary of State Colin Powell said, "I call Taiwan a problem of a success story." He was talking about Taiwan's strong economy and democracy. Taiwan's economic success has given it a good name around the world and helped it become more democratic.

China and most Southeast Asian countries have also started to open up to the rest of the world since the end of the Cold War in the early 1980s. These Asian countries have been working hard to make regionalization of the economy happen. But even though Taiwan keeps trying to join business groups in the region, the PRC's politics keep it on the outside. Before, Taiwan's economic success was mostly due to the island's openness and freedom, but now the island's economic neglect keeps it from getting a fair share of the Asia-Pacific market, which is becoming more open and integrated. Time will tell what Taiwan will do to stay alive in spite of being on the outside of the economy.

A number of macroeconomic measures have shown that Taiwan's economy has been getting worse since the turn of the century. Taiwan's economy grew by 6.42 percent in 2000, then 5.62 percent in 2006, 2.23 percent in 2007, and 2.23 percent in 2013. Since 2011, Taiwan's economy has grown by less than 5% a year. This is especially surprising when you consider that by 2013, most Southeast Asian countries had growth rates of more than 5% a year. Concerns about Taiwan's slowing economic growth include the fact that the contribution of public enterprises to the GDP has been less than 2% since 2004, and that the contribution of government capital to the GDP has steadily gone down from 5.44 percent in 2000 to 4.13 percent in 2008 and 2.86 percent in 2014. These numbers show that Taiwan's economy hasn't grown much since the turn of the century because the government hasn't invested enough in it. This downturn has happened at the same time that Southeast Asian economies have become more connected, while Taiwan has stayed on its own. If Taiwan continues to be economically left behind, it will be very hard for the economy to grow in the future.

Conclusion

Taiwan's economic growth has made it a big deal around the world, and it has definitely helped the country get along better with Southeast Asian countries. Even though the political economy in the region has gotten better, it still faces major problems like diplomatic isolation and being left out of the economy. This chapter looked at what Taiwan is doing to get along with its southern neighbors. The government of President Tsai Ing-wen will need to keep building ties with Southeast Asia. Even though Taiwan's new southward strategy may seem like a good idea, political isolation, economic marginalization, and China's interference and blocking will make it hard for Taiwan to improve its relationships with Southeast Asia. Taiwan doesn't compete with China in the international community, but it can't stop China from forcing the one-China policy, which affects Taiwan's political and economic growth in the future.

From the 1950s to the 1980s, Asian values were practiced, promoted, and used to back political authoritarianism. This could have a big effect on Taiwan's relationships with Southeast Asia and China. This was very different from Western ideals, which seem to be more accepted by everyone today. But China still promotes a culture and set of principles that support Asian values.

Since the end of the 1980s, a lot of Asian countries have changed from dictatorships to democracies. When the People's Power Revolution overthrew Ferdinand Marcos in February 1986, the Philippines became the first country in Asia to switch to a democracy government. After a long time under martial law, which ended in July 1987, Taiwan also began to move toward freedom. President Roh Tae-woo was democratically chosen as the leader of the Republic of Korea in February 1988. This was a big change in politics. Even though Thailand has been a democracy in theory since 1932, it changed its constitution in 1997. But the riots in May 1992 show that Thailand's democracy still has some problems. Since May 1998, when previous President Suharto was removed from power, democracy has also been put in place in Indonesia.

Asia has made a lot of progress toward democracy over the past two to three decades. This seems to be a value that everyone in the region shares. This includes Indonesia, which is a Muslim country, the Philippines, which is a Catholic country, and Buddhist countries like Taiwan and South Korea. Even though Taiwan's international isolation is hard, the island's move toward democracy has been a good example for other countries in the area. China and its officials will also have to deal with this in the future.

Chapter 4
Social Entrepreneurship and Online Platforms in Post-Developmental State Taiwan

In this chapter, I use social entrepreneurship as a way to look at how the relationship between the state and society in Taiwan has changed since the 1990s. I use the typical meaning of entrepreneurship, which includes the ability to find and use opportunities and resources, take risks, come up with new ideas, and make new things of value. Much of the debate in the growing literature on social entrepreneurship, especially from the field of business management, has been about what it is and what it should be. This has been framed by the role of commercial exchange (for example, should social entrepreneurs worry about making money?), the goals of entrepreneurial activities (for example, can social entrepreneurs serve nonsocial goals?), and the hybrid model shown by the Grameen Bank in Bangladesh and other organizations.

Even though these works are helpful for making connections between ideas and policy, it is just as important to put social entrepreneurship in its historical and political context and to look at its connections with other types of entrepreneurship. By doing this, I hope to figure out how much the logic of the state and the market and the logic of social entrepreneurship are the same or different.

This part is mostly about Taiwan after the end of martial law and the end of the developmental state. I will also talk about how the connection between Taiwan and mainland China played a role in the growth of social entrepreneurship.

Taiwan in the Post-Martial Law, Post-Developmental State Era

Most of the time, the interventionist state's policies of industrial restructuring and export upgrading, as well as investments in public education to make a work force that can be upgraded, describe the developmental state. Microelectronics and Hsinchu Science Park have done well in Taiwan, and this is seen as one of the best examples of the country's progress. A lot of the time, an authoritarian government is also a sign of a developmental state. From the 1950s to the 1980s, workers and farmers were mostly quiet during the regime of accumulation, which was marked by high investment, low wages, and large price cuts. This was made possible by the threat of a Chinese communist invasion from across the Taiwan Strait, and by the success of land reform, which got rid of the landed elite in rural areas.

Since the early 1990s, there have been big changes to these four bases of the developmental state: state-led and export-focused industrialization, public education, rural land reform, and authoritarianism. In the 1990s, Taiwan's political system changed from a one-party dictatorship under the Nationalist Party (KMT) to a multiparty democracy. This happened at the same time that social activity grew after martial law was lifted in 1987. Also in the 1990s, Taiwan's microelectronics companies still had an important place on the world market, but they had to deal with new problems and started to move standard production to mainland China. In the early 1990s, public education first took a neoclassical turn. This was done by increasing the number of colleges, which made it easier to get into college. Then, at the beginning of the 2000s, it became more neoliberal, using numbers to measure success in higher education and encouraging private investment in education at every level. Traditional agriculture went through hard times because of the growth of cities and factories, the lack of security from the government, and the World Trade Organization. Some rural areas were able to stay alive by switching to high-value-added farming and leisure businesses, but others got worse. During the time of the postdevelopmental state, these changes were all connected to each other. This created problems, disagreements, and new ways for the state, society, and market to work together.

The way microelectronics changed showed how the relationship between the government and the people in Taiwan has changed in the new era. Since the 1990s, many export-oriented manufacturing industries, including microelectronics, have moved to mainland China. As the issue of Taiwan's growing ties to mainland China continued to dominate political arguments in Taiwan, the government dealt with the problem of industrial hollowing out by diversifying the high-tech sector and by expanding and building new science parks. In farming areas, like Tainan in the south, Yilan on the northeast coast, and Houli in the middle, new science parks were built. The Hsinchu Science Park's sense of victory has given the new parks a lot of symbolic value. Some of the science parks were started by the central government, but many of them were the pet projects of local leaders. This approach of spreading out science parks shows how Taiwan's politics have changed in the postauthoritarian era.

The Democratic Progressive Party (DPP) and the Nationalist Party (Kuomintang, KMT), which were political rivals, competed to keep their supporters by giving public projects to the counties and towns that were most likely to vote for them.

Plans for science parks usually included plans for real estate development. This was done to make sure that projects with both public and private interests would be profitable. Large areas of farmland had to be turned into a science park that could be used for both industry and residential/commercial development.

In 2004, the county government of Miaoli in central Taiwan made a plan to build a science park and use the land around it for real estate projects. Since the proposed park was south of Hsin-chu, it was called Chu-nan (South of Hsin-chu) Science Park to try to get some of the fame of Hsinchu Science Park. One of the subsidiaries of Foxconn, the famous Taiwanese company that makes 80 percent of the world's iBooks, iPads, and Nokia and Motorola cell phones, was looking to move into the proposed park. According to the plan, the farmland of a town called Dapu was one of the areas that would be changed. At first, there wasn't much opposition to the plan because the county governor told Dapu villagers they would get a lot of money for their farms and their homes would stay the same, so they wouldn't have to move.

In 2008, the Foxconn subsidiary asked for a much bigger piece of land in the park so that it could grow in the future. To meet the request, the Miaoli county government chose to take more farmland from Dapu village. As part of the new expansion plan, the villagers' homes would also have to be torn down, so the villagers would have to move. Even more controversial was the fact that the "premium rates" that the governor had promised turned out to be much higher than the pay rates. In response, people in the villages held parades and protests in front of the Executive Yuan and the Control Yuan in Taipei. These are parts of the national government. On June 9, 2010, before farmers and the county government could agree on anything and just as the rice crop was about to be ready to harvest, the county government sent more than twenty crushers into the rice fields very early in the morning. There were 200 police officers and an ambulance with the miners. In the name of getting the land ready for building, a fleet of tractors started tearing up the rice fields in Dapu village.

As the extractors destroyed crops that were full of food, old farmers and women with young children cried out to the operators to stop the monster machines. The cops pushed them back violently and filmed the whole thing. The footage was edited by a citizen journalist who goes by the name Great Tyrannosaurus. The video was then shared on PeoPo (or People's Post), a popular Web site for citizen journalism. When the Excavators Came to the Rice Fields, the name of the video, went popular right away. It led to a large number of farmers, social activists, media workers, students, public thinkers, professionals, and artists from all over Taiwan coming together to protest the government's harsh way of taking land. The Dapu event started one of Taiwan's biggest social movements in recent years. At the end, the head of the Executive Yuan apologized to the people of Dapu, and KMT President Ma Ying-jeou stopped the plan to expand.

There were other problems in Taiwan that made it hard for microelectronics and science parks to grow. Since the mid-1990s, environmental activists and community groups have been trying to stop the pollution made by the microelectronics companies in Hsinchu Science Park. But because the park was part of the state bureaucracy and the sewer and drainage systems were centralized in the science park, environmental protesters went after the management of the science park instead of the polluting companies. Also, most of the complaints came from people who lived in the areas next to the park, where many middle-class science park workers lived. Employees of Hsinchu Science Park and non-employees in the same town had different goals and loyalties, which made it hard for the movement to become more united and gain more followers.

In the 2000s, the fight against high-tech pollution began to grow. The political strategy of giving high-profile science park projects in greenfield areas as a way to build support started to make people more active against high-tech pollution. The voices of environmentalists got stronger as high-tech pollution spread from nearby middle-class neighborhoods to farmers' fields.

In the meantime, the famous Industrial Technology Research Institute (ITRI) and the Electronics Research and Service Organization (ERSO), which were the stars of the government and the center of high-tech research and development in Taiwan in the 1980s and 1990s, have become less important. Since the late 1990s, most high-tech companies have built worldwide technology sourcing and strategic partnerships. Many have also set up their own research centers as the battle over intellectual property rights in the microelectronics industry has gotten worse. Taiwan's pollution of high-tech activists teamed up with activist groups in the United States, especially those in Silicon Valley. They learned from their colleagues in Silicon Valley to go after polluting companies like Acer and Foxconn that were outside the park's boundaries and not protected by the science park management.

Targeting these well-known companies one by one was also a way to get the attention of the media and put more pressure on the companies. There were also protests against pollution in other industries, like the petrochemical industry, which is another important part of the developing state. Farmers, students, public intellectuals, professionals, and environmentalist groups led a persistent and well-connected campaign that forced the government to stop a plan to build a major petrochemical complex in a wetland area in Zhanghua County on Taiwan's southwestern coast in April 2011. This was another big story and a good way to measure the progress of Taiwan's environmental movement.

But not all efforts to bring people together in Taiwan have been successful. What is important about mobilizing people is how they are brought together. The mobilization I described above, along with many other similar events, changed the connection between the government and the people of Taiwan in a big way in the post-developmental state. The microelectronics and petrochemical industries, which were once the showpieces of the developing state, are now both a political risk and an economic driver. Growth-based validity projects were looked at by society from both an environmental and a distributional point of view, and they became a place where people argued with each other.

In the post-developmental state age, there is also a change in how people think about development, which has questioned the idea and ideal of development as economic growth. Along with the rise of social action about labor, the environment, land rights, women's rights, education, and the rights of aborigines, the politics of recognition and representation are also on the rise. The progressive state, which used to focus on growth in size, is now being challenged by a new socioculture that asks who and what development is for.

Since the 1990s, social movements have been based on the question of "who development is for," while religious and spiritual movements have been based on the question of "what development is for." Both types of movements are closely linked to social actions, social ideals, and social entrepreneurship.

Before I talk more about these two types of social entrepreneurship through case studies, I'll give a brief overview of how Taiwan's social movements changed from political entrepreneurialism in the 1990s, which was based on political parties, to social entrepreneurialism in the 2000s, which was based on more diverse and independent ways of mobilizing the public.

Transitioning from Political to Social Entrepreneurship

The DPP, which grew out of Taiwan's democracy movement, won the presidential race in 2000. Taiwan's government went from being ruled by a single party to being a multiparty democracy after it won. The DPP started out as a group that was against the KMT's monopoly. Over time, it grew to include a wide range of political resistance, such as reforms for the legislature, labor, the rights of ethnic minorities, the rights of aborigines, and the rights of women. Chen Shui-bian of the DPP won the presidency in 2000 and stayed in power for two four-year terms. He did this by bringing together a wide range of progressive political groups from the 1990s.

During the election, the DPP and local activists who had become political entrepreneurs worked well together. The grassroots groups gave the DPP candidates political authority and a campaign plan. In return, the DPP backed and funded the election campaigns of movement leaders or hired them at different levels in the government and party bureaucracy. Even though the DPP had political power and social legitimacy, social groups were very dependent on the DPP regime in the 1990s and for much of the 2000s.

But political entrepreneurship isn't just about co-opted radicals or taking advantage of political opportunities. Since the 2000s, social contestation and mobilization has moved from politics of distribution, like labor safety and women's rights, to politics of recognition, like the rights of aboriginal people, religious groups, and gay men and lesbians. But as the number and types of social action grew and changed, the DPP establishment, which had moved from being an opposition party to the center of power, did not support all of them.

Along with the growth and diversification of social movements and agendas, there was another wave of cultural change in the 2000s. It became normal to voice views in public places, to protest and organize, and to network in both real and virtual space. The different kinds of civil organizations and social movements, as well as the culture of protest in both new and old media, created different real and virtual spaces that were shared by people from different classes, such as workers and farmers, community organizers, liberal media workers, student groups, teachers, public intellectuals, academics, white-collar workers and professionals in medicine, law, design, and engineering, spiritual and religious activists, parents, housewives, and older people.

The ability of these groups to organize was very different, and not all of them were "political" in the narrow sense of party and election politics. Some of them said they weren't interested in politics. Still, they all did social networking, which was organized by involved members of the networks, which grew and overlapped with other networks. Taiwanese people have always had a strong sense of the value of networking. Thanks to the widespread IT infrastructure in the age of information, it was now much bigger and stronger.

These loosely or not-so-loosely organized networkers were socially active but not necessarily "political" in the immediate sense. Members were very aware of what was going on in the world and had the ability to get people to work together quickly when needed.

Several Taiwanese observers have said that by the end of the 2000s, social action in Taiwan was moving toward a more independent arena. The new group of social activists and organizers had fewer ties to the DPP or KMT party machines, if any at all. They were smart about politics and knew what it would cost to count on the two main parties. They were less limited by the political and economic goals of the state and had more connections around the world. Even though these activists said they were more interested in helping their communities than in being "political," their networks had strong political implications because they marked the beginning of a nonstate space and could still be used to achieve political goals. Even if it wasn't for specific political projects like election campaigns, activists had well-coordinated social networks that they could use for political purposes. In a recent environmental protest against a plan to build a mega petrochemical complex and a new science park in central Taiwan, student groups, environmentalists, writers, and artists organized, fought, and won the fight.

In the 1980s and 1990s, political mobilization in Taiwan was limited by party politics. Since then, social groups in Taiwan have gone through major changes and have become more aware of the need to keep their own independence in the volatile world of party politics. I call this "social entrepreneurialism" because resourceful and creative social activists have been able to bring people together for social causes, building social meanings and defining social values.

Community Reporting and Public Posts

Information technology has a lot to do with social entrepreneurship in the 21st century. With this in mind, I found a citizen journalist network called People's Post ("PeoPo" for short), which was started in Taiwan in 2007 to look at social entrepreneurship in Taiwan and how it relates to social media.

During the 1990s and 2000s, when Taiwan's democracy was still fairly new and deregulation was a worldwide trend, the number of media outlets grew by a huge amount. Taiwan used to have state-dominated public media that was highly controlled and limited. By 2011, the country had five terrestrial TV networks, nine news channels that were on all the time, nineteen national evening newscasts, 120 cable channels, and more than 85 percent of people had cable TV. For a population of 23 million, there are 4,000 magazines, 2,500 newspapers, and 200 radio stations. Taiwan was ranked fourth in Asia for freedom of the press, but only 1% of people believed what the media said. In 2007, Taiwan Normal University did a poll and found that two-thirds of the people thought that the media was the biggest reason for the chaos in Taiwan. Because there was so much competition for advertising, news programs got more and more shocking, and leaders and political parties bought time on news programs by putting products in them. As distrust of commercial news programs grew, Public Television in Taiwan, a public broadcaster similar to the BBC in the UK, launched People's Post or PeoPo, a multimedia citizen journalism website based on the opensource operating system Linux, in 2007. In Taiwanese slang, the word "tips" sounds a lot like the English word "PeoPo."

PeoPo is different from personal blogs because the stories are more focused on public issues and local community events. Also, the stories are first-hand reports instead of comments on news reports that were written by other people. Unlike South Korea's OhMyNews, which is one of the most well-known citizen journalism projects in East Asia, Taiwan's PeoPo puts more emphasis on grassroots autonomy and doesn't interfere with or edit the materials sent by citizen journalists, as long as they register with the public TV station using their real name to prevent frauds and hoaxes. If someone has a problem with a report, the problem is sent to the person who wrote it, who is then asked to think about it again and change it if they want to. The TV station has the right to take things off the air, but it hasn't found any reason to do so yet. Also, contributors to OhMyNews in South Korea are known to be close to strong political groups like teachers' unions and labor unions. Most PeoPo citizen writers, on the other hand, make their own news. As of September 2011, 55% of the 5,313 citizen writers on PeoPo were women and 45% were men. Most of them were young (70 percent were between the ages of 20 and 40) and well-educated (90 percent had college degrees or higher, while only 36 percent of Taiwan's people over 15 had college degrees or higher). Unlike the BBC, which "welcomes viewers' contributions of photos and videos" but still uses them as "sources," and unlike other social news organizations like ProPublica of the United States, which is mostly a platform for professional journalists who get grants, citizen journalists at PeoPo come from backgrounds other than the media and have a lot of control over their reporting. Between April 2007 and March 2012, 70,000 reports were written by citizen writers, and the number of visitors went from less than 200,000 per month in 2007 to a million per month in 2012.

When Typhoon Morakot hit southern Taiwan in August 2009, it killed more than 700 people and caused widespread damage. A local citizen journalist uploaded the first video report from the disaster area, which alerted the political center of Taipei, which was enjoying the sun that day. With its large and persistent team of video reporters, the PeoPo project shamed the government into sending much-needed aid to the affected areas. Taiwan's president Ma Ying-jeou was criticized for his slow reaction to the disaster and his late call for international help.

As more people started to use PeoPo and become citizen journalists, Public Television started to include PeoPo's work in its news shows. There was a five-minute show every day that talked about the best news items from that day. At least four PeoPo stories were in the main news broadcasts on the weekends. And citizen journalists' stories were not just shown on public TV. Commercial TV stations also reported on stories that were first reported by citizen writers and then became too popular to ignore. Citizen reporters for PeoPo didn't just report from the ground up. They started to make plans for society. Citizen journalists gained credibility that most of the commercial media had long since lost by writing about things that the major media didn't want to cover. And as citizen journalists built up their social credibility, they also improved their political legitimacy. During the 2008 presidential election, PeoPo started a program that chose twelve videos made by citizens out of 300 entries. Each video was thirty seconds long and asked a question to the presidential candidates. These twelve people were asked to take part in the live broadcast of the presidential talks, and each got to ask a follow-up question to the candidates in person.

The link between Taiwan's social entrepreneurship and PeoPo is the ability to strengthen and grow social networks, as well as the ability to build relationships between different types of networks, such as social and virtual networks, personal and institutional networks, and existing and growing networks. In a society with a long and rich history of networking between extended families, friends, businesses, neighbors, and colleagues, the newly open political environment, high computer literacy rates, and the availability of information technologies have laid the groundwork for existing personal and business networks to grow with effective coordination and organization.

Citizen journalists' regular and regular meetings are a good example of how networking, which includes both physical and virtual networks, builds on itself and grows. As a way to keep up the level of reporting, with a strong focus on visual stories, the public television station set up a long training program for its member citizen journalists. In addition to making fifty online training videos and courses, the station has held more than 400 face-to-face workshops, planned citizen journalist gatherings, field trips, and symposiums, given citizen journalist awards, and held summer camps in different parts of Taiwan. Also, Taiwan's community colleges, which have been popping up since the early 2000s and now number 75 across the island, offer writing classes for people who want to become citizen journalists. In the training classes, new and experienced citizen journalists meet, and community workers and social activists share their experiences and talk directly with other like-minded citizens. All of the talks, workshops, and classes are fun and teach useful things. They are for professional training in camerawork, interviewing, writing, and editing, as well as for making friends and growing your network.

Networking also includes making and sharing information, as well as taking action. Another important part of social entrepreneurship is the networks between citizen journalists and social campaigners.

In general, about 80 percent of the more than 60,000 citizen journalist stories written between 2007 and 2011 were directly about public affairs. 23 percent were about social welfare, 17 percent were about education, 12 percent were about the environment, 8 percent were about politics and the economy, 7 percent were about the media, 6 percent were about community reform, 6 percent were about preserving history, 4 percent were about agriculture, 15 percent were about daily life and fun, and 2 percent were about sports and technology.

Even though most citizen writers work on their own, their interest in public issues brings them close to social movements and groups. Most business media are tied to politics and corporations, so they don't usually cover social protests or activities that bring people together. So, social organizers rely on citizen journalists to get the word out and get people to help. Both PeoPo and social groups have grown stronger because they are linked. The 2010 protests over the Dapu incident, which were talked about earlier in this chapter, were started by a video report by a citizen journalist. After activists saw the posting, many groups in Taiwan, like the Taiwan Agriculture United Front, chose to join the farmers' land rights movement that Dapu started. Activists gave the cause the organization and mobilization skills it needed to keep going. The continued mobilization, in turn, gave citizen journalists more things to write about, brought them more readers, and made them want to learn more about the movement. PeoPo is connected to fifteen college news centers, which are generally connected to journalism schools, and more than two hundred nongovernmental and nonprofit groups, for which it holds training workshops. Because of these training programs, people who care about social issues are now not only better at communicating visually and audibly, but they also visit PeoPo often and take part in its activities. A news site with the goal of sharing and giving people a voice from the bottom up has become the best example of how social meanings and values can be made through networking.

The link between interpersonal and mobilizational networks is another example of how different types of networks can work well together. The turning point in the movement against the plan to build a petrochemical complex on the southern coast of Taiwan was when a mainstream news magazine, Business Weekly in Taiwan, chose to cover the story. Before that, all other mainstream news outlets had avoided it. Zhuang Feng-jia said that one of the reasons Business Weekly covered the story was because the executive editor of the magazine went to college with a professor who was a leader in the movement. The latter's college friend persuaded him to do something that other major media outlets chose not to cover. The news was very important because President Ma didn't decide to stop the project until he read about it in Business Weekly. What's also interesting is how community journalism and liberal journalism help each other grow. The story was written by a woman who used to work for a major news organization but now works as a freelancer and is registered as a citizen journalist with PeoPo. She finally won a prestigious national journalism award for the way she kept writing about an environmental issue that was causing a lot of trouble.

To sum up, PeoPo is important because it is a key example of social entrepreneurship in Taiwan during the age of the postdevelopmental state.

First, PeoPo has an odd relationship with both the government and the market. Like citizen journalism in other parts of the world, PeoPo is trusted by the public in a way that business news outlets are not. The connection between PeoPo and the state in the age of the postdevelopmental state is one of the most interesting things about it. Since the beginning, PeoPo has been a part of the Taiwan Public Television Service (TPTS), which means it has never had to think about making money. As one of the results of Taiwan's democratic opening, it could also use the infrastructure and platform of the public TV station. Some North American public journalist platforms, like NowPublic (founded in 2005 in Vancouver), Newsvine (founded in 2005 in Seattle), and Reddit (founded in 2005 in Medford, MA), were run like business startups and were later bought by mainstream media and/or venture capital. PeoPo, on the other hand, was able to stay independent from the market.

There is a cost to having your own money. The head of the TPTS has been chosen by politicians. When PeoPo was first set up at the TPTS in 2007, the general manager of the TPTS was a former student leader who had become a recognized senior journalist in Taiwan's media world. During his time in charge, PeoPo stayed out of politics thanks to his ideas and support. After the general manager left the TPTS, PeoPo went through a lot of ups and downs. During these times, PeoPo had a small budget and a small number of employees. The head of the PeoPo platform said that PeoPo's saving grace was its claim to be a form of "new media." These were the magic words at a time when traditional print media continued to decline and, as we've already said, traditional TV news had lost much of its credibility. PeoPo has also become so popular that it is often shown at foreign conferences about media, democracy, or new media. PeoPo is a good way for Taiwan and the TPTS to show the world what democracy has done for the Taiwanese people, especially when compared to mainland China.

So, the head of PeoPo told me that even though the new leaders of TPTS don't always agree with what PeoPo does, they can't afford to cut its already small budget (less than 1% of the total TPTS budget) even more. The staff at PeoPo is very creative, but they don't get paid much. As a result, PeoPo has found a small, but mostly independent place within the TPTS and has kept party politics at bay.

Second, PeoPo is more than just a high level of expertise. It has kept reporting from being too elitist and has stayed committed to giving grassroots journalists technical training through regular workshops and joint training programs with community schools and social action groups. These training workshops have been very useful for both learning new skills and making new friends.

In the 1990s, Taiwan had good pension plans that allowed many teachers to leave early. These teachers then became citizen journalists. With their wide range of information, good communication skills, and experience with visual presentation, these primary and secondary school teachers were able to learn how to make news quickly. With the help of pension plans paid for by the government, these middle-aged retirees can afford to spend their time and energy on charity work, such as citizen journalism. This is another way that the government and social entrepreneurship are linked.

Third, PeoPo and the network society help each other out. PeoPo is an example of how different types of networks can overlap, join, and grow into larger networks. It is based on a well-developed IT infrastructure on a highly urbanized island with a high population density, and it is part of a society with high computer literacy and dense social networks. Interpersonal, societal, and communication-information networks are all parts of these complex networks. They support each other and create new synergy in a society that only became a multiparty democracy twenty years ago (or eleven years ago, if we use the successful presidential campaign of the oppositional DPP as a baseline). In this case, there seems to be a positive feedback loop between how many social-informational networks there are and how well they work.

Last but not least, PeoPo has important links between its large and wide-ranging communication networks and activities that mobilize people. In a highly commercialized and politically charged country like Taiwan, PeoPo's nonpartisan and noncommercial stance gave it the rarest commodity of all: public trust and social authority. This turned out to be an effective way to get people to work for the public good.

The Internet and Public Confidence in China

The faith that the public had in PeoPo is an interesting contrast to the culture of the Internet that James Leibold and Rongbin Han have written about.

Leibold used Manuel Castells's idea of "networked individualism" to explain the overall mindset of fraud on the Internet. In a piece called "Blogging Alone," he said that "while the Internet has made it much easier for people to get information, it also threatens to make much of this information less accurate and less clear." In China in the 2000s, there are many examples of gossip, false information, and lies spread on the Internet. In the wake of the SARS outbreak in 2003, online rumors said that the virus was a biological weapon made by Taiwan and the US to destroy China. At the same time, stores ran out of vinegar when it was said that it was the only way to treat the infection.

A picture of a tiger is one of the most well-known cases of lying and fakery on China's Internet. Panthera tigris amoyensis, also known as the South China tiger, had not been seen in the wild since 1980. But when a farmer and amateur photographer in the northwestern Chinese province of Shaanxi said in October 2007 that he had risked his life to take more than thirty digital photos of a South China tiger in the wild, the Provincial Forestry Bureau immediately backed up the farmer's pictures as real. They quickly held a press conference to announce the "rediscovery" of the extinct tiger in their area. They did this in the hopes that it would make the place more well-known, get state recognition and funding to set up a protection zone for the tiger like the giant panda conservancy in Sichuan, and increase tourism. But the photos were soon called into question. People on the Internet didn't believe the pictures and said they were fakes. The national Forestry Ministry put together an investigation team on October 24 after people and wildlife experts asked them to do so. However, their report has not been made public. Early in 2008, the Shaanxi provincial government reprimanded the Forestry Bureau for breaking official rules by having the press conference to support Zhou's "discovery" without more proof. The Forestry Bureau later sent out a public letter apologizing for showing the photos, but it didn't say anything about whether or not they were real.

It's interesting that the embarrassing incident didn't stop people from trying the same hoax again. Just one month after the "paper tiger" incident in Shaanxi died down, a fake South China tiger caused another scandal. This time, the person who forged the document was a reporter for a county TV station in Hunan Province, which is also a poor and needy area. The reporter said that he had "accidentally" filmed what he thought was a South China tiger in the mountains of Hunan Province. Again, local officials jumped to back the claims right away. High-level province and city officials went to the place where the tiger was said to have been filmed to check it out. They decided that the recording made by the journalist was real. But just four days later, the provincial Forestry Bureau said that the big cat in the movie was actually a Siberian tiger that had been taken from a circus from another province that was performing in Hunan at the time. In the end, the writer was accused of making the fake to boost his own fame and business interests. Neither the official who helped make the fake nor the reporters who wrote about it were punished.

Even though the South China tiger fakes were found out in the end, many other fakes are still on the Internet. One direct effect of these scandals is that people are now less likely to trust what they read on the Internet. People are safer when they can be anonymous online, but it also makes it easier for scams to happen. Leibold quoted what a Chinese writer said: "Even if you give facts about yourself on the Internet, people won't believe it. They think you're making it up. No one trusts the information on the Internet, so it doesn't matter if you give real or fake information. In the same piece, Leibold talked about a survey that showed the number of people who thought the Internet was reliable went down from 52% to 26% between 2003 and 2007, while the number of people who thought it wasn't reliable went up from 9% to 22%.

Leibold talks about a "regressive" digital society that reinforces and shows the culture of mistrust. Users are excited by the new technologies that let them send and receive messages quickly and widely, but they quickly get tired of them and stop believing in them. In turn, the culture of suspicion haunts internet activism. Han (2012) says that Chinese users have been very worried about each other's identities and motives when they talk online. Netizens might be able to bring down the Chinese Communist Party rule by showing how the state manipulates and distorts public opinion online, but they are just as suspicious, if not more so, of other points of view than those of the party-state. As people who want to change the government use pop activism and make fun of official statements, they are also ready to question the goals and skills of democracy activists. Take the two most well-known leaders of the 1989 Tiananmen student movement as an example. According to Rongbin Han, Chai Ling was accused of putting the lives of other students at risk for her own ambition, and Wang Dan was accused of betraying China's national interests by taking money from the US and Taiwan's pro-independence DPP administration. So, online platforms could be used to shut down public discussions just as much as they could be used to promote them. Han says that people's suspicions and worries about the identities and purposes of others have caused online communities to close themselves off with tight security instead of keeping open networks in cyberspace.

Because of this, there has been a strong call for the government to have more control over the Internet, not less, in order to keep society stable. Nearly 84 percent of people who took part in a poll thought that content on the Internet should be controlled. Violence, malicious rumors, and online chatting were all named as things that should be controlled by 83 percent of people, malicious rumors by 65 percent, and online chatting by nearly 30 percent. Between 2003 and 2007, the number of people who thought the Internet gave people more power fell by more than 50%.

The Influence of the Non-Political: TZU CHI

The goal of this chapter is not to compare social media in Taiwan and China in a more organized way. But one thing that could be looked into more is how trust in the public and politics are connected in strange and complex ways. Taiwanese netizens have set up alternative forums that have a lot of promise to get people involved in politics, but they tend to stay away from overtly partisan politics. Leibold has pointed out that the loss of trust in social media in China has led to more people wanting the government to regulate online, not less.

In this last section, I'll talk about another case of social entrepreneurship from Taiwan to show how the relationship between public trust and politics is paradoxical and how a group that wasn't supposed to be political built the most powerful social organization in Taiwan, which is now also well-established in China.

After military rule There are a lot more religious and spiritual organizations in Taiwan than there used to be. Quite a few Buddhist temples have grown into big, modern organizations with lots of money. Buddhist groups have helped make more welfare organizations, spread the revival movement around the world, and make faith connections between Taiwan and mainland China stronger.

One of the most well-known and biggest Buddhist groups in Taiwan and around the world is the Buddhist Compassion Relief Tzu Chi Foundation, or Tzu Chi for short. In 1966, Tzu Chi began as a small Buddhist charity with more than fifty members in a poor seaside area of eastern Taiwan. By 2009, it had five million fans in Taiwan and around the world. Tzu Chi is also clearly led by women. The leader is a Buddhist Dharma nun named Master Cheng Yan who has a small body but a lot of charm. All thirty of the women who started Tzu Chi were women, and in 2009, about 80% of the most involved followers and volunteer charity workers were women, especially middle-class women in their middle years.

Tzu Chi is different from other religious organizations in Taiwan because it is run by women. It has also shown that it is very good at running a business. In 30 years, the Tzu Chi Foundation went from being a small charity to a big international group with 63 branches in Taiwan, 372 branches in 47 other countries, 800 full-time employees, and five million followers. It is part of Harvard Business School's case study bank. In addition to its religious activities and organizations, Tzu Chi runs charity and disaster relief agencies. These agencies now run three modern hospitals with 900 beds, a television channel, a publishing house, and a secular university with a well-known medical school, several middle schools, and one of the most important bone marrow donation centers in Taiwan. Tzu Chi invests in big projects like hospitals, universities, and schools, but it also runs five thousand recycling centers with the help of 200,000 volunteers all over Taiwan. These centers turn millions of recycled PET bottles into clothes and blankets for crisis relief. By 2010, the company in charge of the recycle-use project made more than $3 million each year.

One of the most important things about Tzu Chi is that it stays out of politics. Master Cheng Yan has told Tzu Chi members very clearly that they shouldn't do anything political. Master Cheng Yan, unlike many celebrities in Taiwan, has never publicly backed a presidential candidate or politician, and members of Tzu Chi must leave if they get involved in political campaigns, elections, or protests. Master Cheng Yan's "ten precepts" include the five Buddhist ones: don't kill, don't steal, don't have sex outside of marriage, don't lie, and don't drink. She has also added five more: don't smoke or use drugs, don't gamble, don't break traffic laws, and don't take part in political activities or protests. For example, Tzu Chi's concern for the environment stayed tied to recycling, which is something that the government also tries to get people to do. Tzu Chi, on the other hand, would not protest against nuclear power plants or particular factories that pollute. In the name of world peace and love, and to stick to the concept of not taking sides in politics, Tzu Chi always tried to avoid any kind of conflict.

This very clear rule about not taking sides in politics was not always a "traditional" Buddhist value, though. In China, Buddhist groups have been spreading for a long time, and they have always done things that were politically charged. These sects often tried to take Buddhism out of the monastery and into the streets, away from complicated ideas and toward deeds that anyone could do. They did this because they believed that everyone could be saved by doing good things in this world.

If we look at Buddhist groups and actions in other parts of Asia, like Thailand, Japan, Vietnam, Myanmar, Sri Lanka, and Tibet, we can see that political involvement is part of the Buddhist tradition. In these societies, monks (mostly monks, not nuns) have not shied away from either small or big political participation. They have protested against secular states, fought against them, or pushed for other sources of authority. In contrast, Buddhist groups in Taiwan, and Tzu Chi in particular, have never had an extreme view of religion and have always stuck to the idea that religion and politics should be kept separate. In Taiwan in the 1980s, Buddhist groups did not take part in the democratic movement, and after martial law was lifted in 1987, they did not take any political sides.

In Taiwan after the end of martial law, Tzu Chi's refusal to take sides in politics has been a form of moral capital. Andre Laliberte has said that Taiwan's politics after martial law were very split. First, a line was drawn between those who were born in mainland China (mostly military and government workers and people who moved to Taiwan when the Nationalists were defeated by the communists in 1949) and those who say they are real Taiwanese (whose ancestors, most of whom were peasants, came to Taiwan from southern China 300 years ago). The difference between "insiders" and "outsiders" was made clearer by how they were thought to feel about Taiwan-China ties. Most "outsiders" were thought to want Taiwan to join mainland China, while most "insiders" were thought to want Taiwan to be independent. When the DPP was an opposition party, its politicians took advantage of this split to unite the opposition and beat the KMT, which had been in charge of Taiwanese mainstream politics for 50 years, in the 2000 presidential race. But Taiwan's identity politics have not led to violent battles like those that have happened in many other parts of the world and throughout history.

This is where "apolitical" Buddhist organizations like Tzu Chi and others come in. In a highly political society with a lively market for ideologies and growing competition for resources from religious and secular nongovernmental and nonprofit groups, Tzu Chi found a place for itself in which it didn't have to make political claims or use political language. Positioned above and beyond secular politics, which was thought to be tainted by money and power, Tzu Chi has members from all ideologies who were looking for a Pure Land in their minds. The more Tzu Chi tried to stay out of politics, the more political power it had over the state bureaucracy and lawmakers from different camps. In a place where most people are tired of politics and too much business, Tzu Chi and Master Cheng Yan stand on a moral peak that few politicians or CEOs can reach. According to anthropologist Julia Huang, the secretariat office of the premier of the Executive Yuan told her that the government treated Tzu Chi's delegate in a special way. Representatives from Tzu Chi didn't have to set up a meeting with the minister's office ahead of time. Often, the former just called from a cell phone when they were only a few minutes away from the Executive Yuan. And these people said again and again that they were "doing good things" when they talked to the minister's office about getting the government's help. Even people in high positions in the government feel they can't afford to upset Tzu Chi. Master Zheng Yan is a religious leader in Taiwan, but unlike other religious leaders there, he has never made a public showing for a presidential candidate. But KMT President Ma Ying-jeou went to one of Tzu Chi's recycling centers as a worker and spent a couple of hours sorting plastic bottles.

Because Tzu Chi is not tied to any political party, it has also been very helpful to the Taiwanese government in its efforts to improve its very weak place in international politics. As a result of China's diplomatic campaign against Taiwan, only 23 countries, many of which are island countries in the South Pacific, accept Taiwan as an independent country. Tzu Chi has become one of the most important places for the Taiwanese government to support its "People to People" diplomacy. This is shown by the fact that Taiwan's Ministry of Foreign Affairs has set up a Committee of Nongovernmental Organizations. And because the issue of unification and independence is so political, Tzu Chi, like other international aid agencies, has said that it is politically neutral in its humanitarian work. This has made it possible for religious and social groups from Taiwan to cross the Taiwan Strait and expand their operations and networks in China. As was already said, Tzu Chi's aid workers have been able to get into mainland China even though the PRC is known for being very careful about taking foreign aid and aid workers. During the 2008 Sichuan earthquake in China, the PRC government gave Tzu Chi permission to be the first outside group to help in the area. After working for 20 years in different parts of China, Tzu Chi became the first and only international nonprofit group to get permission from the State Department to work all over China.

This chapter has looked at how the relationship between the government and society in Taiwan is changing in the postdevelopmental state, as well as how information technology, oppositional politics, and social action work together. What I found most interesting about this three-way relationship was the paradox that social mobilizers in multiparty-democratic Taiwan claimed to be non-political in order to gain public trust, while social media users in single-party China turned to the government to win back public trust. The charity group Tzu Chi is not political, but it is very powerful. It shows how powerful being non-political can be by pushing the limits of Taiwan's diplomatic relationship with the rest of the world and with China. Changes in the relationship between Taiwan and China affect the way the state and culture work in both countries, and the same is true in reverse.

Chapter 5
The Characteristics and Trajectory of Taiwanese Investment in China (1991-2014)
Business Focus, Profit Pursuit, and Depoliticization

In January 1990, the Taiwanese government announced "Measures on Indirect Investment and Technical Cooperation with the Mainland" and officially ended the ban on investment in China. During this time of change, Deng Xiaoping's Southern Tour, which pushed for economic changes, and the Fourteenth National Party Congress's adoption of a socialist market economic system, both in 1992, made China a better place for business and investment. Even so, ties across the Strait will continue to be rocky over the next few years, as Taiwan's industries continue to change and China's economy continues to grow in different ways. In 1994, former president Lee Teng-hui pushed for a "southward policy" to move Taiwanese investment from China to Southeast Asia. In 1996, he came up with the motto "Don't rush, be patient" to encourage a more gradual and careful approach to Taiwanese investment in China (TIC), along with new rules for such investments. In 2000, Lee's replacement, Chen Shui-bian, won the election, and the Democratic Progressive Party (DPP) became the ruling party. Chen's dislike of China and the DPP's support for independence made ties across the Strait very hard, and political exchanges were stopped. But when current President Ma Ying-jeou took office in 2008, the Taiwanese government started talking to China again, and ties across the Strait got much better.

In light of all of this, this chapter will try to answer the following questions: Has the change in political power changed how and how much Taiwanese people spend in China (TIC)? How have businesspeople in Taiwan reacted to the changes in politics? What about TIC has changed since the 1990s, and what hasn't? What has been the general direction of TIC over the past 20 years? This chapter is about TIC between 1991 and 2014, when Taiwan had three leaders and a lot of changes in data availability and political power. Using statistics from both Taiwan and China, this chapter makes the case that TIC has been mostly driven by economic factors and isn't much affected by political situations that aren't stable. TIC is all about taking politics out of business. Even though there has been a lot of political upheaval, Taishang has continued to do well, but it hasn't been able to have a say in how things are run at home. In recent years, TIC has been slowly going down because the business climate on the mainland has been getting worse.

This chapter shows that even though the total amount of TIC has been going up over the past 25 years, its composition has changed a lot because of both internal and external causes. In terms of endogenous constraints, rising labor costs and changing local preferential policies have lowered the benefits and pushed Taishan to either look for new sites with lower production costs or focus on technological and industrial upgrades. In terms of external forces, Taiwanese companies are getting into China's local markets because global markets are unstable and domestic businesses are getting more and more competitive. These trends show that the macroeconomic situation in China has had a big impact on TIC and that political conflicts between Taiwan and China have not changed TIC.

The next part of this chapter goes into more detail about Taiwanese investments in China over the past twenty years. It shows how uncertain policies and changes in power across the Strait haven't had much of an effect on these investments. The third part talks about the role of Taiwanese business owners on the other side of the Strait. Taishang aren't political actors, and they aren't economic hostages, either. They are businesspeople who want more chances and better returns. They are the same as their counterparts in other countries who also do business. The fourth part looks at the "go south" strategy as an alternative for Taishang and TIC to reduce the risk of being too dependent on China. Even though the policies have been in place for 20 years, they still haven't been able to convince taishang to move their investments to Southeast Asian countries. The last part of the chapter talks about the wider effects of TIC and its future. China is now putting its big economic plan into action, and making TIC a part of that plan is a clear political move. Still, taishang's choices about whether or not to invest in China have been mostly based on economic factors. This is especially true now, as China has been slowly getting rid of most of its policies that used to help Taiwanese investors.

Taiwanese Investments in China

People in Taiwan tend to think that the Kuomintang (the Nationalist Party, KMT) is generally pro-China and the DPP is generally anti-China, and that the KMT is more willing to help businesses work with China while the DPP is less willing to do so. Taiwanese society and the media have paid a lot of attention to how the DPP's anti-China views have spread and had a big impact on TIC, especially when Chen was in charge. But this argument is not backed up by either clear proof or statistics. The direction of TIC hasn't always been tied to the direction and changes of government administrations. Instead, it has more to do with business and economic factors. Statistics from the Taiwanese government show that the changes in political power in 2000 and 2008 didn't have much of an effect on the amounts of TIC that were okayed by the Taiwanese government. TIC went up in 2001, one year after the DPP took power in 2000, and down in 2009, one year after the KMT took power in 2008. This goes against how most people think the parties feel about China. That is, the DPP government did not control Taiwanese investments as strictly as was assumed or said to be the case. In fact, economic cooperation across the Taiwan Strait has done well under both parties.

In July 1987, Taiwan's government lifted the ban on foreign exchange and made it easier for money to leave the country. In November of that year, it also made it easier for people to travel to China. These changes in strategy made TIC possible. The Taiwanese government released "Measures on Indirect Investment and Technical Cooperation with the Mainland" in January 1990 to encourage TIC in a limited way. At this early stage, most TIC came from Taiwanese entrepreneurs who ran small and medium-sized businesses and moved their plants to China to get a competitive edge and save money on wages. Taishang set up joint venture and cooperative businesses with Chinese partners because businesses that were run by foreigners alone were not yet allowed. They made money by getting orders in Taiwan, making the goods in China, and then shipping them to the Western countries. This explains why Taiwanese investors wanted to put their money in areas with a high return ratio instead of areas with a lot of resources, like Japan and Korea. Because of limits on the Taiwanese side, the first TIC was small and careful. Based on calculations made by the Republic of China (ROC), Figure 5.1 shows that the Taiwanese government allowed more TIC in 1992-1993 and 1996-1997. The first was a good reaction to Deng Xiaoping's Southern Tour and the Fourteenth National Party Congress's decision to set up a socialist market economy system in 1992. This last trend shows how the Taiwanese government contradicts itself: the amount of TIC it allowed in 1997 was 30% higher than the year before, when Lee was promoting his "No hurry, be patient" policy and putting a lot of new rules on TIC. Since his trip to the U.S. in 1995, which caused a nuclear crisis and froze cross-Strait talks, Lee has been tough on China, but the Taiwanese government has kept giving approved TIC a lot of freedom. Due to the Asian financial crisis in 1998 and 1999, the amount of TIC that was allowed went down by a lot. However, since 2000, it has been on the rise overall, despite some larger fluctuations. Surprisingly, the trend did not reflect the political turmoil caused by Lee's statement in July 1999 that Taiwan and China should have special state-to-state relationships. This was a controversial move, and China quickly responded by canceling the third Koo-Wang talk, which was supposed to take place in Taipei in the fall. Chen was elected president in 2000, and the DPP became the ruling party. The DPP government pushed a "invest in Taiwan" strategy and gave Taiwanese companies incentives to do so, like a low-interest loan fund, tax breaks, and subsidies. Still, in 2004 and 2005, the amount of TIC that was allowed to be used barely changed while Chen was in charge. That is, the DPP government did not make policies that stopped taishang from investing in China or persuaded them to stay in Taiwan. In a strange twist, the amount of TIC fell sharply in 2009, a year after Ma took power, and then suddenly went up in 2010. Since 2011, the amount that has been accepted has gone down because of the global financial crisis and rising labor costs in China. Clearly, the trend in the amount of TIC that has been approved has not usually shown how power has changed in Taiwan.

Figure 5.1. Approved TIC, actual TIC, and the rate (million US$).

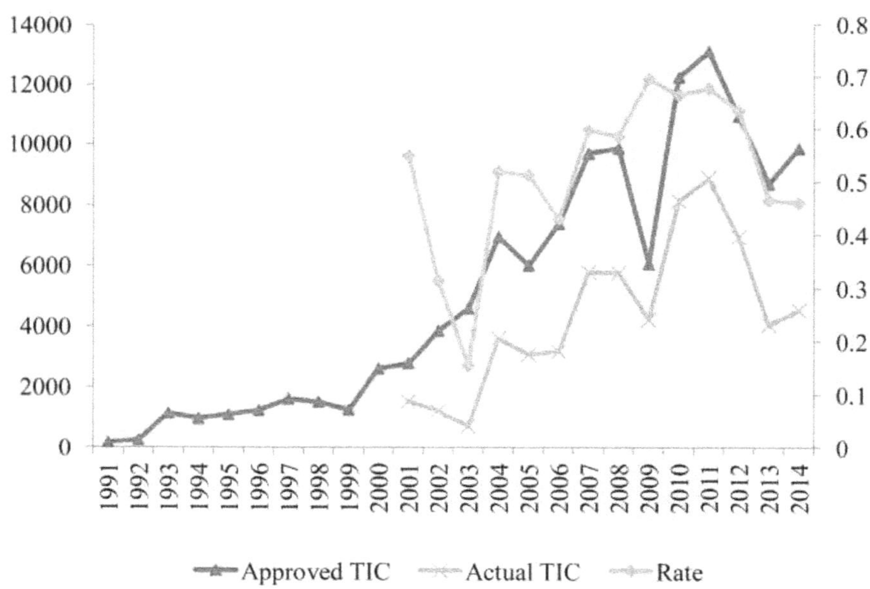

Source: Investment Commission, Ministry of Economic Affairs, ROC, https://www.moeaic.gov.tw.

On the China side, in 1979 the Chinese government released a "Message to Compatriots in Taiwan" proposing an opening up of trade and economic exchanges; this was followed up by the Ministry of Foreign Trade's promulgation of "Interim Provisions Concerning Trade with Taiwan". Later, China's State Council passed the "Special Preferential Regulations on Taiwanese Patriots' Investment in the Special Economic Zones" to make it easier for Taiwanese entrepreneurs to invest in the special economic zones that had been established in 1979. The first wholly owned Taiwanese enterprise was established in Fuzhou in 1984 with the acquiescence of the local government and later received its first approval by the central state's Ministry of Foreign Economic Relations and Trade in 1986. Two years later, the number of TEs grew to eighty with an investment of US$100 million in 1986. By the end of 1989, there were two thousand TEs and the amount of TIC was over US$1 billion. In general, TIC in the 1980s was initially limited because of China's unclear investment environment and the Taiwanese government's restrictions. It followed the development model of "two ends out" (liangtou zaiwai), referring to a pattern in which both the sources of raw materials and the ultimate products were nondomestic. The demand in the foreign market had been rocketing up but that in local market remained quite low. Obviously, for taishang in the 1980s and early 1990s political concerns were more important than economic considerations in their investment decisions. Once the macroeconomic climate had become stable and beneficial to TIC, TIC was less sensitive to political turbulence, and in the 1990s Taiwan's investment rapidly became the second highest in China, second only to Hong Kong's.

Figure 5.2 shows actual TIC as calculated by China's National Statistical Bureau. The amount increased between 1989 and 1996, only slightly decreasing in 1995. This trend reflects the friendly investment environment that the Chinese government created in order to develop TIC. Actual TIC radically declined between 1997 and 2000 (Figure 5.2), but the approved amount declined only slightly from 1997 to 1999 and increased from 1999 to 2000 (Figure 5.1). We find that the deteriorating macroeconomic environment, namely the Asian financial crisis, has had greater impact on TIC than political fluctuations. Although Lee promoted his ideas about jieji yongren, the approved TIC remained relatively stable between 1996 and 1999. In 2001, China, by entering the World Trade Organization (WTO), greatly improved the institutional environment for investment, which strengthened taishang confidence in investing in China. This was reflected in the radically increased amount invested in 2001 and 2002, even though Chen had won the presidential election and had not yet presented clear mainland policies. Nonetheless, the amount of actual TIC declined between 2002 and 2007 while the approved amount rose in the same period. This suggests that what restricted TIC was neither the Taiwanese authorities nor the Chinese state but taishang themselves, who were suspicious of Chen's mainland policy and became more conservative about investing in China even though the door remained open. In August 2002, Chen asserted his "one country on each side of the strait" stance (that the PRC and the ROC were two different countries rather than two political entities within the country of China) and declared that the Taiwanese people would consider holding a referendum to decide Taiwan's future. China rapidly responded with tough comments and suspended interaction with the Taiwanese government. In 2005 China passed the Anti-Secession Law, demonstrating its commitment to unification and adding tension to cross-Strait relations. The law proclaims that Taiwan is part of China and that China may take nonpeaceful action if Taiwanese proindependence forces push Taiwan to secede from China. Surprisingly, Hsu Wen-long, an important Taiwanese entrepreneur and founder of the Chi Mei Group, whose support for Chen had been crucial in the 2000 presidential election, published an open letter to support the law and mentioned that the law made him feel confident about investing in China. Although China could retaliate against Taiwan by imposing clear economic sanctions or issuing tougher regulations over TIC, there was no clear evidence of China taking substantial actions during Chen's tenure. Ironically, Chen's provocative political statement did not inspire China's revenge but instead raised the alarm of taishang.

Figure 5.2. Taiwan's actual direct investment in China (million US$).

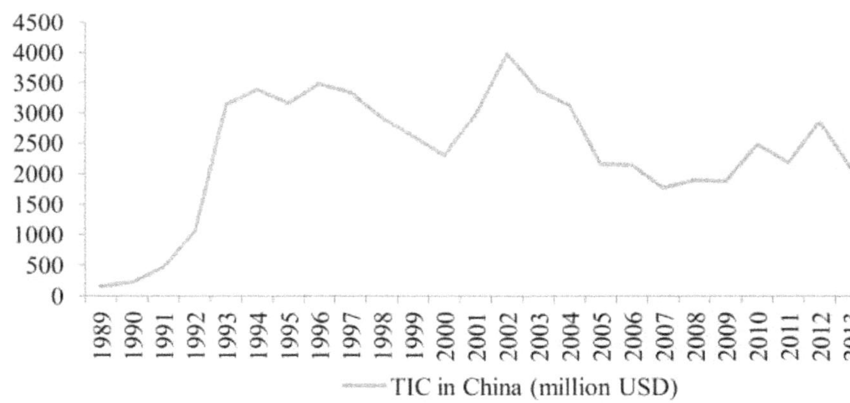

Source: China's National Statistical Bureau, "National Data," multiple years, http://data.stats.gov.cn/.

Even so, China's joining the WTO did pose some problems for TIC. More and more companies from other countries began to invest in China. In the meantime, China's own businesses grew and became more competitive over the course of two decades of economic change. With more institutions and more openness, the Chinese government has been put under pressure to make the market fair for everyone. TIC used to get a lot of benefits that were only available to taishang, but WTO rules and competition from local businesses have made these benefits less important or even gone away. So, the changes in real TIC in the 2000s were more likely caused by changes in the economy than by changes in the political environment.

Figures 3 and 4 show a very different picture of TIC in China as a whole. Between 1999 and 2008, the Taiwanese government allowed more TIC, but data from Chinese authorities show that actual TIC kept going down between 2002 and 2008, and then started going up again after that. One could say that the Chinese government blocked TIC to put pressure on the DPP government and supported it when the KMT was in power. But neither China's policies nor the talks we did with taishang gave us clear proof of this.

People have said that as Taiwan has become more involved in China's economy, it has lost its economic independence and given China more control over Taiwan's future wealth. China has been the second-largest economy in the world since 2010, after Japan. This is because China's economy has grown so quickly over the past 20 years. China has more power over Taiwan's economy because of this, and more than half of Taiwan's overseas investments are in China. However, taishang and TIC have had to deal with more problems from both inside and outside China, and we can't just blame the changes in TIC on changes in political power. Also, statistics show that the amount of TIC is usually going up, and neither the Taiwanese nor the Chinese governments have made clear economic bans and sanctions against TIC. The economy is one of the most important things that affects TIC trends.

Trends Defining the Progress of TIC (Taiwanese Investment in China)

At first, TIC was mostly used in traditional industries that required a lot of labor, like shoemaking, textiles, and plastic goods. Later, it grew to include more manufacturing businesses, like consumer electronics, chemicals, and food and drinks. Over the years, TIC has changed from small factories to big, capital-intensive companies with advanced technology like electrical appliances, precision instruments, and computer hardware. Since 2008, TIC has been used more and more in all areas of the economy, such as real estate, banking, tourism, the media, and many service industries. So, the biggest Taiwanese investors have moved from small and medium-sized businesses to large exchange-listed and over-the-counter (OTC) businesses with investment projects worth more than US$10 million. Instead of sending their goods overseas like their predecessors did, taishang are now focusing on China's huge and growing domestic market. This is because the global market is getting smaller. Also, Taiwanese businesses have been slowly buying more raw materials and semi-finished goods from local companies and importing less from Taiwan. Taiwanese companies are part of China's business chain and have a close relationship with China's economic growth.

In general, TIC has moved slowly from the south to the north, from the east to the west, and from the coast to the interior. Since the early 1990s, the most TIC have gone to the Pearl River Delta area in Guangdong and the Yangtze River Delta area in Jiangsu. This is because Hong Kong and Shanghai are close to those areas. In the past few years, Guangdong has used the "clearing the cage and replacing the bird" and "transferring industries and labor" methods to deal with the global financial crisis and help industries get better. The local government wants to get rid of low-margin, low-tech, labor-intensive industries in the Pearl River Delta area and replace them with industries that require a lot of capital. This desire to change the type of economic activities in the province has a big effect on TIC because many Taiwanese factories were seen as "birds" that needed to be changed. Both Zhejiang and Shanghai made decisions that were similar. Some Taiwanese business owners were told by the government of Anhui Province that they could get more land if they moved their labor-intensive companies there. Some Taiwanese investors negotiated to keep one building or a small piece of land in the original site so they could keep a base there even after moving most of their assets out.

Figure 5.3 shows how the amount of TIC that has been allowed has grown since the beginning of the 1990s in Central China, South China, and especially East China. Since 2010, Jiangsu and Guangdong have lost a lot of TIC, but Shanghai and Fujian have gained more. Since 2005, North China and Southwest China have been open to more TIC. Northwest China and Northeast China have been left behind in economic transitions for a long time because they don't have the right infrastructure. The amount of TIC shows that this is still the case.

Beneficial Policies at Central and Local Levels

The central government of China has put in place a number of measures that help TIC. The "Regulations on Encouraging the Investments of Taiwan Compatriots" were first put out by the State Council in 1988. This paper was very detailed and full of rules about how Taiwanese business owners could invest in China. Less than a decade had passed since China began its economic transition, and the idea of a government change was still full of questions and doubts. China's Taiwan investment regulations tried to boost investor confidence by saying that "the state will not nationalize the investments and other assets of Taiwanese investors" and that "the legal benefits Taiwanese investors get can be sent abroad according to relevant law." In 1994, the Chinese government passed the "Law Regarding the Protection of Investment by Taiwan Compatriots," which made it clear that its goal was to protect and support Taiwanese investment in China and help the two countries' economies grow. The law also gave Taiwanese business owners the right to form business groups. In the same year, the State Council announced the "Decision Concerning Further Development of Economic Issues Across the Strait" and supported the "Priority and Relaxation" principles. After this law had been in place for five years, the Chinese government passed the "Rules for Implementing the Law on the Protection of Investment of Taiwan Compatriots" to give more specific rules. The "Regulation on the Protection and Promotion of Investment of Taiwan Compatriots" was passed by the Jiangsu provincial government in 2012. It is the first and only law at the local level. Some of these laws are out of date because they have never been updated. China said in 2009 that it would start changing the "Rules for Implementing the Law on the Protection of Investment of Taiwan Compatriots," but it hasn't made much progress yet.

Figure 5.3. Taiwan's approved investment in mainland China by region (US$).

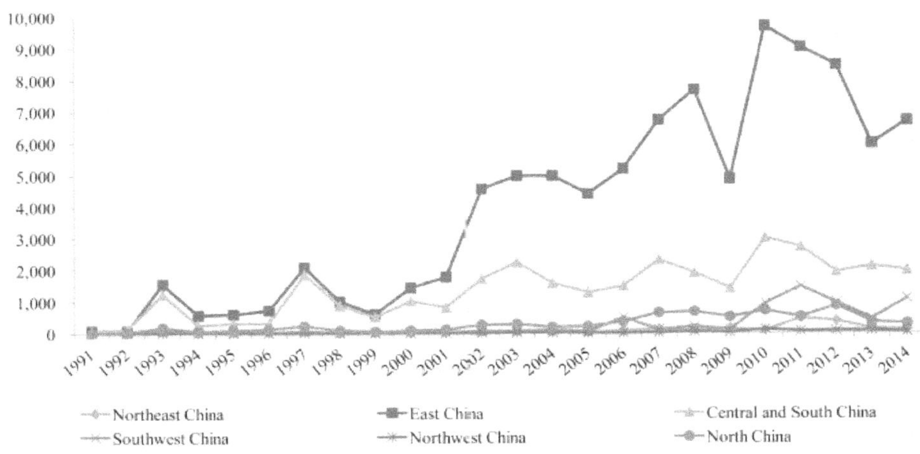

Source: Investment Commission, Ministry of Economic Affairs, ROC, https://www.moeaic.gov.tw. The demarcation of China's regions is different in Taiwan's statistical data. North China includes Beijing, Tianjin, Hebei, Shanxi, and Inner Mongolia. Northeast China refers to Jilin, Liaoning, and Heilongjiang. East China covers Shanghai, Jiangsu, Zhejiang, Anhui, Fujian, Shandong, and Jiangxi. Central and South China includes Henan, Hubei, Hunan, Guangdong, Guangxi, and Hainan. Southeast China includes Chongqing, Sichuan, Guizhou, Yunnan, and Tibet. Northwest China covers Xinjiang, Gansu, Ningxia, and Shaanxi.

The main jobs of Taiwanese business associations (TBAs) are to protect the legal rights of taishang, manage public relations with Taiwanese people in China and take care of them, and improve the economic climate in Taiwan. In 1990, the first TBA was founded in Shenzhen. There are now 142 TBAs all over China.

In 2003, the Chinese government put out a notice called "Interim Measures on Managing Taiwanese Business Associations." This was done so that TBAs could be better managed. TBAs are not official organizations, so they cannot have national offices. Some TBAs worked together in 2007 to set up the Association of Taiwan Investment Enterprises on the Mainland, which is a non-profit group. The Taiwan Affairs Office and the Ministry of Civil Affairs are in charge of the ATIEM, and it can talk directly with the national government. In other words, it's a way for both TBAs and the Chinese government to talk to each other. It sends taishang's messages to the officials and gives entrepreneurs orders from the center.

At the local level, provincial and city governments have offered different types of preferential treatment to draw Taiwanese investment. For example, they have given a wide range of tax breaks and re-invested profits, made it easier to buy cheap land, and lowered bureaucratic barriers. For example, one of the most popular programs is called "Two Free, Three Half." This means that a Taiwanese company that plans to stay in business for more than ten years can get a five-year tax break, with the first two years tax-free and the next three years paying only half the corporate income tax. Still, in December 2014, the central government released Notice No. 62, which tells ministries and local governments to clean up and control favored policies that break the law. Taiwanese investment firms have gotten more help from local governments in China than other foreign firms for a long time, so taishang will have to deal with most of the new rules. In March 2015, after the National People's Congress was over, Premier Li Keqiang told a press conference that China would continue to protect the legal rights and interests of Taiwanese-invested businesses and keep policies that helped them.

In Taiwan, on the other hand, the big question is whether or not TIC is hurting Taiwan's economy. People who disagree say that the problem isn't a lack of money but a lack of chances to invest. They say that upgrading industry is the key to getting the economy back on track. Those who agree say that rising TIC is to blame for the rise in unemployment, the drop in domestic investment, and the growth of manufacturing's share of the gross domestic product (GDP). But there isn't a clear answer yet.

Taishang's Role: Political Operatives or Economic Captives

Under the Chen government, political ties across the Taiwan Strait were put on hold. It was expected that TIC would be affected or even banned by China. According to theories of economic statecraft, China could use economic penalties as a way to force Taiwan to do what it wants. Economic warfare is much more likely to happen across the Strait than military warfare, because China couldn't get what it wants by using military methods. So, if the Chinese government chooses to use economic sanctions as a form of political retaliation, taishang could become hostages or easy targets.

But this point of view doesn't take into account how difficult it is for both governments and Taiwanese businesspeople to work together to get what they want. Instead of using a big stick, the Hu administration used "carrots" by "counting on the Taiwanese people" to put pressure on the DPP administration. Still, this failed attempt to use taishang as political power over Taiwan showed that taishang doesn't have much political importance. During Chen's time in power, official communications between the PRC and the ROC were usually stopped. However, Taiwanese businesses became an unofficial way for the Chinese government to learn about Taiwan. Taishang didn't change the DPP's policies on the mainland, and the DPP wasn't able to talk to the Taiwanese government. When President Ma took office in 2008 and cross-Strait ties got a lot better, the political and economic roles of taishang changed. The KMT government would often get together with taishang, and President Ma would attend and listen to what they had to say. Taishang have been taking part in cross-Strait events put on by both the Taiwanese government and the KMT more and more. But the top leaders of the TBAs and the ATIEM think that the KMT's actions are just lip service and that the situation in the taishang hasn't changed much. In general, taishang are vulnerable to unstable political conditions, but they can't help make decisions. In other words, they are affected by cross-Strait political relations, but they don't have any effect on them.

Voting for the KMT could be seen as a passive response to Taiwanese politics. Taiwanese people depend on this party for a stable and predictable policy toward the mainland. We shouldn't take it to mean that taishang supports China or wants to see more political progress toward unity. In a strange way, they are the ones who know that China can't be trusted. Taishang is finding it hard to do business in China because Chinese companies are getting more and more competitive and the Taiwanese government doesn't help them. When working with other parts of the government, like local governments, the Ministry of Commerce, and the State Administration for Industry and Commerce in China, the Taiwan Affairs Offices in Beijing are often not strong enough to help. People tend to think that Taishang have been more important in cross-Strait ties than they really have been. In short, the taishang are neither political players nor economic hostages. They can't make a good impact on policy, but they haven't been hurt too badly by political upheaval. They are businesspeople who want to do business in China and hope for a safe political climate, just like people who invest in any other part of the world.

Taiwanese Investment in Southeast Asian Countries

In 1993, former president Lee Teng-hui came up with the "go south" plan to help Taiwanese investors spread out their risks and become less dependent on China. "Guidelines for Strengthening Economic and Trade Ties with Southeast Asia," which are now in their seventh version, were released by the government of Taiwan.

During the Asian financial crisis, the Taiwanese government passed more laws called "Measures on Strengthening the Promotion of Economic and Trade Relations with Southeast Asia" to help Taiwanese businesspeople with money troubles. Unfortunately, these strategies did not work very well, and most Taiwanese money left Thailand and Indonesia. In 2002, Taiwan's then-president Chen announced the "go south" strategy again. He said that China was just one part of the global market and that Taiwan shouldn't count too much on it. When the current president, Ma, took office in 2008, he said again that Taiwan had to be a part of Southeast Asia's regional economic union.

Unlike his predecessors, Ma has seen "go south" (invest in Southeast Asia) and "go west" (invest in China) not as zero-sum games but as win-win games, and he has supported Taiwanese investment to flow in both directions. Still, these efforts haven't led to any new ideas or specific plans that would help Taiwanese investment. When the strategy was first put into place in 1994, Taiwanese investments in Southeast Asia went through the roof. But after the Asian financial crisis, it dropped to the same level as in 1993 and stayed there for the next eight years, until 2006 (see Figure 5.4). Between 2007 and 2009, there were a lot of big changes. In general, there isn't a clear trend in capital movements, no matter what the government did to try to get Taiwanese investments to go to Southeast Asian countries. Also, many Southeast Asian countries have strict rules about FDI and usually only want large-scale investments. This makes it hard for many Taiwanese to invest in the area. Southeast Asia is not a good place to spend right now because of its unstable political and economic climate, anti-Chinese movements, and changing local policies. The ASEAN Secretariat says that between 2008 and 2010, Taiwan was not one of the top ten investment countries in ASEAN.

In recent years, though, Taiwanese business owners have started to move their companies from Shenzhen and Dongguan to Southeast Asian countries, especially Vietnam and Cambodia, because labor costs have been going up. Obviously, taishang's focus on making money is more important than government programs in getting them to "go south." Also, in 2012, the Taiwanese government released "Measures on Promoting Taiwanese Entrepreneurs to Invest in Taiwan," also known as the "salmon returns" policy. This policy includes a higher limit of foreign workers and low interest rates for bank loans. It hasn't worked well, though, because land is expensive and there aren't enough skilled workers. In 2014, the amount of taishang income that went back to Taiwan dropped by 55%.

Conclusion

The Taiwanese government has been worried that the country is becoming less important on the world market. Lee and Chen, both past presidents, have mostly failed in their attempts to take trade away from China. The competitive global economy and the fact that Taiwanese and Chinese people speak the same languages and have similar cultures have forced Taiwanese businesses into China's economic orbit. Such exchanges across the Taiwan Strait have not shown that economic liberalization can promote peace, and there is still a chance of political conflict. Taiwanese people have said that Beijing is changing economic incentives to make unification easier. However, neither statistics nor China's policies show this to be true. Strangely, Taiwanese people are unhappy, but they aren't fighting with people from the mainland. Instead, they are fighting among themselves. When you look at how the two sides of the Strait have interacted over the past 20 years, you can see that economic integration has helped keep the peace and eased some of the conflict-intensifying factors that came about when Taiwan became more democratic.

Figure 5.4. Taiwanese investment in seven Southeast Asian countries (million US$). source: Investment Commission, Ministry of Economic Affairs, ROC, https://www.moeaic.gov.tw.

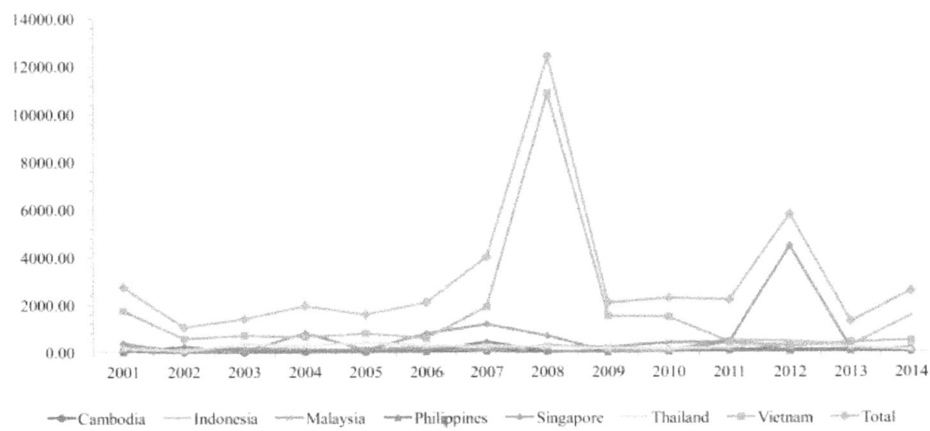

Source: Investment Commission, Ministry of Economic Affairs, ROC, https://www.moeaic.gov.tw.

Without a question, TIC is one of the most important, if not the most important, factors in cross-Strait interactions. It is characterized by three major trends. First, TIC has changed the industries it focuses on. It used to make consumer goods, which required a lot of work, but now it makes high-tech electronics and precision products. Second, TIC has grown from being made up of small and medium-sized factories to being made up of big business conglomerates. Third, TIC has moved from the south to the north and from the east to the west of China. Investors who have left China have moved to Southeast Asia.

Politics haven't been as important as economics when it comes to deciding how much TIC is allowed and how much is actually used. Changes in government haven't stopped the spread of TIC, and the Chinese government hasn't said what it will do to stop it. Politics is not stopping Taishang from putting more money into China. Instead, their economic goals and investor trust are. Southeast Asian countries and Taiwan may not be the best places for taishang to spend right now, but the question of how to fully integrate them into the Chinese economy is becoming more important.

In China, Chinese investment in Taiwan (CIT) is the same kind of thing. Since June 2009, the Taiwanese government has dropped its ban on CIT and made it possible for Chinese business people to invest in Taiwan. As of 2016, a total of US$1.3 billion has been spent on 729 projects that have been given the green light. When compared to TIC, the numbers and amounts of money invested are small. Also, some companies, especially those that are owned by the government, don't think the Taiwanese market is big enough to help their business. Unlike their Taiwanese peers, Chinese businesspeople invest to do political things like improve relations across the Taiwan Strait.

China has been talking about the "One Belt, One Road" strategy, but it looks like the Chinese government is including TIC in the plan to keep it from leaving China. The government of Taiwan is also trying to get Taishang to come back. It could be a good chance for TIC to move upstream to take advantage of cheap land and cheap labor. On the other hand, the Economic Cooperation Framework Agreement (ECFA) between Taiwan and China may be good for TIC, but Taiwan's politics make the matter very controversial for Taiwanese people. We still need more time to see how the problem grows before we can say for sure how it will affect TIC.

Chapter 6
Chinese Youth Nationalism in a High-Stakes Environment

In the first ten years of the twenty-first century, young Chinese people were very angry. In contrast to the angry peasants and workers, who took to the streets because they felt left out of China's economic boom, the furious youth fought for their country. After the 1999 bombing of the Chinese embassy in Belgrade, the 2001 China-US aircraft collision, the 2008 Beijing Olympics, and the 2012 disputes over the Diaoyu Islands, the power of spontaneous mass protest spread like a raging fire to include a huge number of students. This was especially true in September 2012, when the Japanese government bought the Diaoyu Islands, which led to angry protests in as many as one hundred cities in China. Hundreds of thousands of young people took part in huge protests and went out into the streets to fight, damage property, and set fires. In fact, there had been a fight over the Diaoyu Islands before. It had happened over and over again for the past 30 years. After the Americans left Okinawa in 1972, the Japanese government took back control of the Diaoyu Islands. This started a fight that has never stopped. The Republic of China (ROC) publicly said that the Diaoyu Islands are a part of Taiwan for the first time. The islands should have been returned to Chinese control in 1972, but the ROC said that they are part of Taiwan. During the 1970s, a lot of Taiwanese students started nationalist groups to fight Japan's original claim of sovereignty over the Diaoyu Islands. When Japanese right-wingers built a lighthouse on the main island in 1996, protesters in Taiwan and Hong Kong again marched through the streets and tried to land on the Diaoyu Islands.

It was also the first time that the Kuomintang (KMT) government in Taiwan let a big group of students start a movement. Nationalism always led to social mobilization, which, if not kept in check, could easily be used against the authoritarian KMT government. In a way, the KMT brought back the youth nationalism of the 1970s as a way to deal with the fact that Chinese identity in Taiwan was becoming less and less valid. In the 1970s, the People's Republic of China (PRC) took the place of the Republic of China (ROC) as the official name of China. At the same time, Taiwan's economy was growing, and there was more push for big changes in how the country was run. But because the KMT government made it hard for young people to get involved in politics, they had nowhere to talk about their fears and reaffirm who they were. To regain the legitimacy of the KMT and keep the political system stable, the KMT used nationalism with a clear enemy (Japan) as a way to distract young people from the legitimacy problem and get them to support the government. So, the Diaoyu Islands became a shorthand sign for irredentist nationalism, based on the idea that China's land was being taken away by Japan. In 1972, the Diaoyu Islands were made to look like China's lost land with the help of new maps and history books. In short, the Diaoyu Islands movement of 1972 was caused by Taiwan's separation from the rest of the world and its fast-growing economy. This created a state of anomie in which young people felt like they didn't know who they were and had no power in the market economy. So, it seems likely that in the 2000s, the weakening hold of Chinese identity in Taiwan and the Taiwan-centered pedagogy found in school curricula tended to dampen support for the movement to protect the Diaoyu Islands, which the younger generation in Taiwan associated with support for cross-Strait reunification. Before Japan took over the Diaoyu Islands in 2012, we didn't see many online protests by Taiwan's young people against Japan.

The Chinese Communist Party (CCP) stayed out of the argument until 2012. When the first two waves of protests over the Diaoyu Islands happened in 1972 and 1996, big anti-Japanese rallies were held in Taiwan and Hong Kong, but not in Beijing. The Chinese government stopped people from being afraid of foreigners and chose to "shelve the dispute" until it could be solved later. Why did Chinese nationalism about the Diaoyu Islands conflicts start up again among young people in 2012? Some people thought that the building of the state led to the rise of Chinese nationalism. They called the new nationalism of people born after 1980 "official nationalism" or "pragmatic nationalism." It was based on a sense of patriotism that saw the CCP as looking out for the country's best interests. In particular, they saw it as the result of the CCP's "Patriotic Education Campaign" of the 1990s and 2000s. This campaign tried to bolster the party's waning legitimacy by focusing on China's past glory and the "hundred years of humiliation" that followed, which started with the First Opium War in the 1800s and involved repeatedly giving in to foreign powers. They also said that using the U.S. as a point of comparison made people afraid of people from other countries, which helped the communist government stay in power. Other experts thought that the 1990s also saw the rise of a popular nationalism that shouldn't be confused with official nationalism. The CPP couldn't stop the protesters, so it lost control of nationalist speech and had to beg protesters to stop. Scholars are also finding more and more links between local nationalism and the rise of the Internet, which brought the Chinese cyber community together against pressure from outside China. Chinese cybernationalists have been using the Internet as a hub for contact, a place to organize, and a way to carry out their plans.

But without knowing how young Chinese people think, we can't understand why the once-unimportant Diaoyu Islands became such an important part of China to them in 2012. Why did the Diaoyu Islands riots spread so quickly and then become violent? This chapter is split into two parts so that we can look into these questions. The first part tries to figure out how the Diaoyu Islands got into the minds of younger people. Taiwan and Japan were important points of reference for young Chinese people as they tried to figure out who they were. The second part depends on why Chinese youth groups turned nationalist and brought together millions of people in 2012 during the disputes over the Diaoyu Islands. In a lot of ways, China's position was like the Diaoyu Islands crisis in Taiwan in 1972. I think that the "raging youth" phenomenon is caused by a mix of national pride and unhappiness with the CCP. What made people born after 1980 feel both proud and ashamed? This part shows the structural reasons why the youth movements of 2012 were able to happen. After 30 years of economic change, the CCP still has a tight grip on the political system and keeps its legitimacy by keeping the economy growing fast. I will show how China's young people, who were not allowed to form organizations or were watched by the government, used the Internet to vent their anger, share ideas, and take part in social actions, all of which helped them find a sense of national identity. Lastly, we show how the Internet and globalization have worked together to bring back angry nationalism in modern China. People have to come together because of globalization, and this paper looks into why, in an age with more people having access to the Internet, Chinese culture is always defended against a foreign enemy.

Raging Youth

Before we can start to figure out what caused the "raging youth" in 2012, we need to know when and how Chinese youth started to think of the Diaoyu Islands as part of China. As they did in Taiwan in the 1970s, the Chinese government made the Diaoyu Islands a part of the idea of a community for young Chinese people. This was done to give them a sense of legitimacy and help them adjust to the changing foreign and domestic situation.

Setting Aside the Disagreement

In 1968, huge oil reserves were found for the first time near the East China Sea. This brought attention to the Diaoyu Islands. Before that, neither China nor Taiwan had shown any interest in these deserted islands with no people living there. The Okinawa Reversion Treaty, which was signed in 1972, said that the United States had to give Japan the right to run the Diaoyu Islands. This is what started the conflict over the Diaoyu Islands. The main point of disagreement was whether or not the Diaoyu Islands were part of Taiwan in April 1895, when the Chinese government signed the Shimonoseki Treaty and gave Taiwan and "all its islands" to Japan. At the end of the Second World War, the Cairo Declaration of 1943, the Potsdam Proclamation of 1945, and the Treaty of Peace with Japan of 1952 said that all of the land that China had given up had to be given back to China. Both the People's Republic of China (PRC) and the Republic of China (ROC) said that the Diaoyu Islands were a part of Taiwan and should have been returned to Chinese control in 1972.

Japan first claimed ownership of the Diaoyu Islands in 1884 based on the idea of terra nullius. In January 1895, the islands became part of Japan. During the 1970s, a lot of student protests happened in Taiwan and Hong Kong, but, surprisingly, not in Beijing. Between 1966 and 1976, young Chinese people were involved in the Cultural Revolution. During this time, the Down to the Countryside Movement moved many young people from cities to the countryside. Even though schools went back to regular schedules in 1978, revolutionary ideas ruled the curriculum in the 1980s. This was done to restore the CCP's legitimacy. So, the Chinese people who lived during the Cultural Revolution and Reform did not care about the Diaoyu Islands. More importantly, both Japan and the United States were trying to normalize diplomatic ties with China in the 1970s. Deng Xiaoping didn't pay much attention to the sovereignty dispute with Japan in 1972 and 1978 because he wanted the PRC to replace the ROC as China's only legitimate international representative. He did this because he wanted the PRC to replace the ROC as China's only legitimate international representative.

The Influence of Taiwan and Japanese Activities

After being quiet about the Diaoyu Islands for 30 years, the CCP started to say what it thought about them. The territorial dispute between Tokyo and Beijing was kept under control from the 1970s until the mid-1990s by a tacit deal to "shelve the dispute." Still, since the mid-1990s, Japanese politics have become more patriotic, which has made things worse in Asia. In 1996, a group of Japanese nationalists rebuilt a lighthouse on one of the disputed islands. This made Chinese nationalists in Taiwan and Hong Kong very angry. The rise of right-wing nationalism in Japan became clear when Shintaro Ishihara was elected mayor of Tokyo in 1999. In 1989, he wrote a patriotic book called "A Japan That Can Say No," and in April 2012, he announced that the Tokyo Metropolitan Government would buy the Senkaku Islands and fortify them. Since 2000, the Japanese government has sent more police to the contested Senkaku Islands to show that Japan is in charge. As a result of Japan's 2005 textbook screening, there are more references to the Senkaku Islands in elementary and middle school texts. This is to back up an official statement that there is "no territorial problem" between Taiwan and China and Japan over the Senkaku Islands. For the leaders of the CCP, letting Japan win the tug-of-war over who owns the Diaoyu Islands would not only hurt their credibility, but it could also hurt their business interests in the huge oil deposits near the islands.

In the meantime, when Lee Teng-hui won the 1996 presidential election and the Democratic Progressive Party (DPP) won the two that followed, Taiwan's future moved closer to independence. During this time, the Taiwan government didn't say much to defend the ROC's right to rule over the contested islands. As Taiwanese nationalism became the most important part of the political platform, the effort to protect the Diaoyu Islands lost a lot of support. The problem of the Diaoyu Islands, which Taiwan's younger people linked to support for reunification across the Taiwan Strait, was called "politically incorrect." In 1996, when Japan claimed the EEZ around the Diaoyu Islands, Lee Teng-hui said again that the ROC had control over the disputed islands, but he also put the issue of sovereignty aside so that he and Japan could talk about fishing. During the DPP administration (2000–2008), the Taiwanese government was also more focused on negotiating the fishing rights of Taiwanese fishermen in seas that are in dispute with Japan. In 1978, Japanese activists built a lighthouse on the biggest of the Diaoyu Islands. In February 2005, the Japanese government took over the lighthouse. In June, Japan Coast Guard boats chased away Taiwanese fishing boats, which made Taiwanese fishermen and advocates for the Diaoyu Islands angry. In response to the fishermen's anger, Chen Shui-bian sent out patrol ships to protect Taiwanese fishing boats and even set foot on the Pengjia Islet to claim Taiwan's authority over the Diaoyu Islands. At the same time, he said that the Taiwanese government should deal with the fishing rights problem separately from the sovereignty issue so that the situation doesn't get more complicated and tensions don't rise. KMT lawmakers said Chen Shui-bian's reaction was just "making a show," and Taipei's mayor, Ma Ying-jeou, said it showed a lack of courage.

Taiwan and Japan finally made progress on the sovereignty problem in late August 2005, after putting it off for years. The Japanese Diet passed a law that lets Taiwanese people travel to Japan without a visa, but they didn't do anything to make up with China. So, this move was seen as a break from Japan's attempt to keep the situation across the Taiwan Strait in check. China was very upset about Taiwan's sovereignty, especially after Lee Teng-hui said in 1999 that Taiwan and China had "special state-to-state relations" and then said in an interview in 2002 that the Diaoyu Islands actually belonged to Japan. China had to take back control of the Diaoyu Islands because they were directly linked to China's claim to Taiwan and Taiwan's claim to China. After the fall of the Soviet Union, the CCP's credibility was on the decline, so it was important for the country to work together. China's longtime strategy of "putting the dispute on hold" had been weakened by political changes in Japan and Taiwan.

Connections with Taiwan

At the start of the 21st century, the CCP started a public relations effort to make sure that young Chinese people saw the Diaoyu Islands as an inseparable part of China. Like in Japan, texts are at the forefront of China's efforts to make people more patriotic. In 2001, the Ministry of Education of the People's Republic of China (PRC) released the Basic Education Curriculum Reform Outline. This document put Chinese custom and history, as well as national unity and territorial integrity, at the center of patriotic education. Also, the People's Education Press changed its new teaching guides to represent the CCP's new position on its territorial claims. For example, in Geography I, year 8, the topic "Taiwan: Part of the Sacred Territory of China" asks teachers to help students use maps to find places in Taiwan and islands that belong to it, like the Diaoyu Islands. The goal of the high school course "Geography of the Ocean" is to teach students about China's natural ocean riches and make them more aware of their country's sovereignty. To reach this goal, teachers should talk about the illegal taking over of islands in the East and South China Seas and show how this hurts China's interests and freedom of passage. China and Japan are also fighting over maps to prove that the Diaoyu Islands are theirs by history and law. Like other experts on the subject, CCP officials point to a collection of historical maps from the 1600s. For example, the map Coastal Defense Stretching Thousands of Miles shows that the Diaoyu Islands were added to China's maritime defense in 1561. Other maps show that the Diaoyu Islands were used as navigational aids for tributary missions between China and the Ryukyu Kingdom. The Great Universal Geographic Map, which was made in 1767, shows that the Diaoyu Islands were part of the Qing Empire because they were part of Taiwan's fishing grounds. In 1809, when the French geographer Pierre M. Lapie made a map of the states along the coast of the East China Sea, he gave Diaoyu Dao, Huangwei Yu, and Chi-wei Yu the same color as Taiwan. People think that those maps were made with the idea that the Diaoyu Islands were part of China before the 16th century and were not "terra nullius" before 1885, as Japan claims. The Diaoyu Islands, which are part of the Chinese national community, have made their way into the minds of young people through maps.

China also made it clear that the Diaoyu Islands are a natural part of the PRC's property by taking a number of actions that backed up the PRC's claims to the disputed islands. In 2008, soon after Ma Ying-jeou took the oath of office as president of the ROC, a Taiwanese fishing ship called the Lien Ho sank near the Diaoyu Islands after colliding with a Japan Coast Guard ship. The Ma administration demanded a public apology and compensation for the Lien Ho right away. They also put an end to fisheries talks and called back Taiwan's minister to Japan, Hsu Shih-kai, who had been in charge of bilateral relations between Taiwan and Japan for a decade even though there was no official diplomatic relationship between the two countries. The KMT lawmakers even set up a trip to the disputed areas on a navy ship called the La Fayette frigate. DPP lawmakers saw these moves as a way to get closer to Beijing because the first Chen-Chiang summit of cross-Strait talks would be held in Beijing in a week. This would be the first meeting between Taiwan and China in ten years. For China, it was the first step in trying to find a way to work with Taipei on the problem. Four days after the summit across the Strait, China sent two patrol boats to the East China Sea to quest on Japan's effective control for the first time. This move, which was covered to death by China's state-run media, was a turning point in the troubled relationship between China and Japan. It meant that "putting the dispute on hold" was no longer an option. Since 2010, when a Chinese fishing trawler ran into two Japanese Coast Guard boats, China has regularly sent patrol ships to the seas in question.

Since then, China has gotten stronger in its claims about the Diaoyu Islands, and Taiwan's reaction has become less important. In August 2012, to clarify Taiwan's stance on disputed waters, the Ma administration suggested the East China Sea Peace Initiative. This is a plan that wants to put disputes to rest and peacefully resolve disputes in the East China Sea through reciprocal negotiation and cooperative development. The DPP thought that this effort supported the "one-China" idea because it allowed the PRC and Taiwan to work together on the Diaoyu Islands sovereignty claims. The reaction from Beijing, on the other hand, was not very positive. Wang Yi, who is in charge of China's Taiwan Affairs Office, said that China knew about the plan, but that China's position on the East China Sea has always been very clear. Chinese state media and online censors downplayed the effort to show that China was in charge of the Diaoyu Islands.

Research Methods

A week before the 81st anniversary of the Manchurian Incident, on September 11, 2012, the Japanese government bought three of the five Diaoyu Islands. This caused outrage in as many as one hundred places in China and brought one million young people to the streets to protest. Why did a piece of land on a map become a strong and appealing symbol of Chinese pride among young people in 2012? Why did Chinese youth's love for their country turn into a "rage"?

Conceptualization

Before you can answer these questions, you need to define Chinese nationalism, Chinese youth, and Chinese anger. The goal of this chapter is not to look at all of the research on Chinese nationalism, which has different meanings at different points in Chinese history and for different researchers. In this study, "Chinese nationalism" means patriotism, love, loyalty, and dedication to China. Youth refers to the group born after 1980, also called "millennials." These people grew up during China's reform and opening and saw the Tiananmen Square incident and the Patriotic Education Campaign. In theory, a "political generation" is a group of people who grew up together and have "common historical memories" because they were born at the same time and saw the same political and economic changes. Based on this definition, the people of China can be divided into five political generations: the war generation (before 1943), the Cultural Revolution generation (1944–1961), the Reform generation (1962–1980), the post-1980 generation (1981–1990), and the post-1990 generation (since 1991). In this study, "outrage" is described as "righteous anger" that is used to protect China's survival and prosperity.

Data

This chapter uses three types of data that work together to answer its study questions. First, the Strong Nation Forum is an important part of the main study for this chapter. It is a Chinese message board on the website of the People's Daily. It was made in 1999 so that Chinese people could talk about how angry they were that the US bombed the Chinese Embassy in Belgrade. As soon as the Strong Nation Forum went online, it quickly became the most popular place for nationalists to talk online. In 2008, the Liao wang dong fang zhou kan (Oriental outlook) did an online poll that showed that 68 percent of Internet users on the Strong Nation Forum were between the ages of 20 and 40. In this way, the Strong Nation Forum can be used as a good way to study how Chinese youth are becoming more nationalistic. This study looks at comments and talks on the Strong Nation Forum from 2008 to 2015 and analyzes them to learn about the rise of Chinese youth nationalism and how it changed into anti-Japan nationalism in 2012. For the research, we looked for posts on the Strong Nation Forum that used the word "Diaoyu Islands" as a key word. Repeated and similar posts by the same Internet users were deleted to cut down on spamming or stop well-known users from trying to spread their own views. There were 1,355 true posts about the Diaoyu Islands that were collected to be looked at. This text-based data set was also looked at through the lens of content analysis. In this study, the posts were read and recorded by hand to avoid the problems that come with automated (fully computerized) content analysis, which tends to make random connections between words and phrases and miss the context of each post. We took as much information as we could from each post and linked it to major themes. We then put the information into categories like reason, solution, attitude toward the CCP, Japan, the US, Taiwan, and so on (see Table 6.1). Content analysis is prone to coder bias, so two coders coded the same data and checked it against each other to make sure the results were accurate. Two other sources of information were used to help with this study. First, it looked at the results of an internet poll about patriotism and nationalism that the People's Daily did in 2012 and 2013. Several things about this type of data worked well for this study. Most obviously, the poll asked people born after 1980 about their freedom and ability to think for themselves. The World Values Survey, which looks at how values and cultures change over time, did face-to-face conversations in China in 2012. These interviews were the last source of data. The people who were the focus were Chinese people over the age of 18. By looking at these three sets of data, we were able to find out what Chinese nationalism is and why it erupted among Chinese youth in 2012.

Limitations of the Data

Concerns about selection bias were raised when we used the Strong Nation Forum as our unit of observation. Possible bias is caused by two things. The first is that only about 27.5 percent of China's rural places had Internet access in 2013, while 62 percent of China's cities did. Because of this, there were not enough rural kids in our sample. Even though just over half of the rural population uses the Internet, more than half of them are between the ages of 20 and 40. In 2013, this group made up almost two-thirds of the rural population, just like it did in cities. In this way, the first worry about selection bias can be ruled out. The second selection bias is that the People's Daily, which is part of the CCP's Central Committee, is in charge of the Strong Nation Forum. The general rules of the Strong Nation Forum say that people can't try to overthrow the government, start separatist groups, or do anything else that is illegal. Messages about sensitive subjects like Tiananmen Square and Falun Gong can't show up. If talks go too far, webmasters will delete all of the posts and block the IP addresses and registered names. Some people aren't free to say what they want on the Internet, which can change how people think. But the government hasn't done much to stop internet conversations that criticize its policies but appeal to nationalist feelings. The rate of loss is thought to be between 1 and 1.5 percent. Also, as the number of online political forums run by privately owned media like SINA, Tianya, and many others has grown, the CCP is less likely to turn against Internet users by cracking down hard on the Strong Nation Forum. In general, the Strong Nation Forum is a good place to see a lot of Chinese youth nationalism, so it might be a good place to study it. A self-selection bias could also happen if the online survey is used as study data. Since people can choose whether or not to take part in a study, certain groups, like young people, people from the middle class, and people with college degrees, are over represented. Because of this, the people who answer online surveys will not be a good representation of the whole community. But we can lessen this worry about self-selection bias because the goal of this study is to look at young people, not the whole community.

Diaoyu Island Incident

Why did young Chinese nationalism come back and get worse in 2012? Even though the Chinese government said they couldn't, Chinese Internet users started a large campaign on the Web to boycott Japanese goods. This led to a drop in sales of Japanese cars, which made Toyota and Honda stop making cars in China for a while. Did the movement just come from a made-up community or hate from the past that was brought up in textbooks, or did it come from national pride in China's rapid economic growth and a desire to escape oppression?

Influenced by Mixed Feelings toward the CCP

The empirical study shows that the "raging youth" are torn between being proud of their country and being disappointed in the CCP. As shown in Table 6.1 of the Strong Nation Forum, about 8.5 of the Internet posts said that China has had clear ownership of the Diaoyu Islands since ancient times, but Japan is now illegally living on them. In 2012, the World Values Survey (Table 6.2) showed that 91.4 percent of people born after 1980 were proud of China and 84.1 percent would fight for China in a war. This was an average of 15% more than the two generations before them. But when the Diaoyu Islands event happened in 2012, the Strong Nation Forum (Table 6.1) was full of messages that were ashamed of and disappointed in the CCP. About 16.6% of the posts said that the CCP was "too soft" on Japan and that government officials and experts were not doing enough to reclaim control over the islands. About 3.8% of the posts agreed that the government was doing the right thing by sending patrol ships to a contested area, but they were worried that the goal was to distract people from the slowing economy. One user said, "Sending patrol ships is just tiptoeing around the issue." What made people born after 1980 feel both proud and ashamed?

At the beginning of the 1990s, China's move to a market economy and the sudden fall of the Soviet Union caused people to look for a new philosophy. Jiang Zemin started patriotic education in 1991, and it was fully running by 1994. He did this to fill the spiritual void. The main topics of patriotic education in China, which was meant to bring back loyalty as a replacement for fading socialism, were Chinese culture and history and national unity and territorial integrity. Since 2001, patriotic education and education changes have made sure that Chinese people born after 1980 are committed to protecting China's sovereignty and territorial integrity. The Chinese youth's sense of national identity wasn't just based on a "nationalism of despair" that reminded them of a past greatness that had been lost after a "century of humiliation." Built on thirty years of economic changes and opening up to the rest of the world, China's amazing economic growth has boosted national confidence to a level that has never been seen before. This has led to a new period of Chinese nationalism. Michel Oksenberg called it a "confident nationalism" that was patient and moderate and based on the belief that China could someday get back to being a great country through economic growth. Since 1980, most Chinese have believed in a strong China and the thought that "China can say no" to US hegemony and stand up to other countries that try to dominate it. Since the Diaoyu Islands are an important part of the country, many people on the Internet have called for stronger steps to protect them. Even though 4.3% of the posts on the Strong Nation Forum called for a peaceful settlement through talks or economic sanctions, 6.9% called for war to be declared against Japan (see Table 6.1). "It's easy because we have nuclear weapons," he said. About 2.8% of the posts said that China should get the islands back no matter what, and 2.6% said that war was going to happen anyway. Some posts (4.3%) said that the fact that Taiwan is an inalienable part of China was at the heart of the territorial conflict between China and Japan. "It would make things easier to help cross-Strait unification happen." When all the messages were added up, 12.3% of them were in favor of using force to solve the problem. As a result of patriotic education and China's rapid growth, Chinese youth are becoming more and more proud of their country's rising status and feel a strong need to protect China from unfriendly outside forces.

Table 6.1 Opinions on the Diaoyu Island Dispute

Theme	Percentage	Subcategory	Percentage
Sarcastic messages	19.2	Controversial figures	4.1
		Mockery of the CCP	5.0
		Boasting, bragging of plans to seize islands	3.5
		Others	6.6
Disappointment with CCP	16.6		
Awareness of patrol vessels	3.8		
Diaoyu Islands as insepa-rable from China	8.5		
Resolution by force	12.3	Declaration of war	6.9
		Retrieve at any cost	2.8
		Inevitable war	2.6
Resolution by talk	4.3		
Taiwan factor		Unification as crucial	4.3
		Taiwan must act to signal control over Diaoyu Islands	4.2
Japan's responsibility	6.5	Japan's provocation	1.9
		Japan's ambition	4.7
US's responsibility	12.3	Obama's foreign policy pivot toward Asia	6.1
		Occupation of Okinawa	6.2
Ethnic slurs	5.8	Against Japan	3.7
		Against US	2.1
Criticizing attitudes of Chinese netizens toward Japan and US	5.9	Calling pro-Japan and pro-US attitudes unpatriotic	2.1
		Calling anti-Japan and anti-US attitudes irrational	3.8
Others	11.3		

Source: Strong Nation Forum, bbs1.people.com.cn/.

Table 6.2 Level of Patriotism in China

			Generation				Total
			War generation (before 1943)	Cultural Revolution generation (1944–61)	Reform generation (1962-80)	Post-1980 generation (1981-90)	
How proud of nationality	Very proud	N	41	124	212	123	500
		%	33.9	24.2	24.9	23.2	24.8
	Quite proud	N	68	313	557	362	1300
		%	56.2	61.1	65.3	68.2	64.5
	Not very proud	N	11	72	75	41	199
		%	9.1	14.1	8.8	7.7	9.9
	Not at all proud	N	1	3	9	5	18
		%	0.8	0.6	1.1	0.9	0.9
	Total	N	121	512	853	531	2017
		%	100.0	100.0	100.0	100.0	100.0
Willingness to fight for your country	Yes	N	88	392	740	470	1690
		%	70.4	70.8	81.6	84.1	78.8
	No	N	37	162	167	89	455
		%	29.6	29.2	18.4	15.9	21.2
	Total	N	125	554	907	559	2145
		%	100.0	100.0	100.0	100.0	100.0

Source: World Values Survey in China (2012). WVS [World Values Survey],Wave 6 (2010-2014), China 2012, conducted by the Research Center for Contemporary China (RCCC) at Peking University in 2012. Data can be retrieved from www.worldvaluessurvey.org/WVSDocumentationWV6.jsp.

note: % in the parentheses is the row percentage.

Still, since China is now part of the global economy, it is hard for China to say no. Most people agree that China's fast integration into the global economy has made tensions between countries worse. Beijing's leaders are finding it harder and harder to keep patriotism high and put economic growth first at the same time. In a speech at Harvard University in December 2003, the Chinese president, Wen Jiabo, used the phrase "peaceful rise." Since then, economic growth and a calm rise to power have been the two main goals of CCP leaders. The party has shown that it is peaceful by being involved in international groups, hosting the

Olympics, and negotiating trade deals with as many as twelve other countries. At the 18th CCP meeting in 2012, Xi Jinping, the new general secretary of the CCP, was put in a tough spot by pressures from the market and calls from the majority of the public for tough responses to Japan. The continuing territorial disputes over the Diaoyu Islands have slowed down the progress of the China-Japan-South Korea Free Trade Agreement (FTA) talks, and the United States' return to the Asia-Pacific region has made China's political and economic power much more difficult to control. In particular, since 2010, talks have been going on to create the Trans-Pacific Partnership (TPP), which will be the world's biggest free trade zone and is being led by the US. This is being done to stop China's rise. Because of these efforts, it is even more important for China to work hard to get FTAs with Japan and South Korea that lower trade barriers. This will help China take advantage of the huge trade possibilities in ASEAN and around the Pacific Rim. China is very aware of how much it would cost to push Japan to go to war. Even though China sent a marine surveillance plane and patrol ships into the disputed seas to show that Japan didn't have sole control over the islands, the CCP hasn't tried to land on the islands or put any economic sanctions on Japan since then. Christopher Hughes says that a lot of young Chinese people see the CCP's patrols and foreign moves as "shows of defiance." So, the group born after 1980 has been pushed into action by their mixed feelings about the CCP.

Emergence of Network Society

How can this proud group lessen the worries that come from feeling both pride in their country and disappointment that the CPP hasn't lived up to its nationalist promises? Psychoanalysts say that existential worry and uncertainty about what we are have made it harder to find stable identities. Anxiety and uncertainty often lead to aggressive behavior and radical groups. China's protests by young people also show these patterns. Even though the economy has changed a lot over the past 30 years, the CCP still has a firm grip on political power. Young people don't have many ways to get their anger out because the state only allows or watches a small number of organizations. Even though there won't be direct elections or party changes in the near future, young people also don't have a public place to voice their unhappiness. Chinese youth can switch from virtual reality to group action to get to a stable point where they all have the same ideas about the Diaoyu Islands.

To get a big group, like a country, to work together, you need two kinds of tools: effective institutions that bring people together to work toward a common goal and unifying ideas that show people they all have the same fate. For the first tool, the spread of the Internet in China has a mobilizing effect by making it easier for people to get involved in politics and share their thoughts. In the 21st century, modernization in China has led to a change in how people communicate. With the rise of Internet-based communication comes a new type of communication: mass self-communication, which is "self-generated in content, self-directed in emission, and self-selected in reception by many that communicate with many." People build their own systems of mass communication and asynchronous talk using BBS, blogs, Weibo, Tencent QQ, and other social media. This has made it easier for people to get involved in their communities and opened up new ways for ideas to spread. In China, the number of Internet users has grown a lot in the last ten years. In 2014, there were more than 600 million users. Nearly two-thirds of Internet users in China are born after 1980. For them, the Internet has become a virtual society. So, the Internet gives young Chinese people a way to talk about and share their feelings about their country. It also brings together people who don't know each other well and encourages them to protest.

Concerning the second tool, unifying ideas, China's fast-growing educational system goes even further to create unified fields of communication by using standard languages and homogenized contexts to support a common discourse of nationalism. Statistics from 2014 show that China's higher education is growing all the time, with over 2,000 universities and 7.27 million college grads. Education does more than make people loyal to the state and the ruling party or build a made-up community that includes the Diaoyu Islands. It also makes people smarter and more open-minded, making them better able to check the truth of information, be skeptical, and question authority. Evidence from the People's Daily online poll showed that 70% of people born after 1980 thought they were more independent thinkers than people born before 1980. In an online poll about populism, also done by the People's Daily from October 21 to October 31, 2012, 42.8 percent of people born after 1980 supported radical groups for the sake of patriotism, while only 32.4 percent of people born before 1980 did. These results explain why the government's requests for quiet and restraint were ignored when Japan bought the Diaoyu Islands in 2012. In other words, education has both positive and negative affects. Education doesn't just make young people more patriotic; it also gives them ways to change the government when they think it's going in the wrong direction. On the streets, young protesters shouted things like "Never forget national humiliation" and "Protect China's inseparable territory." They also showed their anger at the Chinese government, calling it "shamefully weak" and telling it to "take Japan down."

Strengthened by a Perception of Crisis

Lastly, why did the Diaoyu Islands riots turn violent? A strong sense of danger can help explain why angry Chinese nationalism came back in 2012. Many people who posted on the Strong Nation Forum thought that the United States was an even bigger threat than Japan ("Of first importance now is the need to check the United States") and that it was the reason for Japan's rise to power. On the thread (Table 6.1), 6.5 percent of the posts said that Japan should be blamed for the conflict, while 12.3 percent said that the US should be blamed. About half of the posts that blamed the U.S. (6.1% of the total sample) said that Japan's decision to take over the Diaoyu Islands was part of a plot by the U.S. to make things worse between Japan and China so that it could move forward in the Asia-Pacific. They used the Treaty of Mutual Cooperation and Security between the United States and Japan and joint military drills between the US and Japan to back up the fears of the posters. They said that Japan would not risk war without the support of the US. The other half of the posts (6.2% of the total) looked to history to show why the US was to blame. For these Internet users, China's claims to the controversial Diaoyu Islands were mostly based on international agreements like the Cairo Declaration from 1943, the Potsdam Proclamation from 1945, and the San Francisco Treaty from 1951. But the islands were never given back to China because the US was in charge of the Ryukyu Islands after the Second World War. "The US bombed the Diaoyu Islands to satisfy their own greed," many Internet users wrote. Many people also thought that in the 1971 Okinawa Reversion Treaty, the US left the question of who owns the Diaoyu Islands unsettled and unclear. They thought that this was done on purpose so that the US could move into Asia.

China may have been worried about the US threat right away because of how the US treats Asia now. In 2011, the Obama government said that the U.S. would move back to Asia. This was a big blow to China's political and economic power. Obama went to the 2011 Asia-Pacific Economic Cooperation (APEC) summit to support the Trans-Pacific Partnership (TPP), which would create a path to free trade in the Asia-Pacific and include 40 percent of the world's GDP. The requirements to join the TPP were based on American ideas about labor rights, intellectual property rights, and protecting the environment. This would keep China from joining the biggest free trade zone in the world. Not surprise, all of the hundreds of comments on the Strong Nation Forum saw the TPP as a way to stop China from getting too powerful. Many people on the Internet saw it as a "revival of US imperialism" and "US hegemony over the world." In 2012, when tensions with China over the Diaoyu Islands were getting worse, the US convinced Japan to join TPP talks. This made the power struggle between the US and China even more difficult. At the same time, the US made it clear in a statement that the Diaoyu Islands were covered by the bilateral Treaty of Mutual Cooperation and Security, which required the US to protect them if they were attacked with force. Later that same year, the US and Japan started doing armed drills together. Concerns about an unstated US goal to block China grew after the US military involvement in Japan's conflict with China grew. This was especially true after Japan's Liberal Democratic Party won a landslide victory in the House of Representatives elections in December 2012, which pushed the new Japanese prime minister, Shinzo Abe, to push the Diaoyu Islands issue more strongly. In 2013, the government of Prime Minister Abe said that joining the TPP would make Japan safer. He kept working on reinterpreting Japan's law to give people the right to self-defense as a group.

The economic and military containment policies of Japan and the United States are seen by young people in China as an immediate danger to China's existence. Their sense of crisis comes from the shared memory of China's humiliation and isolation during the Cold War. From this sense of danger and disaster come two things that strengthen their national identity and make them act in more extreme ways. The first enemy is easy to pick out. Identity is about how you fit in with your own group, what you have in common with them, and what makes you different from others. So, the first and most important step in figuring out who you are is to identify "others." It takes putting up a line between "us" and "them," where the differences between the two groups can be seen. But it's hard for young Chinese people to get a clear sense of "us." A huge number of cultural treasures and traditional ideals were lost during the Cultural Revolution. Lucian Pye said that China doesn't have the building blocks for a strong sense of identity because the symbols and ideals of the society are in such bad shape. The content of modern Chinese nationalism seems to be very thin, with no shared ideas or good ideas that can motivate people. Also, China's move from communism to capitalism has led to a state of anomie in which young people don't believe in socialism and feel helpless in the market economy. So, the new generation has a closed-off mentality and loses real connections with other people. So, the Chinese identity of people born after 1980 was already unstable because it was built by the state through patriotic schooling and state propaganda. Still, as international conflicts get worse, Chinese youth become more aware of being part of the Chinese country because they see it as being threatened and need to work together to fight enemies. They start to become more Chinese in order to stand out from Japan and the United States, which are clear foes.

The second thing that a sense of threat and disaster does is make people want to work together to fight back. Since the 19th century, the Chinese have been fighting against deep-seated questions about the worth of their people. Even though China has done well economically, the story of the "century of humiliation" has been told again and again in history books and official papers to remind people of the pain and shame caused by foreign aggression. Young Chinese people think that the Japan-US alliance is meant to stop China's rise. This alliance threatens not only China's rise, but also its national pride. Gordon Allport says that when an enemy threatens people's good values, it makes them more stubborn and makes them overstate how good their cause is. In the same way, Chinese youth nationalism comes from working together against Japan and the U.S., which are both seen as enemies. This is especially true now, when Internet access is growing quickly. Verbal violence on the Internet is the easiest way to make yourself feel better about yourself by making others look bad. A small number of posts on the Strong Nation Forum (Table 6.1) said bad things about the United States and Japan. They called Americans yang gui-zi, which means "foreign devils." They also made up a new word, mi-guo, which means "rotten country." They also called the Japanese "dogs," "little Japan," "gui-zi," and, most of all, "wokou," which means "dwarf bandits" and is a very insulting way to talk about a group of people. Even though the movement started with peaceful protests, it is easy for large-scale nationalist organizations that aim to let out xenophobic feelings to get out of hand. Even though there were calls for peaceful protests and a ban on the boycott, Chinese Internet users started a large campaign on the Web to get people to stop buying Japanese products. This led to a drop in sales of Japanese cars, which forced Toyota and Honda to temporarily stop making cars in China. Why did the pride of young Chinese people become a risk? From many transitional states, it is clear that fear and insecurity, not hatred, are behind racial violence. When a person feels less safe, he or she acts more violently. As a result of the immediate danger and the need to stop the US-Japan alliance from moving across the Pacific, China's xenophobic nationalism spread faster and more widely than ever in 2012, and shockingly, youth movements have almost caused riots in big Chinese cities.

Conclusion

Before the 81st anniversary of the Manchurian Incident in 2012, when the Diaoyu Islands were taken over by Japan, there were a lot of angry protests against Japan. This made things worse between China and Japan. This event got people all over the world talking again about what causes Chinese pride. This study went further than the highly contested question of whether Chinese nationalism came from the top down or the bottom up. It has looked into the psychological factors that make young Chinese people more nationalistic. By looking at the content of the statistics from the Strong Nation Forum, it has found three main reasons why Chinese youth nationalism in 2012 had become more violent.

In 1972, when the US gave Japan the right to run the Diaoyu Islands, this led to disagreements. Both China and Taiwan were very firm about who owned the Diaoyu Islands, and both thought they were part of Taiwan. So, when the Second World War ended, both the Diaoyu Islands and Taiwan should have been turned back over to China. In the meantime, after the PRC replaced the ROC as China's UN representative, the weakening of Chinese identity led the KMT to look for a new set of policies to keep its credibility. The Diaoyu Islands disputes were used by the KMT government as a way to get young Taiwanese to join nationalist groups during times when the public wasn't very active. At the same time, diplomatic ties between Japan and China were getting better. Even though disagreements led to angry protests and riots in Taiwan and Hong Kong, the CCP leadership stayed out of the way during the 1970s, 1980s, and 1990s. But since the mid-1990s, the rise of Japanese and Taiwanese nationalism has made China change its long-standing strategy of "putting the dispute on hold." Faced with new threats in international affairs, the CCP brought back nationalism among Chinese youth to replace socialism, which was becoming less popular. At the start of the 21st century, the CCP started a patriotic education program to show that Taiwan and the Diaoyu Islands were part of China. By learning about geography and history in school, Chinese kids have grown up with the idea that they should protect the unity of their country's land. A propaganda war against Japan is making China's young people see Taiwan and the islands it has taken over, called the Diaoyu Islands, as a natural part of China.

Then, we want to know why the 2012 protests against Japan's claim to the Diaoyu Islands went violent. The first reason is that people feel both pride in their country and sadness in the CCP. The generation that was born after 1980 grew up believing in a strong China and a mission to protect national unity. This was made possible by patriotic education and China's amazing economic growth. The 2012 World Values Survey showed that people born after 1980 are more happy to be Chinese than people born before 1980 and are more willing to be loyal to their country. But in 2012, when the trouble with the Diaoyu Islands was still going on, China, Japan, and South Korea were about to start talks on an FTA. In the meantime, economic interests and national pride were pulling the CCP in different ways. Many young Chinese people thought that the CCP's protests were just for show and that the CCP really put economic interests ahead of national pride. The Strong Nation Forum was full of posts that were upset with the CCP and called for tough answers to Japan. Without a way to show their anger through elections, Chinese youth took to the streets to talk about how they felt and to calm their fears about their feelings. Even though the government tried to stop them, there were a lot of protests after the Internet and schooling made people smarter. Lastly, the "raging youth" nationalism in China is made stronger by its fight against common enemies. In 2012, young people protested because Japan took over the Diaoyu Islands. However, many people on the Strong Nation Forum thought that the United States was to blame for Japan's aggressive nationalism and the 2012 Diaoyu Islands episode. China is worried about the US danger because the US is trying to keep China in its place with the TPP and a military alliance with Japan. In 2012, when tensions over the disputed islands were at a high, the US convinced Japan to join the TPP. This was the peak of the conflict between China and the US. A shared memory of China's humiliation and isolation for a century during the Cold War has made people feel like China's survival is in danger right now. Chinese youth tend to be more proud of being Chinese because Japan and the United States are clear foes. The threat problem is also a reason for people to work together to fight back. Having a common enemy brings a country together. China's xenophobic nationalism spread quickly in 2012 because of the immediate danger and the need to stop the US-Japan alliance from moving across the Pacific. In the end, the stranger was shown to be wrong about the Chinese youth.

Chapter 7
Reconstructing Chinese National Identity

Soon after Mao Zedong said on the Tiananmen Square stage that the Chinese people had stood up, it seemed like the People's Republic of China (PRC) was almost done building a nation, a process that had been sped up by a century of national humiliation and frequent foreign invasions. At the time, Taiwan was the only exception, since Chinese Nationalists had been in charge of Taiwan since 1945. Over the past 70 years, there have been two Chinese cultures on opposite sides of the Taiwan Strait, each with its own government. From the point of view of the Chinese mainland, the people who live in Taiwan, or "Taiwanese," are part of "the Chinese." This includes both the Han Chinese majority and the small number of Taiwanese aboriginals, who are considered one of the 55 minority ethnic groups in China.

Even though cross-Strait relations have been getting better over the past eight years, the growing feeling of Taiwanese identity on the island has shown how little Chinese national identity there is. People on the mainland have worked hard to rebuild the idea of one China through political communication, economic integration, social exchange, and cultural assimilation across the Taiwan Strait. This is because more people on Taiwan now identify as Taiwanese instead of Chinese or both. "Two shores, one close family" and "both sides [of the Strait] realizing the Chinese Dream" are two new political slogans that have been added to "a community of shared destiny across the Strait" and "the great rejuvenation of the Chinese nation."

This chapter talks about what Beijing is doing to rebuild the national character of China in relation to Taiwan. In theory, the Chinese national character is both natural and made up. Over the course of history, government growth and cultural mixing have made the old idea of the Middle Kingdom richer and richer. From 1949 to 1979, the Chinese people on the mainland were taught to free the poor people on Taiwan and bring the island back to China. This was done during times of political conflict and military stress. Since 1979, Taiwan's growth and the growing number of cross-Strait civic exchanges have helped mainlanders think about modernization and national identity in a new way. Based on what has happened in the past, it seems that rebuilding a Chinese national identity that spans the Taiwan Strait depends not only on economic modernization and integration, mutual cultural exchange and assimilation, and reinterpretation of contemporary Chinese history and political relations between the two entities before China's reunification, but also on improvement of public governance and political engineering on the mainland.

The Role of Taiwan in China's Remolding of National Identity

The land mass The Chinese government is clearly afraid that if most Taiwanese people see themselves as Taiwanese and want independence, this could make unification much less likely in the future. Taiwan's final unification with the mainland has become even more important for China's rebirth since Hong Kong and Macau went back to the home. This doesn't mean that Taiwan is the last lost region that will be taken back by the motherland, ending a century of foreign powers making China feel bad about itself. From Beijing's point of view, the question of recovering lost land has been settled since the end of World War II. As Hu Jintao, the boss of China, once said:

> *Although the mainland and Taiwan have not been reunited since 1949, the circumstances per se do not denote a state of partition of Chinese territory and sovereignty. Rather, it is merely a state of political antagonism that is a legacy—albeit a lingering one—of the Chinese civil war waged in the mid- to late-1940s. Nevertheless, this does not alter the fact that both the mainland and Taiwan belong to one China. For the two sides of the Strait, to return to unity is not a recreation of sovereignty or territory but an end to political antagonism.*

From this point of view, Taiwan's rebels are like those in Tibet and Xinjiang, even though Tibet and Xinjiang are already under the control of the PRC and Taiwan hasn't been united yet. Beijing has put these three areas together as part of its plan to strengthen national identity in a practical way to protect national sovereignty and territorial integrity. In the past few years, Chinese academics have suggested that their country's national identity should be changed for the new age by strengthening institutions, improving government, and making democratic progress. He Donghang and Xie Weimin point out the problem with China's process of building a national identity: the development of public identity has fallen behind the development of ethnic identity. Yao Dali says that, in a country like China with many different ethnic groups, it is important to speed up the process of democratizing the government in order to build and strengthen a sense of national identity. Yao thinks that the spirit of the modern nation-state and the main concept of democracy are the ideas of sovereignty and equality among people from different classes. Jin Taijun and Mi Jing say that political ideas like democracy, freedom, and human rights, as well as organizations based on them, are most important to national identity, especially in a country where people have different identities and multiple affiliations because of globalization. Lin Shangli says that identifying with state institutions, which are very important for building modern countries, is the most important part of national identity. In modern society, democracy is the political basis of a country's sense of itself.

In the case of Taiwan, however, political talk on the mainland has focused more on cultural similarities, ethnic equality, and economic interests shared by people on both sides of the Taiwan Strait and less on so-called institutional identity, which means accepting the identity of the economic and political system on the other side of the Taiwan Strait. Obviously, this is because most Taiwanese people are Han Chinese, and Beijing's "one country, two systems" plan for unification makes it unlikely that institutions on both sides of the Strait will merge. A lot of people in Taiwan would say that they are Taiwanese politically but Chinese culturally. Assuming that "blood is thicker than water," the Chinese mainland government offered people-to-people exchanges with Taiwan as early as 1979, when Beijing's unilateral announcement ended the political and symbolic military confrontation with Taiwan. Since then, Beijing hasn't said that it wants to "free miserable Taiwanese compatriots" from the cruel rule of the KMT. Instead, it has asked Taiwan for peaceful unification, pinning its hopes not only on the Taiwanese people but also on the KMT officials led by Chiang Ching-kuo. Blood ties, hometown ties, and ethnic ties were all used to rebuild a link between the two cultures that had been separated for a long time. Liao Chengzhi, who was a minister in the Chinese Communist Party Central Committee and in charge of the United Front, wrote an open message to Chiang Ching-kuo in July 1982. In the letter, Liao told Chiang Ching-kuo, "Brothers are still brothers, even after a painful fight between them, and they can easily forget their mutual hatred with a smile when they meet again." The story behind this sad letter was that Liao's father, Liao Zhongkai, was a top leader of the KMT in the 1920s and helped the KMT-CCP United Front fight against the Northern Warlords government. After this open letter, leaders from both sides kept in touch by mail, and in 1987, former PRC president Yang Shangkun said that Taiwan's leaders should respect the "overall national interest" of China and have peace talks with Beijing about unification. On the other side of the Strait, Chiang Ching-kuo even thought about sending his official representative to Beijing for preliminary political talks before he died in January 1988. Although peace talks on China's reunification between the two ruling parties on each side of the Taiwan Strait did not happen in the 1980s, Chiang Ching-kuo did decide in November 1987 to allow cross-Strait family reunions for old soldiers who had followed Chiang to Taiwan. Beijing's open-door policy and appeal for peaceful unification to the island, as well as Taipei's choice in 1987, have led to more people-to-people exchanges between the two sides, both for business and for family, hometown, and ethnic reasons. From the mainland's point of view, if the two sides can't have a real political conversation, cultural and economic factors can help stop separatist movements on the island, which has been out of PRC control since 1949. Both Jiang Zemin's "Eight Points" (1995) and Hu Jintao's "Six Points" (December 2008) have talked about how Chinese culture and economic cooperation help connect the two sides of the Taiwan Strait, despite the ups and downs of cross-Strait ties over the past 30 years.

"Two Shores, One Close Family"

When he met Lien Chan, the honorary chair of the KMT, on February 18, 2014, Chinese leader Xi Jinping pushed the idea that "compatriots from the two shores of the Taiwan Strait are one close family" in an effort to bring the two sides closer together on the issue of national identity and to build a Chinese identity that includes people from both sides of the Taiwan Strait. Xi Jinping said that people on the Chinese mainland and in Taiwan would always have blood ties to each other. This idea comes from the fact that the two countries share a similar past, culture, and ancestry. Cross-Strait links are not between neighbors, friends, or even enemies. Instead, they are between family members. Xi Jinping tries to get across the idea that both the mainland and Taiwan are part of one China and that both can "strive for China's reunification" by using phrases like "both sides fulfilling the Chinese Dream." He has stressed that unification is a goal shared by people on both sides of the Taiwan Strait and that it can only be achieved through China's rejuvenation. So, peaceful unification depends on both sides' peaceful growth and the "great rejuvenation of the Chinese nation."

Chinese mainland leaders have used a call to a shared culture with Taiwan for a long time, but it has become more common since the mainland's economy took off and its culture was rebuilt in the 1990s. In 1995, when the former leader of Taiwan, Lee Teng-hui, said that Chinese culture was the basis for cross-Strait exchanges, he was more confident about Taiwan's role in preserving and rebuilding Chinese culture than he was about mainland China's part. In fact, Taipei's 1991 rules for national unification said that cultural sinicization was one of the four things that had to happen first. The other three things were economic liberalization, political democratization, and social pluralism. Many people in Taiwan, including some supporters of the pro-independence Democratic Progressive Party (DPP), have said that Chinese culture is better preserved on the island than on the mainland, since Taiwan was not affected by the iconoclastic May Fourth movement and the Cultural Revolution, which happened on the other side of the Strait. Since the 1990s, however, cultural reconstruction on the island has come a long way. Some Confucian morals and ways of acting work well in the modernizing Chinese society, and the culture industries have grown quickly. The building of the China Art Museum at the Shanghai Expo in 2010 is a good example. It was a mix of traditional and modern styles. Taipei's efforts to stop being Chinese while the DPP was in charge just made the mainland realize how important Chinese culture is as the cultural link between the two sides.

Since the KMT came back to power in 2008, cultural contacts have come a long way, thanks to Ma Ying-jeou's love for traditional Chinese culture and the Chinese people. The Cross-Strait Cultural Industries Fair began in 2008 and has happened every year since then. In 2009, the fifth CCP-KMT forum was held in Changsha, Hunan. Culture and education were the main topics, with a focus on: 1) keeping Chinese culture alive and encouraging innovation; 2) promoting cross-Strait cooperation in cultural industries; and 3) increasing cross-Strait exchange and cooperation on education. In the same year, Fujian held the first Strait Forum. Since then, it has been held every year, with the goal of promoting social and cultural exchanges between the two sides. For example, at the 2010 Strait Forum, there was a cultural week about Mazu, an ancient sea goddess that people in southern Fujian and Taiwan used to worship. There was also a cultural festival for Zhu Xi, a famous Confucian scholar who was born and lived his whole life in Fujian, and a forum about Hakka culture. All of these events were meant to bring attention to parts of Chinese culture that people on both sides of the Strait have always shared. On the mainland, Taiwanese people took part in cultural events like worshiping the Yellow Emperor's ancestors in Shanxi and Henan Provinces and an arts festival for Chinese calligraphy in Beijing. Even though the two sides of the Taiwan Strait were not able to sign a deal on cultural exchanges during Ma Ying-jeou's first term, cultural exchanges continued during his second term. Cultural exchanges have covered a wide range of topics, including education, publishing, libraries, exhibitions, media interactions, religions, music, dance, theater, secular arts and customs, and local culture. In 2012, there were Cross-Strait Cultural Friendship Weeks and the Cultural Exhibition on the mainland, as well as Cross-Strait Intangible Cultural Heritage Month and the Cross-Strait City Arts Festival in Taiwan. The books were changed from simplified Chinese to traditional Chinese and reprinted on the island so that young people in Taiwan could read them. In the same year, 1,858 young people from Taiwan came to the mainland to study, and 951 people from the mainland went to Taiwan to study full-time. The Department of Culture under the PRC State Council said that 10,802 people from both sides of the

Taiwan Strait took part in 324 cultural exchange events in 2013. In 2014, there were 500 events and 12,593 people took part. Liu Xiangping says that culture identity is one of the most important parts of national identity. Ethnic identity and state identity are the other two. When it comes to cultural identity, the two sides are more alike than different, but when it comes to national identity, the differences have grown.

Lowell Dittmer points out that one of the things that helps people feel like they belong to a country is its history. This includes a shared understanding of difficult times in a country's history when fundamental questions about its purpose were brought up and settled in some way. The government on the mainland knows very well that different views of history can hurt national identity. As Xi Jinping told Lien Chan on February 18, 2014, the painful feelings that Taiwanese people have about political events from the past are shared by Chinese mainlanders. This is a tragedy for the whole Chinese country. Xi says that a strong nation can bring good luck to all Chinese people, while a weak and chaotic nation can only bring them bad luck. Because people's memories of the past are a big part of how they feel about their country, mainland media and academics have been talking about how the CCP and the KMT worked together to fight the Japanese invasion in the 1930s and 1940s. This has been shown in movies, newspapers, and academic journals. In particular, Tengchong, a frontier city in southwestern China that was a famous battleground between Japanese troops and the KMT military with US help, has become a popular place for academic conferences that include experts from Taiwan, including some from the Green (pro-independence) camp. The mainland wants to make sure that Taiwan and it share historical memories, even if young Taiwanese people who have nothing to do with the old KMT government may think that historical events in Tengchong don't matter to them. For the same reason, the mainland has told the story of the famous Wushe uprising (also called the Wushe incident) by the aboriginal Wushe people against Japanese colonial rule in the 1930s. This is done to show how both sides suffered during a bad time in China's past. In fact, Japan's violent response to the Wushe uprising and its killing of the people of Nanjing both happened in the same decade on the other side of the Taiwan Strait. The uprising happened on October 27, 1930, in a place called Wushe in Nantou County. The people who took part were called Seediq. At the time, they were thought to be a subgroup of the Atayal tribe, but in April 2008, they were recognized as Taiwan's fourteenth native tribe. The Seediqs rose up because British officials treated them badly. Under the leadership of Mona Rudao, the Seediqs rose up against the Japanese occupiers in an armed revolt that lasted fifty days and killed more than a hundred Japanese. In response, the Japanese killed about a thousand Seediqs. About 80 years later, in September 2008, the

Taiwanese director Wei Te-sheng planned to start making a movie called Warriors of the Rainbow: Seediq Bale. He ended the movie three years later. People on both sides of the Taiwan Strait and around the world, especially on the Internet, had different ideas about what happened because of the movie. Most people on the mainland, though, thought that this happened because Chinese people on both sides of the Strait fought against Japanese rule or attack.

2015 was the 70th anniversary of the Chinese success in the Chinese People's War of Resistance against Japanese Aggression and the Second World War. To remember this victory and strengthen national identity on both sides of the Taiwan Strait, there were many events on the mainland. On September 2, the day before Victory Day in China, President Xi Jinping gave medals to veterans who fought in the fight, including representatives for "eight hundred brave soldiers" of a KMT troop. In his speech, Xi stressed that both frontline soldiers led by the KMT and rearguard soldiers led by the CCP added to the final victory and that people fighting on different battlefields were all national heroes. On September 3, as planned, a gathering, a military parade, a reception, and an evening gala were held in Beijing to honor the anniversary. Thirty leaders of countries and officials from nineteen countries and ten organizations were there. Some retired soldiers from the KMT troops took part in the military parade. Former KMT chair Lien Chan, New Party chair Yu Mu-min, People First Party general secretary Chin Chin-sheng, and a few other important people from Taiwan also attended the commemorative events. In his speech at the rally, Xi said that the Chinese people had fought hard for fourteen years before winning a great victory in their War of Resistance against Japanese Aggression. He did not say who led that war, the KMT or the CCP, but he did say at the reception after the parade that the war had been led by the "United Front of Resistance against Japanese Aggression Initiated by the CCP." Also, Xi included the 50-year fight of the Taiwanese people against Japanese rule as an important part of the war of resistance of the whole Chinese country. Yu Zhengsheng, the head of the Chinese People's Political Consultative Conference, told Lien Chan the day before when they met that more than 50,000 Taiwanese came to the mainland in the 1930s and 1940s to fight in the War of Resistance against Japanese Aggression. During his talks with Xi and Yu, Lien Chan said very similar things.

But Lien's actions in Beijing were not supported by many people in Taiwan, including KMT leaders. Ma Ying-jeou and Hau Pai-tsun, a top general and the father of the former mayor of Taipei, Hao Lung-pin, both criticized Lien for going to the event in Beijing. For them, the War of Resistance Against Japanese Aggression (WRAJA) was led by the Republic of China (ROC), so it should get the credit. From the point of view of the KMT, the war was an important part of ROC history. The DPP, on the other hand, thinks that Taiwan had nothing to do with the War of Resistance. In fact, more Taiwanese were recruited by Japanese troops during the war, and local Taiwanese were hurt by US bombing near the end of the war. Lee Teng-hui is a good example of this kind of thinking. Before 1945, he freely said he was Japanese and said that Diaoyu Island belonged to Japan. It's interesting to know that Lee and Lien ran together for president and vice president in the 1996 election, and that they won. Some Taiwanese who were born and raised there miss the days when Japan ruled as a colony, especially the last few decades. Through political socialization, these feelings were passed on to some young people, who felt uneasy about calling the time between 1895 and 1945 the "occupation" by the Japanese, as the new teaching outline backed by the Ma government did. This led to protests against kegang in August 2015. In hindsight, the migration of people from the mainland to Taiwan after the war ended in 1945 has created different "ascriptive categories" of national identity in Taiwan. This is an important social factor that needs to be taken into account when making political decisions and rewriting the history of the War of Resistance against Japanese Aggression on the island. For the mainland, it is very important to build national unity that people on both sides of the Taiwan Strait remember the war in the same way. So, Beijing has used historical memories, along with cultural parallels and ethnic equality, to strengthen the idea of "a community of cross-Strait shared destinies."

In December 2014, a public memorial was built for both People's Liberation Army (PLA) soldiers and Nationalist troops who died in a fight on Jinmen Island in October 1949. This is a good example of how history is reconstructed. The PLA troops, which numbers around 9,000, attacked Jinmen and held the island for three days. However, the Nationalist military, which had more troops and a better air force, was able to beat them. On both sides, several thousand people died. The political goal of the memorial is to ease the historical grievances of people on both sides of the Chinese Civil War and to cherish cross-Strait peace from the perspective of "two shores, one close family." As one retired soldier from Shanghai said during the event, he came to Jinmen to remember his old colleagues who died on the battlefield but ended up feeling respect for all who had died there, no matter which army—the PLA or the KM. At the end of the event, it was interesting to see that everyone gave a military salute to the PLA and Nationalist troops who had died in the anti-Japanese war. By doing this, they changed the memory of the terrible civil war into the memory of how all Chinese soldiers fought bravely against the cruel Japanese attack before 1945. In the 1950s, Jinmen was a military border between Taiwan and the mainland. In the "one-China" framework, it was a link between the two sides because both the Nationalist government on Taiwan and the PRC government on the mainland claimed sovereignty over it. This showed that China's civil war wasn't over yet. Jinmen has been a peace border in recent years, starting with the three minilinkages (xiao santong) between it and the island of Xiamen, which is run by the PRC, when Chen Shui-bian was in charge. Since then, more and more mainland tourists have been going there. The public media tell a good story about how kitchen knives were made in Jinmen using artillery shells left over from the bombing of Jinmen between the late 1950s and the 1970s, when more than a million shells were fired on the small island. This story is meant to encourage the peaceful growth of cross-Strait relations. People from the mainland buy a lot of Jinmen kitchen knives and Jinmen Gaoliang, which is a strong liquor. In May 2015, Zhang Zhijun, director of the Beijing-based Taiwan Affairs Office (TAO) of the State Council, and Xia Liyan, chair of the Taipei-based Mainland Affairs Council (MAC), met there for an official meeting. This brought attention to the role of Jinmen in bringing the two sides of the Taiwan Strait closer together. Since Jinmen is much closer to the mainland than to Taiwan, the two sides have agreed to speed up the signing of a contract to send water to Taiwan by the right departments in Fujian and Jinmen. In the past few years, Jinmen and Xiamen have talked about working together on other projects, like a bridge and an electricity grid that would connect the two islands.

Shared Fortune

People on both sides of the Strait also think that economic integration and trade are important for building community. Neoliberal or neofunctional ideas say that economic integration will finally lead to political accommodation and even political integration. The European Union has shown that this is true. Karl Wolfgang Deutsch's idea of a "security community" says that growing functional interdependence will make war too expensive for both sides to wage. In the 1980s, business between the two countries was done in a roundabout way. Since 2008, however, it has become more clear and thorough. Cross-Strait trade, for example, went from $129 billion in 2008 to $188 billion in 2015, which is about 30 percent of all of Taiwan's foreign trade. Taiwanese direct investments on the mainland that were allowed by the island's government went from $1.9 billion in 2008 to $2.8 billion in 2012, but dropped to $1.5 billion in 2015. In the same time period, the number of tourists from Taiwan to the mainland went from 4.37 million in 2008 to 5.5 million in 2015, while the number of tourists from the mainland to Taiwan went from less than 0.28 million to 4.14 million. Yung Wei pointed out a decade ago that this growing economic dependence has led to "linkage communities" on both sides of the Taiwan Strait. During the 2012 Taiwanese elections, a number of big business owners publicly supported the KMT idea of "one China, different interpretations." This is similar to Beijing's idea that there is only one China and that only one government can legitimately represent it, but it is very different from the DPP's idea that the PRC and the ROC should have "state-to-state" relations. On the other hand, it could be said that most Taiwanese people have not directly benefited from the growing merger of the economy. Even though Beijing's "benefit-offering" policy in economic talks across the Strait, such as the signing of the Economic Cooperation Framework Agreement and the Cross-Strait Service Trade Agreement, has led to the Economic Cooperation Framework Agreement and the Cross-Strait Service Trade Agreement, cross-Strait exchange has not led to much economic growth in Taiwan or in people's daily lives. Social divisions in Taiwan between the rich and the poor and between the upper and lower classes have contributed to the strong opposition to the progress of economic and social exchanges across the Taiwan Strait. The Sunflower Movement, a group of students who protested the Cross-Strait Service Trade Agreement in March 2014, was a good example of this. Due to the social divides in Taiwan, Beijing has paid more attention to what Taiwan's grassroots people and young people have to say. These groups have felt frustrated and taken advantage of during the process of regional economic union.

In the spirit of neofunctionalism, Beijing's Taiwan policymakers want to rebuild a shared Chinese national identity across the Taiwan Strait by taking care of "economic and easier issues first, and political and difficult issues later." After 2006, most of the CCP-KMT forums on economic and cultural exchanges across the Taiwan Strait focused on economic cooperation. The 2009 forum, on the other hand, was mostly about culture and educational exchanges and cooperation across the Taiwan Strait. During Ma's time in office, the most important political goal for Beijing was to sign a peace deal with Taipei and agree on how the two countries' governments would work together before China reunified. In 2013 and 2014, Beijing worked harder to get Taipei and the government to talk about these problems in a "one China" framework. From Beijing's point of view, if the two sides can have political talks within the framework and resolve the issue of Taiwan's participation in the international arena in a fair way, political relations between the two sides will improve and Taiwanese political identification with the mainland will grow. In May 2015, when Xi Jinping met with KMT chair Chu Li-lun, he suggested that the two sides of the Taiwan Strait work together to build a community with a common goal. Xi came up with five ideas for how to do this. First, for cross-Strait relations to grow peacefully, both sides would have to stick to the 1992 Consensus and oppose Taiwanese independence. The 1992 Consensus says that Taiwan and the mainland are part of the same China, but the two sides disagree about who is the country's rightful leader. Second, the goal of supporting the peaceful development of relations across the Taiwan Strait would be to bring the interests of the mainland and Taiwan closer together, find creative ways to help both sides win, and make people happier on both sides of the Taiwan Strait. Third, exchanges across the Taiwan Strait would be between people, and heart-to-heart contacts would be the most important. Both sides would need to strengthen their sense of who they are as an ethnic group, a culture, and a country. Fourth, both the CCP and the KMT, as well as both sides of the Taiwan Strait, would need to understand the big picture and treat each other with respect. They would have to not only try to find common ground while having different points of view, but also work hard to reduce differences while increasing the number of people who agree with each other and trust each other politically. Fifth, the great rebirth of the Chinese people would need both sides to work together. In response to Xi Jinping's call, the PRC's TAO made it clear that Taiwan was welcome to join the infrastructure development of the so-called "One Belt and One Road" (a network of railways, roads, pipelines, and utility grids connecting China to West Asia, Central Asia, parts of South Asia, and Europe) and to take part in the Asian Infrastructure Investment Bank, which was started by Beijing, in a way that made sense.

Taiwan's political changes have stopped Beijing's plans to build a cross-Strait community with a shared future. As the Sunflower Movement protests on March 18 and the results of Taiwan's local elections in November 2014 showed, the January 2016 presidential elections gave power back from the pro-status quo KMT to the pro-independence DPP. Because the ruling DPP doesn't want to accept the 1992 Consensus, official and semiofficial ties between the two sides have been broken. This means that the Association for Relations across the Taiwan Strait on the mainland and the Straits Exchange Foundation in Taiwan can't come to any new agreements for economic and cultural exchanges. Just like Xi Jinping said a year ago, if the foundation of the 1992 Consensus was broken, cross-Strait ties would go back to the chaotic and unstable state they were in before.

This doesn't mean that Beijing will have to attack Taiwan with the military. Beijing's grand policy of "peaceful development through reform and opening" has made the mainland more dependent on the rest of the world, especially the Asia-Pacific area. This is a big change in China's international standing. The mainland's ability to use either hard or soft tactics has grown as its national power has grown. This has made hard tactics harder and soft tactics easier. Without a political agreement between Beijing and the new leaders in Taiwan after Ma, it is possible that Taiwan's small diplomatic friends will switch to the mainland. From the point of view of the mainland, the problem of Taiwan's participation in international events can only be solved within the "one-China" framework. As long as Taipei doesn't try to change the status quo of cross-Strait relations in general and its diplomatic allies in particular, Beijing doesn't need to cut off all of Taiwan's external links during the transitional period before China's reunification. Even though Taiwan's foreign relations don't depend on its twenty or so diplomatic friends, getting rid of them would be a big deal on an island where the two main parties are in a very heated fight with each other. If this happened, Taipei might take a strong stand against Beijing in some way, which would bring back problems that were there before.

In this situation, Beijing is sticking to its policy of engaging with Taiwan's two main parties in different ways, favoring the KMT over the DPP. So, in addition to the current CCP-KMT platform, city-to-city and people-to-people exchanges are the major ways for people on both sides of the Strait to get along. But a trip to the mainland in September 2016 by local officials from one city and seven counties controlled by the "Blue" camp (parties like the KMT that are more open to reconciliation or eventual unification with China) shows that Beijing doesn't want to have city-to-city exchanges with Green (more pro-independence parties like the DPP) mayors and magistrates unless they agree to the "one-China" framework. At a lower level, city areas and neighborhoods, towns and townships, and social groups can become important units for exchange and cooperation. By making these kinds of links, the mainland government hopes that the benefits of its economic exchange with Taiwan will be felt by both big businesspeople and regular Taiwanese people, especially young people. Zhang Zhijun, head of the TAO, said on September 19, 2016, that Beijing will stick to the 1992 Consensus, fight against Taiwanese independence, support the peaceful growth of cross-Strait relations, and urge people on both sides of the Taiwan Strait to share feelings and benefits.

Mutual Respect for Social Systems

The fact that the two sides have different political institutions is another thing that affects national political identity. Beijing has tried to fix this structural issue by making the unification plan more appealing to Taiwan. Based on the idea of "one country, two systems," Taiwan could keep its own economic, political, and social systems after union. Even though China would still be a unitary state after unification, Taiwan's executive, legislative, and judicial powers would stretch the limits of a unitary government. This would make the relationship between the mainland and Taiwanese governments more like that of a federal authority to a state authority. In Taiwan, unlike Hong Kong, political autonomy comes from the law, not from basic rules handed down from the central government. After unification, Taiwan would still have some independent powers, but it would give up others, like national defense and diplomacy. This would make the relationship between Beijing and Taipei similar to a federal one.

"One country, two systems" is linked to two problems that a rising China has to deal with: building the country and building institutions. Most studies done in China about "one country, two systems" have focused on the first problem and ignored the second. Will the two different economic, social, and political systems always coexist? How can they get along and work together? By living together for a long time and learning from each other, will the two systems be able to close the structural gaps between them?

In the long process of modernizing China, the PRC has gone through several steps of building institutions. From 1949 to 1978, the government thought that the socialist system was much better than the capitalist system and would eventually take its place. Since reform and opening began in 1979, Beijing has leaned more on how China is different from other countries to defend socialism and socialist democracy on the Chinese mainland. In 2005, the Chinese government published a white paper called "Building Political Democracy in China." It says that there is no single, absolute, and universally applicable form of democracy in the world. In the new party policy, getting rid of class exploitation and social division is no longer seen as one of the most important parts of socialism. Also, socialist and communist ideas are seen as good for China, but not as the only way for people in other parts of the world. At its Eighteenth National Congress in 2012, the party asked people to keep believing in socialism and its ideas and institutions. However, it still described socialism as something that works for China and not as the universal truth for all people. Jiang Zemin realized ten years ago that different social systems can coexist and learn from each other. Beijing's "one country, two systems" formula, which came out of the reform era, seems to fit well with its view on institutional growth in the modern world.

"One country, two systems" has been the standard model chosen by Deng Xiaoping and followed by successive Chinese leaders. Xi Jinping has tried to make it acceptable to Taiwan by repeating that the Taiwanese model of "one country, two systems" is different from the Hong Kong model. This is especially important in the wake of protests in Hong Kong against the 2017 electoral formula approved by Beijing. In February 2014, when Xi met with Lien Chan, he said that he knew the Taiwanese people were proud of their social system and the way they decided to live. Even though the term "social system" here covers both economic and political systems, the word "cherish" suggests that these systems are good for Taiwan and should be appreciated for that reason. Xi says that the mainland respects Taiwan's social order and way of life and also wants to share the opportunities for development on the mainland with the people of Taiwan. In his opening comments at the Sixth Strait Forum, Yu Zhengsheng, chair of the Chinese People's Political Consultation Conference, said that Beijing respects the Taiwanese social system and way of life. He also added values and ideas to the list. In June 2014, TAO head Zhang Zhijun told Kaohsiung mayor Chen Chu what Xi had told Lien Chan. The same thing could be said about what Xi said about "one country, two systems" when he met with several pro-unification or pro-integration delegates from Taiwan in September 2014.

Many Taiwanese politicians have said that the two sides of the Taiwan Strait don't have a shared identity because they have different social systems. Taiwan is more democratic than the mainland, which is not, and these politicians have stressed the importance of Taiwanese democracy as a defense against pressure from the mainland to unite. Lin Xinhua from Taiwan, on the other hand, says that it is very strange that about a million Taiwanese businesses live on the mainland, which has a different social system than Taiwan. This suggests that institutional differences alone can't keep people from coming together. Institutional differences between the two societies shouldn't be a problem, says Li Peng of Xiamen University, as long as each side can look at these differences in a humble and honest way.

This doesn't mean that the subject of institutional differences, let alone conflicts, can be completely ignored. As was already said, one of the most important parts of national identity is official identification. Since the two sides have different political, economic, and social systems, they need to find more similarities in their institutions, especially in how they are run. In fact, the economic system on the mainland has changed a lot over the past 35 years, going from a planned economy to a market economy. This has made the theoretical differences between capitalism and socialism in China less and less important, and Taiwanese businesspeople on the mainland feel less and less out of place. With the rise of civil society, social organizations, and human rights on the mainland, the institutional gap between the two sides of the Taiwan Strait has shrunk a lot. In recent years, the mainland has been trying to improve state governance, and Taiwan's experience with governance and public policy can help. The idea behind "one country, two systems" is that different societies can have their own institutions. However, in order to have two systems in one country, social links have to overlap to some degree. As a first step, Taiwanese neighborhood officials and mainland officials at the same level in Shanghai have visited each other's offices and talked about their job. This may help close the gap between the two sides' institutions at the local level. Through learning from each other, city-to-city exchanges have also helped improve the way government works and the level of municipal services on the mainland.

Conclusion

Taiwan's growing sense of national identity, both on a cultural/ethnic and a political/civil level, has made it harder for the mainland to rebuild China's national identity in the modern world. From a social and political point of view, most people in Taiwan say they are Taiwanese, and a large number, though less than one-quarter, would like Taiwan to be independent sooner or later. Beijing is well aware of the gap between Taiwanese culture and the idea of Taiwanese freedom. It has done its best to fit Taiwanese culture under the big umbrella of Chinese culture. The fact that almost everyone in Taiwan knows they are a part of the Chinese country seems to be a good sign for a confident Beijing. But more people in Taiwan want freedom than unification, and most of them would not accept unification with the mainland even if the mainland had democratic institutions like Taiwan.

Even though Beijing is trying to build economic, cultural, social, and political foundations for peaceful growth of cross-Strait relations as a step toward its ultimate goal of unification, it still has a long way to go. Taiwanese attitudes toward economic benefits from the mainland are neutralized by social unrest on the island. Similar historical and cultural backgrounds of the two sides were interrupted by Japanese colonial rule and long-lasting separate governments after that, and crises have interrupted times of political detente. All of these problems have shown the mainland that rebuilding a shared Chinese national identity across the Taiwan Strait requires not only economic modernization and integration, mutual cultural exchange and assimilation, and a reinterpretation of modern Chinese history and political relations between the two entities before China's reunification, but also better public governance and political engineering on the mainland. In other words, rebuilding the national character of China is a long-term project that involves everyone on both sides of the Taiwan Strait.

Chapter 8
Evolution of Identities in Taiwan during Ma Ying-jeou's Era

Since the late 1980s, when Taiwan started to become more democratic, people's identities on the island have changed a lot. Then, most people who lived in the Republic of China (ROC), which is the official name for Taiwan, thought of themselves as Chinese. Only a small number of people thought of themselves as Taiwanese. The last part of society was mostly found in and around the Democratic Progressive Party (DPP), a resistance group that had just been made legal. Today, the situation has changed: less than 5% of ROC citizens think of themselves as Chinese, 60–70% think of themselves as Taiwanese, and the rest say they are both Taiwanese and Chinese. In other words, all political parties have become "Taiwanized." This includes the Kuomintang (KMT), which for a long time was the only party in power and dreamed of reuniting China under its rule. But many ROC citizens are happy to say that they are politically Taiwanese but culturally Chinese. This shows that, like in many modern societies, having more than one identity is becoming more normal and doesn't always cause social or political problems. Only the most extreme pro-independence, or "Green," Taiwanese would try to draw a clear line between Chinese and Taiwanese societies, putting the focus on how different and unique Taiwanese culture is.

At the same time, after Ma Ying-jeou was elected president of Taiwan and the KMT came back to power in 2008, he, the KMT, and what is known in Taiwan as the "Blue camp" (fanlanjun, a coalition of the KMT, the People First Party [PFP], the New Party [CNP], and the Minkuotang [MKT]) tried to bring back a more traditional Chinese and ROC political and cultural identity. They did this to help the rapproche At the same time, business and social ties across the Taiwan Strait have grown quickly, leading to more interactions between people from the ROC and the PRC.

These two trends can have opposite effects: they can help bridge the gap between mainland Chinese and Taiwanese and convince the latter that, in the end, there isn't much that separates them from the former; but they can also highlight the differences between the two societies and, in a protective reaction seen elsewhere, convince most Taiwanese that, even though they share some cultural traits with PRC citizens, like the written language, they belong to a different society.

My guess is that Taiwanese political or civil identity, which is closely tied to the island's move toward democracy and democratic life, will continue to grow stronger. The Sunflower Movement in the spring of 2014, the KMT's crushing loss in the local elections in late November 2014, and, most importantly, Tsai Ing-wen's win and the DPP's return to power (and for the first time control of the Legislative Yuan) since 2016 all show this trend. At the same time, there are more ways than ever to be a Taiwanese person, leading some to identify with the local culture, the building of a new Taiwanese nation, and even the search for formal independence from China, and others to identify with a democratized, sovereign, and de facto independent ROC on Taiwan.

Evolution of Political Identities in Taiwan Pre-2008

We start this part with some big, well-known trends: National Chengchi University's Election Study Center, one of the most respected and reliable polling organizations on the island, says that in June 2016, 59.3 percent of the interviewees thought of themselves as Taiwanese, compared to 17.6 percent in 1992 and 43.7 percent in 2008; 3.4 percent of them see themselves as Chinese (25.5 percent in 1992 and 4.1 percent in 2008); and 33.6 percent of them see themselves as both Taiwanese and Chinese (46.4 percent in 1992).

The first and most obvious thing to learn from this survey is that Taiwanese identity has totally pushed Chinese identity to the sidelines. The second is that the number of Taiwanese who say they have more than one identity has been steadily decreasing since Ma Ying-jeou was elected in 2008. This makes some people question how well the KMT's plan to "resinicize" the island is working. But the third conclusion, which is often overlooked, is that in 1992, when Taiwan started to become more democratic, people who said they were Chinese were already a minority. This minority would shrink quickly in the middle of the same decade, falling behind people who said they were only Taiwanese and becoming the smallest group by 1995 (20.7% vs. 25%). In other words, when Taiwan was just starting to become a democracy, almost half of the island's people saw themselves as both Taiwanese and Chinese, and almost two-thirds saw themselves as either Taiwanese or Chinese.

Even though this kind of poll is helpful, it has a major flaw: it doesn't tell the difference between cultural and political identities. But Taiwanese identity has always been both a political or social and a cultural thing from the start. It started as a reaction to the February 28 Massacre, which was an uprising against the KMT-led government in Taiwan in 1947 that was violently put down by the ROC military and killed an estimated 10,000 people. It was also a reaction to the KMT's policy of forbidding and punishing Taiwanese students for speaking their native language at school (mostly Hokkien or Minnan, which is called Tai-oan-oe or Taigi in Taiwanese), As early as the 1960s, political activists like Peng Ming-min talked about a Taiwanese identity that was closely tied to their calls for democratization. In the 1970s, this identity also grew as a result of the "nativization" (henluhua) of literature and the arts, which was a reaction to the KMT's dominance of traditional Chinese culture and cultural production. Even though martial law was in place, the KMT had no choice but to become "Taiwanized" (66 percent of its members were Taiwanese in 1986). This process reached its leadership in 1986 (when mainlanders made up 55 percent of its powerful Central Standing Committee, and then 48 percent two years later), just before President Chiang Ching-kuo legalized the DPP and ended martial law in 1987, starting Taiwan's democratic transition. Since the early 1950s, local and (partial) national elections have been allowed. Starting in 1969, the number of seats for national elections was increased. Since then, opposition (or dangwai) candidates have been more likely to use Taiwanese instead of Mandarin in their campaigns. This has helped promote a political-cultural identity that the KMT has either ignored or tried to downplay. Since the 1970s, Taiwan's scholars and intellectuals, and later the general public, have become more aware of the ethnic diversity of the island. This led to the idea of "subethnic" groups (zuqun) to describe its major parts: the Hoklo (fulao) or South Fujian immigrants (70 percent of the population), the Hakka (kejiaren, 15 percent), the mainlanders (waishengren, 0.3 percent), and the aborigines (shand During the same time period, more Taiwanese have given themselves a different meaning of what it means to be Chinese. They now call themselves huaren, which means ethnic Chinese, instead of zhongguoren, which has come to mean PRC citizen. In other words, Taiwan's cultural identity and arguments about cultural identity have always been very political and have a lot to do with democratization. So, for a long time, both the people being interviewed and the general public thought that Taiwanese polls on identity had a strong political or, more accurately, civic dimension. In other words, they were seen as signs of a new Taiwanese "civic identity."

Another, more controversial question is whether there is a direct link between identity and country, between political identity and national identity, and between Taiwanese identity and the fight for Taiwan's legal or de facto independence. This is a clear link: Christopher Hughes has said that "civic nationalism" is growing in Taiwan. But people still have different ideas about the nature and content of the country that has been under construction since democratization and even since 1949 when China split into two separate states. Taiwanese civic and national identities sometimes overlap, especially for those who want formal independence or a permanent break from China. Other times, they don't, like for those who want to keep the ROC constitutional envelope or "order," to use a phrase from President Tsai Ing-wen's inauguration speech in May 2016, or the "one-China" (ROC) principle as defined by the KMT-inspired phrase "one China, different interpretations." And, as we'll see below, the gap between the desire to build a separate and new Taiwanese nation and the geopolitical reality and political choices that can be considered is growing. Because of this, Taiwanese nationalism is always unclear and has its limits. In other words, the relationship between identity and nationalism has stayed complicated in Taiwan more than anywhere else. This is because of well-known foreign restrictions.

Taiwan has done a lot of research on identity politics. This part is not the place to show or talk about all of this great writing. Because of Taiwan's strange history, diverse subethnic makeup, unrecognized statehood and international status, and long dominance by the 1.5 million mainlanders or "outsiders" (waishengren, who arrived in 1945–50, as opposed to Taiwan's "natives" or benshengren), democratization has had a direct effect on the central role of identity politics and the rapid consolidation of Taiwanese civic and, to a large extent, national identity. So, since the early 1990s, all parties have been affected by identity politics. It has caused a painful change in the KMT and contributed to the new internal cracks that appeared under Lee Teng-hui (1988-2000) between the "mainstream faction," which supported the president's Taiwanization process, and the "nonmainstream faction," which had leaders like General Hau Pei-tsun, who was prime minister from 1990 to 1993. The latter wanted the party to keep its strong Chinese character and traditions from the mainland. One of the fights that happened during this time was about changing the history books and putting out the "Get to Know Taiwan" series. During his first term as KMT chair, Lee Teng-hui found a good balance between his desire to support Taiwan's identity, uniqueness, and statehood and the need to make deals with the more conservative leaders of his party. Taiwan's United Nations bid, which began in 1993, was a good example of the middle path that was taken at the time. Taiwan offered to return to the UN under the name ROC instead of Taiwan, which is what the DPP wanted. And in its 1994 white paper on relations across the Taiwan Strait, Taiwan's government stuck to the idea that there was only one Chinese nation while asking Beijing to accept that it was split into two "political entities."

But after he was re-elected by all Taiwanese voters in 1996, Lee slowly moved away from this path. In 1999, he advocated a two-state approach to cross-Strait relations, which showed that building a Taiwanese nation separate from both the PRC and China in reality was his top priority. By doing this, he was trying to stop the DPP from becoming more popular by using its issue against it and to move the KMT in the way he wanted. Many KMT officials were affected by this change, including Ma Ying-jeou, who ran for mayor of Taipei in 1998 and said that, even though he was born on the mainland, he was a "new Taiwanese" In any case, it is interesting to note that the number of ROC citizens who said they were only Taiwanese went up from 25% in 1995 to 39.6% in 1999, while the number who said they were Chinese went down even more (from 20.7% in 1995 to 0.2%) and the number who said they were both Chinese and Taiwanese stayed about the same (42.5 in 1995 and 47 in 1999).

The DPP went through a simpler but no less confusing change. Since its founding in 1986, we know that the major opposition party has been united in its goal to make Taiwan more democratic but divided in its desire for formal independence. Then, the Formosa group was seen as more moderate and willing to work within the ROC than the New Tide faction, which wanted to make the Republic of Taiwan a new country. In the end, all DPP factions agreed in 1999 to adopt a self-determination plan that clearly said Taiwan was not a part of China but also accepted the ROC institutions and the formula "ROC = Taiwan." In other words, by the end of the 1990s, the unity of Taiwanese identity paved the way for a new Taiwanese national identity and even nationalism, which helped DPP candidate Chen Shui-bian win the 2000 presidential election.

The KMT's loss in the election of 2000 was a turning point in Taiwan's policies about who they are. Chen Shui-bian pushed the ROC to become more like Taiwan once he was in charge. He added "Taiwan" to the ROC passport, insisted that the island be recognized as a separate state after 2002, and supported a new historical story and many cultural activities that emphasized Taiwan's unique identity, especially its non-Chinese or aboriginal parts. For example, he tried to spread Shi Ming's view of Taiwan's history as a 400-year fight for freedom and independence. He did this by putting Zheng Chenggong, the Ming general who "sinicized" Taiwan in the 17th century to help it resist the Qing invasion, on the government website (GIO) as the leader of this movement. He talked about how Taiwanese many cultural practices or habits are, even though they are also found on the Chinese mainland, especially in southern Fujian, where the Taiwanese language came from. And he talked about Taiwan as a melting pot where each outside impact had the same amount of power. Many of these changes were made to keep up with the changes Lee had already made. They were meant to strengthen Taiwan's sense of community and national security. In hindsight, though, the most extreme parts of this new Taiwanese nationalism look like convenient replacements for the independence-leaning policies Chen wanted to put in place but couldn't, not only because of China's opposition and threats, but also because the US government, especially President George W. Bush, was getting more and more annoyed after 2003. These symbolic exaggerations led the KMT and the Blue camp to say that Chen was "desinicizing" Taiwan. This was right around the time that KMT chair Lien Chan made his famous trip to China and started talking to the Chinese Communist Party (CCP) again. In a way, you could say that the Chen Shui-bian administration helped move the KMT's story to a darker blue stance by pushing a "dark green" story. During those years (2004–2008), political polarization also helped spread two very different stories and identities on the island. But it is important to look into the link between the KMT's promotion of Taiwan's Chinese identity and its policy of rapprochement with the PRC. This is possibly where the Nationalist Party's attempt to return to its roots and original values on the mainland can be found. In any case, this brief overview of Taiwan's identity politics before 2008 shows the background of Ma Ying-jeou's attempt to restore what can be called a more traditional "ROC Chinese" identity, as well as the negative reactions it has caused in Taiwanese society, even though or because China and Taiwan are getting closer together.

The KMT's Contemporary Chinese Nationalism

After Ma took power in 2008, the KMT brought back some of its old-fashioned and traditional Chinese nationalism. This nationalism once again put the unity and future unification of the Chinese nation/race at the center of its ideology. This new/reborn story was meant to criticize and stop what the KMT and Beijing called Chen Shui-bian's "desinicization" policy. It was also meant to counter Lee Teng-hui's earlier attempts to "localize" or "nativize" the KMT and the ROC by making them more like Taiwan. By doing this, Ma brought back a story and way of talking that was popular during martial law. This brought back bad memories of the authoritarian period and the KMT's undemocratic tendencies in the thoughts of older Taiwanese. Even though Ma didn't agree with the dark blue view that Taipei has only been the temporary capital of the ROC since 1949 and that unification should happen quickly, he and the KMT tried to make Chinese culture and identity more important. This put pressure on their brand of Chinese nationalism and the need to build up Taiwanese identity and voters. In other words, Ma and the KMT's new message didn't bring Taiwanese people back together, which was their stated goal. Instead, it made society more divided.

Before he was elected for the first time in 2008, Ma wrote a book called Native Spirit: The Model Story of Taiwan. In it, he argued against the "four hundred years of tragedy" story and emphasized how Qing leaders like Liu Minchuan and ROC leaders like Chiang Ching-kuo helped modernize Taiwan. In this book, he played down the part of the Japanese and lied about how many

Taiwanese joined the Chinese resistance against Japan. Most Taiwanese who fought in the war did so on the Japanese side. He also said that the DPP's idea of "nativization" was a chauvinistic and dividing way to get rid of Taiwan's Chinese identity. After he became president, Ma made a number of changes that showed what he really wanted to do. In his inaugural address, he said that people on both sides of the Strait were part of a zhonghua minzu (Chinese nation), where minzu meant a shared racial and cultural identity. He also changed the name of Taiwan's mail service from Taiwan Post to China Post, which was its name before Chen Shui-bian was president. He also brought back the tr More importantly, he pointed out that Taiwan and the old ROC have the same institutions and territories, and he insisted that the legal meaning of the ROC includes Taiwan. He also said that there was only "one China," according to the PRC and ROC's 1992 Consensus that the phrase "one China" could mean different things depending on which government was the rightful leader of that China, and, later in 2012, according to the formula "one country, two areas" (yiguo liangqu). Lastly, he spoke very confidently about his country's territory claims in both the East China Sea (Diaoyutai) and the South China Sea (Spratlys), and he played with the idea of working with the PRC against other claimants on these issues. In other words, as Stephane Corcuff has pointed out, Ma, who was born on the mainland but raised in Hong Kong, started a policy of "de-Taiwanization" and tried to "resinicize" Taiwan in order to "justify his own legitimacy as a leader," as Chris Hughes has said.

The KMT's new or revived Chinese nationalism was also clearly aimed at tying Taiwan to the Chinese nation, bridging the gap with the PRC, opposing Taiwan's independence, favoring reconciliation and eventually unification between the two sides of the Strait (with strict conditions), and legitimizing its own policy of getting closer to Beijing. In 2008, Ma Ying-jeou and his party did say that they didn't want reunification to happen in the near future. And it's true that one of the goals of their strategy was the gradual democratization of mainland China, but they didn't do much to reach that goal, and they were very careful around PRC dissidents. For example, Ma refused to meet the Dalai Lama or blind activist Chen Guangcheng when they came to the island, and he also wouldn't give a visa to the president of the Uighur World Congress, Rebiya Kadeer. In any case, what counted to the Ma administration was Taiwan's economic integration with the PRC. They saw this as the best way to boost the economy, keep Taiwan from being left out, and embrace regionalization and globalization. The cozy relationship between the KMT and the CCP made more and more Taiwanese, not just DPP members, doubt Ma's policy of rapprochement.

Between 2008 and 2016, things on both sides of the Strait changed in ways that had never happened before. For example, direct air and sea links were set up, 23 agreements were signed, and the number of Chinese tourists visiting the island rose to over 4.3 million in 2015. Clearly, these events have made it easier for both states and both societies to work together. But have they changed who Taiwanese people are?

Consequences and Resistance to Ma's Chinese Nationalism

The answer is no, or to be more precise, yes, but not in the ways you might have thought. As we mentioned at the beginning of this chapter, Ma's efforts to improve relations between Taiwan and China on the political and economic fronts have, if anything, made Taiwan's identity stronger. And this is even more true for young people. The Taiwan Brain Trust is a "Green" think tank that does fair surveys and polls. In August 2014, 78 percent of people between the ages of 20 and 29 said they were Taiwanese, compared to 52 percent of people between the ages of 50 and 59 and 48 percent of people over 70. Women are more likely to feel Taiwanese than men are (67 percent vs. 54 percent). People with at least a bachelor's degree feel more Taiwanese than those with a bachelor's degree or less (63 percent vs. 57-59 percent). Also, in a three-option survey (independence, reunification, and status quo), support for independence is much higher among young Taiwanese: 44 percent for ages 20 to 29, compared to 8 percent for ages 50 to 59 and 19 percent for those over 70. The numbers for supporters of the status quo are 45 percent, 64 percent, and 54 percent, and the numbers for supporters of reunification are 2%, 8%, and 8%.

It is easy to figure out why this is happening. After Mas was elected in 2008, most Taiwanese backed his policy toward the mainland. However, over time, a large number of them began to criticize it for going too far to make Beijing happy without bringing the results he had promised. Ethnic representations were still talked about and pushed in the public sphere, especially on the Internet. Late in 2011, there were the first signs that the KMT's plan to simplify things was not going as planned. Then, after Ma was re-elected in 2012, he had to give up on his plan to start formal talks with the PRC because most Taiwanese were against it. When KMT chief Wu Bo-hsiung proposed the "one country, two areas" plan in China in March 2012, it was seen as too close to the now-infamous "one country, two systems" idea, and only 33% of Taiwanese agreed with it, while 55% disagreed. But it was during Mas's second term that tensions started to rise. They reached their highest point in March 2014, when some KMT lawmakers tried to ratify the Cross-Strait Service Trade Agreement (CSTA), which Taipei and Beijing had signed in June 2013. The DPP said that there hadn't been enough discussion in parliament about the agreement's content. This bad choice led to the 23-day Sunflower Movement protest, which was one of the biggest acts of civil disobedience in democratic Taiwan's history. Even though its political and economic reasons were both many and complicated, this movement was a clear sign of Taiwan's sense of civic identity. Between March and June 2014, the number of Taiwanese who said they were Taiwanese went up from 58.2% to 60.5%. In other words, Ma's Chinese nationalism was not in line with what was going on in Taiwanese society. This made the KMT's talk and policy toward the mainland weaker and made Taiwanese identity stronger on the island. More importantly, Ma's speech and policies made the Taiwanese even more angry. They were already upset about their stagnant standard of living, the slowing economy of the island, and growing social inequality. In a broader sense, Ma's Chinese nationalism made it less likely that the KMT would stay in power after 2016. The November 2014 local elections were a clear loss for the KMT and a huge win for the DPP. This showed, among other things, that Ma's Chinese nationalism is not popular. So did Tsai's clear win over KMT candidate Eric Chu Li-luan (with 31% of the vote) and People's First Party candidate James Soong Chu-yu (with 13% of the vote) in the January 2016 presidential election, and the rise of the "Greener" and more pro-independence New Power Party (shidai liliang) from the Sunflower Movement (five legislators, 6% of the vote).

Taiwan's efforts to keep its own character can also be seen as a reaction against globalization, which is happening all over the world, even in Europe. In this way, it's not nearly as strange as it might seem. In the case of Taiwan, however, it also shows that national identity is not shaped by the state (the ROC) but by larger political and social trends, such as "the practice of sovereignty through the ballot box and the evolution of multi-party politics in the context of a thriving, pluralistic civil society in which identities shift, interact, and compete." In the case of Taiwan, the consolidation of a separate identity is also a response to the PRC's growing military threat and ability to influence Taiwan's society, business people, media, and elites. In other words, it is a response to the growing imbalance in cross-Strait relations and an attempt to make up for it and rebalance things.

The next question is, of course, if Taiwan's claim to a separate identity is not doomed to fail in the long run. The uneven process of merger between Taiwan and China may already be having an effect on identity politics and, perhaps more importantly, is slowly breaking the link between identity politics and policies on the mainland.

Evolving Taiwanese Identity

It is clear that Taiwan is not Hong Kong and that, unlike the former British colony, which has agreed to reintegration into the PRC as long as it happens within the "one country, two systems" framework, the ROC is a de facto sovereign state whose future cannot be decided without its permission. But in terms of identity politics, there are some similarities between the two civil societies. For example, both are emphasizing the local over the global, and both are trying to protect their own interests in the face of a powerful force—the rise of China. In the summer of 2014, a lot of young activists from Hong Kong went to Taiwan to learn from those who were involved in the takeover of the Legislative Yuan. Some of those Taiwanese activists then went to Hong Kong to help the Occupy Central movement. Since the Sunflower Movement in the spring of 2014 and the Umbrella Movement that followed in Hong Kong for 79 days in the fall of 2014, these similarities between the two movements have become even clearer: both show a desire to fight back and a sense of crisis. At the same time, another part of this crisis is that Taiwan and Hong Kong's strong local identities are becoming more and more disconnected from the choices that political parties can offer their citizens and that people, especially young people, can think about for their lives and careers.

As far as Taiwan is concerned, Ms. Tsai Ing-wen has worked very hard to keep things the same in the Strait since she took office in May 2016. She has done this despite Beijing's clear lack of cooperation and demand that she sign the so-called 1992 Consensus. During her election campaign and her trip to the U.S. in June 2015, she made it clear that, if elected, she would keep the "status quo," keep the "ROC constitutional order," and, unlike Chen Shui-bian, not give any bad "surprises" to Washington or Beijing. The DPP has become much more cautious because Taiwan's culture, elites, and ways of thinking have changed over time. For example, it's clear that more and more young Taiwanese are tempted to start or continue their careers in China, where salaries and job opportunities are much better than on the island, even though most of them would rather stay in Taiwan (40 percent versus 32 percent, according to a recent survey). Also, before 2008, Taiwanese who wanted to have tighter political and business ties with the mainland were usually part of big businesses or companies that supported the KMT. This is no longer true. Today, more and more small businesses in Taiwan, including those in the "Green" South (Kaohsiung, Tainan, and Chiayi), have a stake in keeping ties with China stable. For example, their economic dependence on Chinese tourists has become clearer, especially since 2012. The drop in Chinese tourists since early 2016 has led some of them to protest against the new ROC government and even ask it to back the 1992 Consensus. So, since Tsai took office, she has been pushing for a "New Southbound Policy" that aims to make Taiwan less dependent on China's economy and build closer ties with ASEAN, South Asia, and Australia. However, Tsai has also made it clear that she will not break any of the agreements made by the Ma administration with Beijing or stop Chinese tourists from coming to Taiwan. And even with this new policy priority, Taiwan is expected to continue to be economically dependent on China.

So, even though Taiwan's identity is getting stronger, it is becoming more limited by these facts and less related to Taiwan's goal of becoming a full state or even formal independence. Even though Taiwanese culture still helps protect Taiwan's political independence, it can't stop the island from being too dependent on China. Taiwan has to accept and deal with its dependence on China, even as it works to reduce it. In other words, Taiwan's identity is becoming more "Hongkongized," or limited, by Beijing's "one-China" theory and request.

Taiwan is a de facto state and a democracy, while Hong Kong is neither a city-state (even though some young Hong Kong activists now want it to be) nor a full democracy. This means that Hong Kong and Taiwan still have very different identities. But it seems that more Taiwanese, especially young people, are taking a more relaxed and realistic view of who they are. It also seems that identity politics is losing steam and may become less of a problem in elections in the future.

Identities and Political Choices

As Taiwanese culture becomes more connected to the rest of the world, it also becomes more diverse. And new ways of expressing politics and culture in the postmodern era have helped downplay the value of identity as a whole. Several studies have shown, for example, that young Taiwanese have a more flexible and practical view of the PRC. As was already said, their professional careers often involve at least a temporary move to the mainland, since the local job market is still slow and doesn't offer as well-paid jobs. Most people would rather leave than be forced to fight for the survival of the ROC in a war, and they are becoming more open to the idea of unification and other long-term solutions to the cross-Strait conflict.

The slow loss of the Minnan language in Taiwan, especially in the north and center of the island, is another cultural irony of the rise of Taiwanese identity. Even though it is still used a lot in election campaigns, young people tend to speak or even understand it less. For example, Sunflower Movement participants mostly talked to each other in Mandarin or guoyu or negotiated with the government in those languages. And instead of fighting for Taiwanese identity, this movement fought for Taiwan's interests as a whole, as a political community, and especially for the social groups that haven't gotten the benefits of the growing cross-Strait economic integration or have been left out of it. In other words, cultural differences and fights have been replaced in some ways by new social and economic divides. Some of the social movements that have started since 2008 are based on identity, but they are becoming more and more focused on specific issues like the environment (like the protest against the

Fourth Nuclear Plant), farmers' rights, human rights (like getting rid of the death penalty), and gender inequality.

In this situation, promoting a fully Taiwanese national identity has become harder and less convincing. People who live in postmodern or globalized societies don't see themselves as having a unique character. Most Taiwanese still recognize and accept the similarities between Taiwanese and Chinese cultures, as well as the strong influence of Chinese culture in Taiwan, as long as that culture isn't understood in the same way as the official, neoconservative Chinese culture pushed by the communist government of the PRC. Because of this, only a few militants still try to Taiwanize all parts of the local culture, and even fewer people agree that there is a Taiwanese race that is different from the Chinese race, despite the fact that many Hokkien or Hakka migrants have married local aborigines over the past 400 years. In any case, the different cultures and languages of the Native Taiwanese (Hoklo, Hakka, and the 14 recognized aboriginal tribes) and the presence on the island of about 600,000 Southeast Asian workers, mostly from the Philippines, Thailand, and Vietnam, make it impossible to build a Taiwanese culture or nationalism around the still dominant Hoklo subethnic group and its language.

The growing number of PRC spouses and other residents in Taiwan and taishang (Taiwanese business people) on the mainland also have an effect on the identity of the Taiwanese people that is not always easy to measure because there is still a lack of thorough study on them. About 350,000 mainland Chinese people have married Taiwanese people in the last twenty years or so. About 320,000 of these people live in Taiwan, while the rest mostly live in the PRC. Because of this, it is hard to know how many PRC citizens live on the island as a whole. The number of illegal PRC citizens is also going up, and it is hard to keep track of them. On the other hand, between 1 and 2 million Taiwanese live on the mainland, and some of them have married people from the mainland. In any case, these two different but growing communities and their children have already started to change Taiwan's view of the PRC (and China's view of Taiwan), just as mixed marriages and the growing number of mainlanders living in Hong Kong (10–15 percent of the population) have been slowly changing the social fabric there. The sheer size of these exchanges can't be thought of as small, especially in a society where the number of births per woman has been going down steadily since 2000 (1.12 in 2016, down from 1.76 in 2000). Even though this may not have any immediate effects yet—Taiwan and Hong Kong's local civic identity has been getting stronger—it is likely to make it easier for Beijing to promote unification under the slogan "one country, two systems" and to change both places' sense of identity in relation to China in the long run.

Most studies of the taishang show that most Taiwanese people who work in China have kept a strong sense of who they are as Taiwanese. One easy reason is that most of them are from Taiwan and not the mainland. They tend to stick together, live in the same places, and speak Hokkien instead of Mandarin among themselves. It can also be said that the way the PRC has handled them administratively since the start of the reform era (1979)—"Taiwanese compatriots" with a special travel and identification document, the taibaozheng, has not made them more Chinese. Instead, it has kept them outside of local Chinese society, much like how Hong Kong business people, who have had a "hometown return permit," or huixiangzheng, since the beginning of the reform era, have stayed outsiders. Estimates show that about two-thirds of them are likely to vote for KMT or Blue camp candidates, but most of them still say they are Taiwanese (50 percent, compared to 62 percent of those who don't work in China). Even though more of them say they have two identities than people who don't work in China (40 percent vs. 32 percent), fewer of them see themselves as only Chinese (6 percent vs. 4 percent). Moreover, most taishang continue to identify with the ROC, not the PRC; they believe nearly as much as the rest of the Taiwanese population that Taiwan is a "sovereign, independent country" (59 percent vs. 65 percent for those who do not work in China); they remain massively in favor of the status quo in the Taiwan Strait (56 percent vs. 59 percent); and they even continue to prefer independence (25 percent against 26 percent) to reunification (11 percent vs. 6 percent). Overall, the taishang have become what I would call "agents of accommodation," but they are not yet, and probably will not become, "agents of unification."

The Erosion of Identity-Based Politics

It seems like a contradiction to say that Taiwanese identity is getting stronger while identity politics are getting weaker. But there is some sense to this strange situation. Since most ROC voters were born and raised in Taiwan, the difference between locals and people from the mainland is becoming less important. For most people on the island, being Taiwanese is now a given.

It is true that Ma, who is from the mainland, helped bring a lot of mainlanders into the government and other state bodies. This helped bring the debate back up. But by doing this, he also helped to divide his own party and make Taiwanese KMT leaders dislike him. From this point of view, you can see the difference between Ma and Legislative Yuan speaker Wang Jin-pyng, who is from Taiwan and was a key mediator in the calm end of the Sunflower Movement and the occupation of the Legislative Yuan by some activists. But in the last few elections, bread-and-butter problems, public policy, and social issues have been more important than identity politics. For example, during the campaign for the January 2016 election, Tsai Ing-wen and the DPP were careful not to bring up identity politics while promoting Taiwan's aboriginal roots and multiculturalism. They knew that identity politics is a dangerous tool and an argument that may not appeal to most voters, especially young voters.

The Ko Wen-je incident also shows how identity politics are becoming less important in Taiwan. This surgeon ran as an independent and beat Lien Chan's son, Sean Lien Sheng-wen, who was running for mayor of Taipei for the KMT. He was elected mayor of Taipei in November 2014. Even though he is backed by the DPP, he represents the emergence of a new political force that many Taiwanese, including those in the Sunflower Movement, have been waiting for to end the crippling polarization between the KMT and the DPP and between mainlanders and natives.

Both the DPP and the KMT have had to change because of this. They have also had to put identity politics on the back burner, if not completely. On the DPP side, Tsai Ing-wen has been more interested in reassuring voters that her party can fix the economy and come up with a good policy toward China than in pointing out that it is Taiwanese. Even lawmakers and think tanks that support Taiwan's independence now agree that Taiwan's relationship with China is unique. For example, dark Green leader Ku Kuan-min suggested in 2013 that both sides of the Strait become "brotherly states" or, more correctly, brotherly entities within the same confederation. He did this even though he didn't like how moderate Tsai was.

On the KMT side, Chinese culture is becoming less important as a new generation of leaders takes over, even though Hung Hsiu-chu, the daughter of a mainlander from Zhejiang and a dark Blue leader, became party chair in March 2006. The fact that the KMT replaced Hung as its presidential candidate in October 2015, just three months after handpicking her, because she was too close to the PRC with New Taipei City mayor Eric Chu, a more popular figure (and KMT chair from January 2015 to January 2016), shows that the party wants to get closer to the voters and become more Taiwanese again. Eric Chu comes from a mixed family background, but he has a strong Taiwanese identity thanks to his father-in-law, his wife, and his mother. He speaks excellent Hokkien, and his father-in-law, Kao Yu-jen, was promoted by Chiang Ching-kuo in the 1970s and 1980s and was the speaker of Taiwan's Provincial Assembly from 1988 to 1989. He is close with both local KMT and DPP elites. But more importantly, Eric Chu has been aware that his party needs to stop focusing on identity problems and instead focus on social and economic issues. He has done this by separating himself from "unificationists" like Wu Poh-hsiung and "Chinese nationalists" like

Ma Ying-jeou or Ms. Hung. Because of these things, it is unlikely that Hung will be able to bring the Nationalist Party back together around a credible policy plan and let it take power again.

This drop in identity politics shows that there are many different ways to be Taiwanese, that local identities are getting stronger in different parts of the island, and that, to some extent, people can hold on to more than one identity, which is a trait of most postmodern and free societies. As was already said, it also shows that Taiwanese culture is no longer questioned. In other words, the fall of identity politics is a sign that Taiwanese democracy is getting older and maybe even getting stronger.

Conclusion

Because Taiwan's move toward democracy and political life are closely linked, Taiwanese identity is likely to keep getting stronger while Chinese identity and even dual identity get weaker on this island. The Sunflower Movement in the spring of 2014 and the KMT's big losses in both the local elections in November 2014 and the national elections in January 2016 have shown this trend in some ways. But at the same time, there are more ways to be Taiwanese than ever before. It has made some people identify with the local culture and language and with building a new Taiwanese nation that is de facto, if not de jure, and forever independent from China. It has also made some people identify with a democratized, sovereign, and de facto independent ROC on Taiwan, and it has made some people, though a small minority, imagine a future in which Taiwan is eventually reunified with the mainland (probably after the PRC becomes more democratic). The gap between Taiwanese identities and their political options for the future is likely to get bigger. This is because most Taiwanese are very proud of their unique culture, but they also know that the only solution for their country is the ROC institutional framework, the status quo in the Strait, informal but reliable US protection, and growing communication and cooperation with the PRC. Even so, most Taiwanese now, unlike in the 1990s and early 2000s, associate the ROC with Taiwan and don't want the mainland to be legally part of their own government. Even if they feel part Chinese, they see the PRC as a different country, even though they feel part Chinese. In other words, there is no longer any difference between state identity and national identity. Today, Taiwanese municipal identity is only connected to the ROC or Taiwan, or what Lee Teng-hui liked to call in the late 1990s, the Republic of China on Taiwan. This is a form of national identity for most Taiwanese.

Some Taiwanese will always see themselves as a whole, both politically and culturally, and this will affect every part of their lives. But this group is likely to get smaller as Taiwan becomes more and more connected to China, but also as the world becomes more connected and as social and economic differences get worse. Because of this, groups and identity politics will have less weight in Taiwan. But as long as Taiwan is militarily threatened by the PRC, which denies its existence even under its official name, the ROC, and wants to annex it, Taiwanese identity, understood as a political or civic identity, is likely to survive and remain, along with democracy, one of the most natural barriers to Beijing's imperial dream of reunification.

Chapter 9
U.S. Security Relations with Taiwan and the Outlook for Stability in the Taiwan Strait

US security links with Taiwan, especially the sales of weapons to the island, have been a source of tension between the US and China for a long time. The People's Republic of China (PRC) thought it was wrong that the US kept selling weapons to Taiwan even after relations between the US and PRC improved in 1979. The Taiwan Relations Act, which made clear that the US would keep selling weapons to Taiwan, made Chinese leaders even more angry. In a 1982 communique, Washington agreed "to gradually reduce its sales of arms to Taiwan" and promised that future arms sales to Taiwan "would not exceed, either in terms of quality or quantity," those of the past few years. However, the history of US arms sales since then suggests that the communique hasn't had much of an effect on how the US acts. In turn, when the US sells arms to Taiwan, China often gets angry and responds with harsh words and symbolic actions, like briefly stopping military-to-military talks between the US and China. Even though ties between Taipei and Beijing have been much better since Ma Ying-jeou was elected president of Taiwan in 2008, US arms sales to Taiwan have continued to cause problems between the US and China. At the beginning of 2010, for example, PRC officials were "strongly indignant" after hearing about an arms sale. They called the sale a "gross intervention in China's internal affairs" that would have a "serious negative impact" on bilateral relations.

China's fast rise as an economic and, more and more, a military power is changing the security situation in East Asia in a big way. In recent years, influential people in both Washington and Beijing have called for a change in how their countries deal with the relationship between the US and Taiwan. Several scholars and former US officials have called for the US to cut back on its security pledge to Taiwan and stop selling arms to Taiwan. People who agree with this point of view say that a smaller US commitment would help improve ties between the US and China. In the meantime, some people in the PRC have asked for a stronger response to US arms sales, such as economic sanctions. People who want to take a tougher stance say that the US would have to rethink its commitment to Taiwan if it was ready to respond more harshly. This chapter takes a hard look at both of the suggested policy changes. In the pages that follow, we give you a simple way to think about how US arms sales affect the cross-Strait relationship as a whole. In turn, we use the framework to show how changes in US or PRC policy on the arms sales problem could affect the chances of peace between China and Taiwan and the way they negotiate. Our main conclusion is that both proposed policy changes—less arms sales from the US to Taiwan and a tougher reaction from the PRC to arms sales—carry significant risks, some of which are surprising, for the country that would make the change.

First, we show that a choice to end US arms sales to Taiwan could make things worse between the US and Taiwan in ways that previous studies haven't fully considered. In particular, a smaller US commitment to Taiwan could help change the general structure of relations across the Taiwan Strait from one based on deterrence to one based on force. But we want to point out that stopping arms sales to Taiwan could have other, stabilizing effects, and that under the right conditions, a change in US policy like this could actually make it less likely that there will be a military clash in the Taiwan Strait. Second, we show that a tougher reaction from the PRC to US arms sales could show a stronger US commitment to Taiwan than was previously clear. This would give Taiwan more freedom to go against Beijing's wishes. In other words, both of the proposed policy changes would have a high chance of backfiring because they could lead to results that are totally different from what the policy change was meant to do. We say over and over that these unexpected results might not happen, but that they are real possibilities that should make both Washington and Beijing cautious.

In the next part, we'll take a quick look at the recent debate in the US about how to keep Taiwan and the US safe. Then, we draw a simple model of cross-Strait ties and use it to figure out what would happen if the US stopped selling arms to Taiwan. Next, we'll talk about calls in Beijing for the PRC to be tougher on US arms sales to Taiwan and how a change in PRC policy could affect ties across the Taiwan Strait. We end with a few short suggestions for policy.

The US Debate

Because US arms sales to Taiwan cause tensions and anger in Beijing, some people in the US want Washington to stop selling weapons to the island or at least cut back. Proponents say that doing so would take away a major source of tension between the US and China and improve trust and cooperation between the two countries. People who want the US to have less of a pledge to Taiwan say that this would help make it less likely that there will be a war in East Asia.

Charles Glaser makes the best case for this point. He says that ending the US commitment to protect Taiwan would have two big benefits for the relationship between the US and China. First, it could improve ties between the US and China because such a change in US policy would take away a major reason why China doesn't trust the US. Second, if the US stopped helping Taiwan, it would take away the most likely cause of a military clash between China and the US. This would make the US and China less likely to go to war with each other. Glaser suggests a "grand bargain" in which the US would stop supporting Taiwan if China agreed to "resolve its maritime disputes on 'fair' terms" and let the US keep a security presence in East Asia for a long time. Others say that the US can't keep supporting Taiwan as long as China's military power keeps growing. For example, Chas Freeman warns that a continued US commitment to Taiwan is incompatible with (a) the US's declining power in the region and (b) how important the PRC thinks the problem is to them. If the US doesn't change its policies to fit the new geopolitical realities, there could be a military clash in the future over an issue that is very important to China. In a similar way, John Mearsheimer says that if China continues to become a great power, the existing US security commitment to Taiwan will become less and less possible to keep up. Taiwan will have to give in to China s growing power in the end.

Proposals to cut back on security links between the US and Taiwan are, however, controversial, and many scholars have written well-thought-out arguments against the idea. Most of the time, these reviews have made a few important points. First, it's not clear that cutting security ties with Taiwan would change the US-China relationship. The interests of the two countries may conflict on many other issues, such as North Korea, maritime disputes in East Asia, and economic issues, and it's not clear why Beijing would give up on these other issues if the US only changed its policy on arms sales, which, from Beijing's point of view, the US had already agreed to follow in the 1982 join communique. Second, the image of the United States in the area could be at risk. Some people worry that breaking a promise to Taiwan would send a bad message to the US's other friends in East Asia. Beijing might also see US concessions on Taiwan as a sign of weakness and think that Washington is unlikely to challenge the PRC on other problems in the region. Third, stopping arms sales would make Taiwan feel even less safe, which could make Taipei less willing to talk politics with the PRC. It's not clear that a smaller US pledge to Taiwan would help find a peaceful solution to the dispute. Lastly, and this is connected, stopping arms sales would probably weaken Taiwan's ability to protect itself, which could lead the PRC to treat the island with more force.

Even though we think these counterarguments make sense, we think the reasoning behind them needs to be broken down more. This is especially true when people talk about the chances of peace in the Taiwan Strait. For example, we think it's likely that if arms sales stopped, Taiwanese leaders would feel less sure about their ability to negotiate with the PRC. But it's not clear why this should make them less likely to talk with Beijing. It's also possible that Taiwan's leaders would feel they had no choice but to negotiate with a more powerful PRC in this case. Also, a change in the balance of power across the Taiwan Strait would make it easier for Beijing to use military force, but it's not clear that this would make the relationship less stable. For example, it's possible that Taiwan would respond with more accommodating policies that would make it less likely for Beijing to use military force. In short, it's not clear how a change in the military balance of power across the Taiwan Strait would affect stability in the Taiwan Strait. In the next part, we'll look at the topic in a more organized way.

Reassessing the Consequences of Halting Arms Sales to Taiwan

In this section, we say that ending the US's security pledge to Taiwan, and especially stopping the US from selling arms to Taiwan, could make things worse. As other people have said, stopping US arms sales would probably change the balance of power in the Taiwan Strait in a big way. We think that a big change in the balance of power could change the way people talk across the Taiwan Strait. This could make the relationship between the PRC and Taiwan go from one of threat to one of force. In turn, this could make it more likely that there will be a military clash, for reasons we explain.

We also want to point out that US arms sales to Taiwan and the overall relationship between the US and Taiwan are only one of many things that affect how much Beijing thinks a war in the Taiwan Strait will cost. If other things make Chinese leaders think that the costs of war are high enough, then even big changes in the balance of power across the Taiwan Strait won't make things worse. In fact, fewer arms sales could make Beijing think that war will be more expensive. For example, if those who want Washington to cut back on arms sales are right that this will lead to better relations with Beijing, it could give the PRC a bigger stake in a stable relationship between the US and China, which would likely be hurt if the PRC started a military conflict with Taiwan.

In short, it's not clear what stopping arms sales to Taiwan would mean for security in the Taiwan Strait. Instead, coming to a conclusion in this area takes a careful look at the specific ways in which arms sales affect stability in the Taiwan Strait and how those causes work. We want to do this kind of research by making a simple model of how people get along across the Taiwan Strait. Then, we look at how US arms sales to Taiwan affect key model factors and how stopping those sales would change the chance of a war.

A Basic Framework for Cross-Strait Relations

The main thing that the PRC and Taiwan disagree about is whether or not Taiwan is an independent country. The PRC claims sovereignty over Taiwan and disagrees with the idea that the Republic of China (ROC) government on Taiwan reflects an independent, sovereign state. Beijing still sees formal unification with the island as a major state goal. So, any effort on Taiwan that tries to weaken the political and historical ties between Taiwan and mainland China is met with resistance in Beijing. The PRC refuses to stop using force against Taiwan and has vowed to fight a war to stop Taiwan from officially breaking away from China. In the meantime, Taiwan's view on the subject of sovereignty has changed a lot over time. After the Nationalists fled to Taiwan, the ROC government still thought it was the legal government of all of China for many years. The PRC, on the other hand, was a "bandit" regime that didn't have any legitimacy. As Taiwan became more democratic in the 1980s and 1990s, its government started to move away from the idea that both sides of the Taiwan Strait were "one China." Under President Lee Teng-hui's "pragmatic diplomacy," Taiwan tried to get more involved in foreign politics as a separate political entity from PRC. Lee talked about ideas like "one China, two political entities." In 1999, he called the link between the two sides of the Taiwan Strait "state-to-state, or at least special state-to-state relations." Later, President Chen Shui-bian (2000–2008) did a lot of symbolic things to show how different Taiwan is from China. Chen often called Taiwan a "independent, sovereign country," and while he was president, he pushed for a new constitution that was more "suitable" to Taiwan's needs than the ROC constitution, which was written before the Nationalists moved to the island. During the Lee and Chen administrations, ties across the Taiwan Strait were often tense, and Beijing often said it would use force to stop Taiwan from making its independence official.

After Ma Ying-jeou was elected president of Taiwan in 2008, the relationship between China and Taiwan became much more stable. As president, Ma had a "three no" policy: no independence, no unification, and no use of force. He also tried to work with the PRC in areas like trade, business, tourism, and extradition, and he was mostly successful. But even though Ma was more flexible than his predecessors when it came to sovereignty problems, the main question of Taiwan's status was still not answered. Progress on this front doesn't seem likely in the near future. Ma's successor, Tsai Ing-wen of the Democratic Progressive Party, has been less flexible than Ma on sovereignty issues, and the detente that existed between China and Taiwan after 2008 has mostly disappeared. In short, the relationship across the Taiwan Strait hasn't changed much at its core, because there are still disagreements about Taiwan's sovereign position.

So, we believe that Taiwan's status as a sovereign country is the main thing that the PRC and Taiwan are (explicitly or implicitly) negotiating about. For simplicity, we assume that Taiwan's position can be shown on a single dimension, with formal unification with China (U) on one end and formal independence (I) on the other (see Figure 9.1). Assume also that Taiwan's leaders want a result closer to I and China's leaders want a result closer to U, and that China's utilities run from 0 for formal independence to 1 for unification. The PRC and Taiwan have very different ideas about whether they want to join together or stay separate. In our model, we assume that the status quo point is somewhere between U and I, and that Taiwan could offer a different status quo at any time. The PRC can either accept the new status quo as set by Taiwan or use force to try to get what it wants most (U). Assume that if the two sides went to war, China would win with a chance of p, and that victory would allow Beijing to force Taiwan to join China, which is what Beijing wants. Lastly, let's say that the costs of fighting the war, which are shown by cc for China, would lower the expected benefits each side would get from the war. So, the expected value of war for China is p - cc, which is shown in Figure 9.1 by the point R. R is the reversion point for the PRC. As long as Taiwan picks a level of sovereignty to the right of R, the PRC prefers to let that happen. But if Taiwan picks a rank to the left of R, the PRC would rather start a war. War would be very expensive for Taiwan, so the people in charge there have strong reasons to choose an amount of sovereignty to the right of R. In other words, R is the best thing that can happen for Taiwan.

Concerning the possibility of instability in the Taiwan Strait, analysts of the China-Taiwan relationship have said that a "revisionist" Taiwan trying to formalize its independence (or taking steps in that direction) would be the most likely cause of a cross-Strait conflict, which would lead to a PRC military response. A president who really wanted Taiwan to be recognized as an independent country might, for example, change the island's official name to the Republic of Taiwan or try to get a new constitution made just for Taiwan passed. Figure 9.1 shows that this situation could lead to war if the new status quo was to the left of R, China's reversion point. Why would Taiwan cross such a red line, knowing that a war with the PRC would be very expensive? If Taiwan knew for sure where R was, it would set its level of sovereignty just to the right of R and leave it at that. Unfortunately, Taiwan doesn't know for sure where R is because it doesn't know for sure how China thinks about p and c. Also, it's hard for Beijing to get this information across to Taiwan in a credible way, because the PRC has a clear reason to exaggerate its power and resolve in order to convince Taiwan's leaders that R is further to the left than it really is. Taiwan, on the other hand, is sure to know that Beijing has a reason to lie.

Figure 9.1. A model of cross-Strait relations.

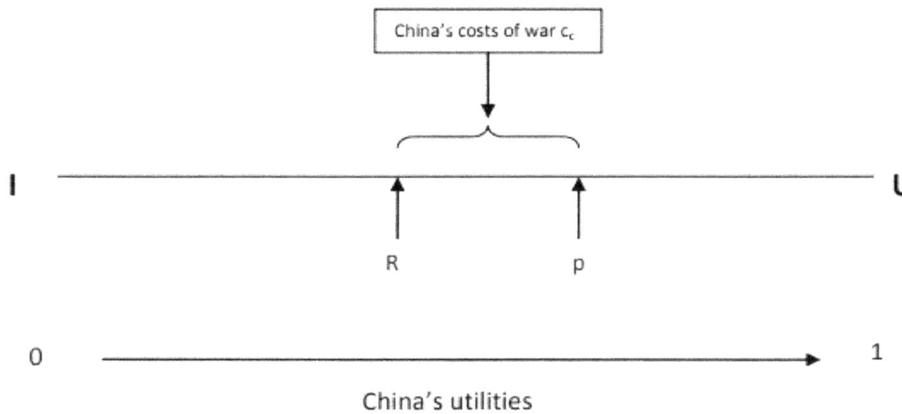

So, in the last few decades, the main problem in cross-Strait ties has been the problem of deterrence. The PRC tries to stop Taiwan from taking steps toward formal independence, but Taiwan may not be sure how serious these threats are. During the Lee and Chen administrations, it was most clear how important deterrence was. Both presidents tried to change Taiwan's relationship with the PRC in a way that went against Beijing's goal of eventual reunion. The PRC tried to stop Taiwan from going too far on sovereignty issues by showing that it was ready to use force to stop Taiwan from becoming independent. Here are some examples: the PRC's increasing number of military drills after Lee Teng-hui visited Cornell University in 1995; its warning in a white paper in 2000 that it wouldn't wait forever for national unification; the PRC's repeated claims during the Chen administration that it would "pay any price" to stop Taiwan from becoming independent; and the passage of the anti-secession law in 2005. After Ma Ying-jeou was elected in 2008, the relationship between the two countries became much more stable. Ma did not push sovereignty issues as hard as his predecessors, so Chinese leaders did not have to show their resistance to Taiwan independence as strongly as they did before. But deterrence is still the most important part of the bond. In fact, the PRC's threat to use force seems to be the main reason why Taiwan's people aren't more in favor of independence to begin with. And now that Taiwan's Democratic Progressive Party is back in power, it's possible that the PRC's threats to stop Taiwan will once again become more frequent and clear.

US Arms Sales to Taiwan Might Lead to Destabilization

How would a smaller US security pledge to Taiwan change the chances of a conflict across the Taiwan Strait? What would actually happen if the United States stopped selling guns to the island? Remember that in our simple model, there is conflict if Taiwan claims an amount of sovereignty to the left of point R on the I-U continuum. How, then, would stopping the sale of arms change the chances that Taiwan's claimed standing would be to the left of point R? Here, we'll start by looking at the most obvious and direct ways that changing the amount of arms sales to Taiwan could change the model's parameters and the results of that. In the next part, we'll talk about some of the less obvious and indirect effects of stopping arms sales, which will help us understand the points made in this section.

From what I can tell, US arms sales to Taiwan have a clear effect on both the costs (cc) that China would expect to pay in a military conflict across the Taiwan Strait and the chances (p) that China would win such a conflict. At the very least, arms sales should make Taiwan's military stronger compared to that of the PRC, which will lower p and raise c,. p and cc aren't just based on the balance of power between China and Taiwan. They're also based on what the US is likely to do in the event of a cross-Strait war: At the very least, US involvement would make it much harder for the PRC to win a war across the Taiwan Strait, and it would almost certainly raise China's predicted costs of such a war. So, a higher chance of US involvement means that p is smaller and cc is bigger. Arms sales to Taiwan, on the other hand, may show how much the US cares about the island. Insofar as US arms sales to Taiwan do increase confidence in Beijing and Taipei that the US is likely to step in if there is a conflict across the Taiwan Strait, continued US arms sales to Taiwan imply a smaller p and larger cc than if the US didn't sell weapons to Taiwan.

Because of these direct effects, stopping arms sales should lower China's projected costs of war and make it more likely that the PRC will win. R should then move to the right. This makes sense: if the balance of power in the Taiwan Strait favors the PRC, we might expect Beijing to be more demanding on sovereignty issues (and less tolerant of results that are far from its ideal point of unity). If R moved to the right of Taiwan's actual status, the model suggests that the PRC would rather fight a war than accept a continuation of the status quo. If Taiwan didn't change its status to reflect this new reality by pushing the status quo back to the right of R, there would be a military conflict. Given how high the costs of war would be for Taiwan, costs that would likely be even higher if the US didn't help protect the island, leaders in Taipei would have strong reasons to try to avoid this outcome by giving in to new power realities and making some concessions to the PRC on sovereignty issues.

But there are some reasons to think it would be hard to find a solution in this case. Remember that the biggest strategic problem in cross-Strait ties over the past few decades has been a problem of deterrence. The PRC has been trying to stop Taiwan from trying to change its sovereign status in a way that goes against PRC hopes for unification. But if R moved to the right of where it is now, the model says that the relationship across the Taiwan Strait would be marked by a problem of coercion. Here, a war could happen not because the PRC fails to stop Taiwan from making unilateral changes to the status quo, but because the PRC fails to force Taiwan to change the status quo in a way that is more to Beijing's liking (remember that once R moves to the right of the status quo, Beijing's expected war payoff is greater than its utility for staying with the status quo). But commitment issues could make it harder to find a peaceful solution, even if Taiwan knew that R had moved to the right of the status quo and was happy in theory to give up some of its sovereignty. The reason is that the problem being negotiated, Taiwan's sovereign status, could affect the two sides' ability to negotiate in the future. In other words, giving up some of Taiwan's sovereign status to avoid war in the short term could make Taiwan's ability to negotiate with Beijing even weaker in the future.

Even if the U.S. stopped selling guns to Taiwan and stopped being responsible for its safety, Taiwan would still be different from places where the PRC has direct control. It would still be self-governing and democratic, it would still have armed forces, and, for all intents and purposes, it would still be like an independent country in every way except that it would not be recognized by international law. But the fact that Taiwan is still different in this way leaves the door open for the US to get involved in a war across the Taiwan Strait, even if the US decides to stop providing security for Taiwan. Leaders in Washington, for example, might change their minds about the PRC after an attack on Taiwan, especially if the PRC made a promise in exchange for the U.S. giving up its security guarantee. So, even if the US stopped selling arms to Taiwan and stopped providing security for the island, the chances of the US getting involved in a conflict across the Taiwan Strait would not go down to zero. This is in contrast to the chances of the US getting involved in other parts of China, like Tibet or Hong Kong. But the more Taiwan gave in to PRC requests by becoming more like Hong Kong or Tibet and less like an independent country, the less likely it was that the US would step in, just like it does in other places where the PRC has direct control. This kind of intervention would be clearer and clearer to be in a civil war, not an international conflict.

So, any deal that involves Taiwan giving up some of its sovereignty should also lower Beijing's predicted costs of war, which would move R even further to the right. Because of this, it would be hard to believe that Beijing would stick to such a deal, because once it was in place, Beijing would have a reason to ask for an even better deal (and Taiwan wouldn't be able to say no). Fearon comes up with a similar model in which states negotiate over strategic land and the result of the talks changes the balance of power. This change in the balance of power happens because the result of the negotiations gives land to a rival state, which makes that state better at fighting. When this kind of dynamic is at play, it's hard to reach a settlement because the change in power that comes with a settlement may be less desirable than fighting and not negotiating. Even though a hypothetical deal between the PRC and Taiwan is not about strategic land, it is possible that a similar dynamic is at work when the PRC and Taiwan talk about Taiwan's sovereignty. Since giving authority to the PRC makes the PRC more powerful in negotiations, Taiwan may decide that risking war is better than negotiating with the PRC over unification. In other words, Taiwan might decide that it would be better to risk going to war with China right now than to accept the terms of an outdated deal that would make it a lower-ranking part of a united China. So, in the same way that negotiating over strategic land is hard because any deal could have strategic effects, negotiating over unification can be dangerous because it could affect the PRC and Taiwan's ability to negotiate in the future.

In conclusion, stopping arms sales to Taiwan could make the Taiwan Strait even more dangerous. A change in US strategy like this could change the balance of power in the Taiwan Strait, which could change the strategic dynamic from one of deterrence to one of coercion. On the other hand, there are reasons to think that a relationship between China and Taiwan in which China tried to force Taiwan to take steps toward unification would be more prone to conflict than one in which the PRC tried to stop Taiwan from taking steps toward independence. This is because Taiwan might have trouble making credible commitments, which could make it hard for Taiwan to adjust to new power realities.

Ending US Arms Sales to Taiwan Would Not Inherently Lead to Destabilization

Based on the study above, stopping arms sales to Taiwan would be unstable if it changed p and cc enough to move R to the right of where it is now. But there are some reasons to doubt that stopping sales would have such a big effect. On the one hand, the balance of power in the Taiwan Strait keeps moving toward China, and it's not clear that the arms themselves have a big effect on this. Whether or not the sales have a big impact in this way also depends a lot on what kinds of weapons the United States is willing to sell to Taiwan and what kinds of weapons Taiwan is willing to buy. For example, some analysts have said that Taiwan's efforts to buy expensive and high-profile packages like the F-16C/D fighter aren't worth it because the PRC's air capabilities are getting better. These analysts think that Taiwan would be better off buying more common (and cheaper) systems to counter the PRC's capabilities. So, whether or not stopping arms sales has a big impact on p and cc will depend in part on what kinds of weapons the US would sell Taiwan if arms sales kept going.

In the same way, it is not clear how much selling guns sends a message. As we'll see in the next part, when it costs the US a lot to sell arms to Taiwan, this is the clearest sign that the US backs Taiwan. But it's clear that not only do the sales not seem to cost Washington a lot, but also that many people in the U.S. gain financially and politically from them. In 2011, when the Obama administration was thinking about selling the F-16C/D package, a lot of US senators signed a letter to the president urging the sale to go ahead. Many of the senators who signed the letter were from states that would benefit economically from more people buying fighter jets. In other words, as long as China's actions against the U.S. for selling weapons don't get too bad, the strategy doesn't seem to cost Washington very much. So, it doesn't seem to us that selling arms to Taiwan is a very strong sign of US support for Taiwan. If the US stopped selling arms to Taiwan, it wouldn't necessarily cause Taiwan and China to have a very different idea of what the US would do in a cross-Strait war.

It is also important to note that the value of p and cc is affected by many things other than US arms sales to Taiwan. These include Taiwan's own military capabilities, the capabilities of the PRC, the amount of economic integration across the Taiwan Strait, and so on. In recent decades, economic integration and cooperation across the Taiwan Strait have grown quickly. This, along with China's general integration into global markets, suggests that a military confrontation across the Taiwan Strait would likely cost China a lot, even if the PRC won. Compared to these prices, a drop in arms sales could have a very small effect on cc.

Lastly, and this might be the most important point, stopping arms sales to Taiwan could actually make cc better in some ways. Critics sometimes say that stopping arms sales might just make China want more and make it want to make more claims on the U.S., but supporters like Glaser say that stopping arms sales could lead to a big improvement in the relationship between the US and China. Also, whether the US gives weapons to Taiwan or not, it is hard to see how a strong relationship between the US and China could stand up to PRC pressure on the island. So, if the PRC wants a stable relationship between the US and China, and if ending arms sales to Taiwan does lead to a better relationship between China and the US, then the PRC will have more to lose (in terms of a strong relationship between the US and China) if it starts a conflict in the Taiwan Strait. If this kind of effect is bigger than the direct effect that stopping arms sales would have on China's war costs, then stopping arms sales could help to keep things as they are.

In the end, even in our highly stylized and simplified model of cross-Strait relations, changes in US policy have complicated and uncertain effects on security in the Taiwan Strait. Analysts should realize that stopping arms sales to Taiwan could cause a lot of instability. Such a change in US policy could help change the relationship between the two sides of the Taiwan Strait from a safe deterrence relationship to an unstable compellence relationship. But stopping arms sales might not have this effect, and it might even help keep the Taiwan Strait calm by making China more invested in keeping things the same. We hope that our model will help people think about this important topic in a more organized way by showing how different kinds of effects fit together.

Stringent PRC Policy on Arms Sales

In the same way that people in the US have asked for a change in US policy on arms sales to Taiwan, people in Beijing have asked for a change in PRC policy on the same problem. As was already said, when Taiwan buys weapons, Beijing gets very angry. When the US announced a US$5.8 billion weapons package to Taiwan in 2011, official Chinese media called it a "despicable breach of faith in international relations." One general wrote that the US was "cheating and making a fool of the Chinese people." This kind of response isn't new. In 1992, when the Bush administration said it would sell 150 F-16 fighter jets to Taiwan, the Standing Committee of the National People's Congress released a statement saying it was "extremely angry" about the US's "wanton interference" in China's internal affairs.

Even though China gets angry when the US sells arms to Taiwan, the real policy response to these sales has usually been mild. Aside from the tough talk, most of the response has been symbolic. For example, when the PRC sells arms, it often stops talking with the other country. In the past few years, the PRC has put a temporary stop to military-to-military talks after decisions were made about arms sales. In 1992, because of the F-16 deal, the PRC stopped talking about human rights. At times, the PRC has hinted that it might respond more strongly. For example, in 1992 and 2010, Chinese officials said that the PRC might respond with economic measures. But there isn't much proof that China has followed through on these kinds of threats so far.

Some Chinese analysts and military officials are upset that China won't respond more strongly to US arms sales. They have sometimes called for a tougher, "tit-for-tat" reaction. At the beginning of January 2010, retired Rear Admiral Yang Yi, a well-known defense analyst, called for tougher sanctions against US companies that sell arms, and well-known scholar Shi Yinhong said that China should charge the US more because of arms sales. Soon after, when the US government announced a new package of arms sales to Taiwan at the end of January, PRC government officials did in fact threaten penalties, saying that China would punish the US companies involved in the arms sales to Taiwan by putting them on a blacklist. Several well-known scholars and analysts, such as Yang Yi and Wang Yong from Beijing University, were quoted in the Chinese media as saying that they supported such a strategy. Reports from the media also showed that many Chinese "netizens" supported a stricter strategy like this. To be clear, these ideas are not new. People in China have been calling for a tougher PRC reaction to Taiwan's arms sales for a long time. John Garver says, for example, that military leaders wanted a strong response to the sale of F-16s to China in 1992. Some of them called for economic sanctions on US exports to China, such as wheat and other agricultural goods. Garver says that Deng Xiaoping was the one who finally shut these people up.

There are two main reasons for taking a tougher stance. First, a tougher approach would make it more expensive for the United States to keep selling arms to Taiwan as it does now. Because of these higher costs, Washington might rethink how useful the status quo is and decide that the benefits of arms sales no longer justify the costs. In short, sanctions could give the PRC more power to negotiate in the Taiwan Strait by making it more possible that the U.S. will reduce its support for Taiwan. Second, even if the US didn't change its policy, a tougher approach would at least make it easier for the PRC to show, both at home and around the world, that it is unhappy with the way things are. Jia Qingguo of Peking University has written that the Chinese Communist Party is finding it harder and harder to defend its "weak" responses to U.S. weapons sales, such as verbal protests, because domestic pressure is growing. The CCP thinks it needs to show its courage with concrete acts of retaliation.

But China faces big risks if it gets stricter about selling weapons. Clearly, threatening or punishing US companies with sanctions could make things worse between China and the US and could even start a trade war. But more importantly, think about what will happen if the US keeps selling the weapons even though the PRC will fight back. In this case, it would be clear that Washington would have to pay more to sell weapons. By keeping up with the sales despite the higher costs, the US would basically be showing that it cares about Taiwan's security. It would be much harder to say that US arms sales to

Taiwan were motivated by a cynical desire to help US companies and create a few jobs in the US. In response to US arms sales, the PRC has to make a big choice. If Chinese policymakers think that the United States is selling weapons to Taiwan for mostly cynical economic and political reasons, it makes sense to get tough. The United States would be more likely to back down in this case, which would open the door to an end to US arms sales. But if the PRC thinks that US decisions to sell weapons are based on genuine worries about Taiwan's safety, a tougher policy reaction could backfire. The U.S. isn't likely to back down, and by staying solid in the face of PRC sanctions, the U.S. would show both the PRC and Taiwan that it cares more about Taiwan than before. Also, the tougher reaction would probably cause more trouble in the relationship between China and the United States.

Conclusion

One of the main sources of conflict in the Sino-American relationship as a whole is that the US still cares about Taiwan's security and continues to sell arms to Taiwan. In the past few years, experts in both Washington and Beijing have come up with new ways to deal with the problem. Some people in the US have said that the US should stop selling weapons to Taiwan and think about pulling out of its pledge to the island as a whole. Some people in the PRC have said that a stronger stance should be taken by a growing China in response to US arms sales. We have argued that both of the planned changes to policy carry big risks. In the case of the US, stopping arms sales to Taiwan could make it more likely that there will be a war in the Taiwan Strait by changing the relationship between the two sides from one of deterrence to one of force. In the case of China, being tougher about US arms sales could fail by showing that the US cares more about Taiwan's safety than is currently thought. In turn, if the US showed a stronger commitment, Taiwan might be less willing to give in to the PRC on sovereignty problems.

Chapter 10
Shifts and Persistence in the Identity of Taiwanese in Mainland China

Identity has been the most important problem in Taiwanese politics for the past 20 years. Identity problems are at the heart of social divides and political competition within a country. Some people have used Taiwan's government change to argue that it is not Chinese. Almost everything Taiwan has been doing on the outside has something to do with protecting its national identity. Taiwan's attempts to figure out its foreign policy with China, the U.S., and other countries have also been based on identity politics. But "the Taiwanese identity project" may have a weak spot: the Taiwanese who live on the mainland. Since China's post-Mao reforms, the coming together of the Kuomintang (KMT) and the Chinese Communist Party, and the rise of global production and outsourcing networks, the mainland has become the top place for Taiwanese foreign investments. Taiwan is also one of China's main sources of foreign direct investment (FDI). Close economic ties caused many people to move from Taiwan to the mainland in waves. Some figures say that there are between 300,000 and 400,000 Taiwanese people living in China.

This is a pretty big share of the people who live on the small island. They and their close families add up to about 2 million people, or about 10% of Taiwan's total population. How these Taiwanese see themselves is a very important question. Are they adopting a Chinese identity, or do they still hold on to their Taiwanese identity? If the first is true, they may be a strong and growing "fifth column" in Taiwanese politics, but most taishang would be saddened to think that their fellow countrymen saw them this way. So, in Taiwan, the identity of Taiwanese in mainland China has always been a point of contention. Some experts see these Taiwanese as immigrants and look for signs of assimilation, while others see them as expatriates and focus on their mobility (they go back and forth between the mainland and Taiwan) and their psychological stability. But empirical research has not fully supported expectations of assimilation that are based on theories of migration (like Fong Xiaoqian's and Shu Keng's). This is because it shows how hard it is for migrants to keep ties to their original culture and resist pressures to adopt a new identity. Researchers have been looking into this topic for more than a decade, but they still can't agree on anything.

Our own study on this topic began in 2002, and since then, we've added more information from interviews and surveys. In this chapter, we'd like to make a final comment on the topic to explain the current situation of Taiwanese identity in China and give some reasons for it. There are five parts to the chapter. The next one talks about who the Taiwanese are and asks why they don't call themselves Chinese even though they settle down and fit in. In the third part, I try to explain why Taiwanese people try to keep their own culture. We say that this is because of how easy it is to move. Taiwanese can keep their strong ties to Taiwan by being able to move, which makes it easier for them to live in mainland China. The fourth part asks why Taiwanese people have been so reluctant to take on a less "exclusive Taiwanese identity." In this part, we look at how the political and social cultures of Taiwan and China are different and sometimes at odds with each other. In the last part, we come to the conclusion that the identity of Taiwanese people who live on the mainland is a good example of identity in a globalizing world. Globalization brought people from Taiwan to the mainland, and the changes and the things that stayed the same show transnationalism, cultural conflicts, and the way national identity is made up of many different parts.

Establishment and Integration without Altering Identity

As was already said, scholars have made different claims about who Taiwanese people are who live on the island. This could be because of the political backgrounds of the scholars, but it could also be because they are focused on different aspects. In other words, depending on where you look, you get different results. The trouble comes from the idea of "identity." Identity in this chapter means "social identity" or "identity of the related person," especially how the person identifies with a social category or group and how much the person thinks of himself or herself as a part of the social category or group. In terms of cross-Strait ties, Taiwanese people could choose between being Chinese or Taiwanese to describe who they are. But the difference between "Chinese" and "Taiwanese" may not be clear when the idea is used in different ways. It could mean "Chinese in a cultural sense" or "Chinese in a nationalistic sense." In Taiwan, most poll questions have three possible answers: being Chinese, being Taiwanese, or being both. This could help make things clearer. Based on these kinds of questions, we can tell that Taiwanese people have either a "inclusive Taiwanese identity" (where they say they are "Chinese" or "both") or a "exclusive Taiwanese identity" (where they say they are only Taiwanese).

There are a few things to keep in mind before talking about identity among Taiwanese people who live in mainland China. First, the question of identity only comes up when planning a job for people who want to settle down and stay put. Second, the question of identity only comes up in social life for people who want to reach out and make friends outside of their racial group. We can then separate three parts of the identity question: (1) psychological settling, which is shown by questions like "bringing over the whole family" and "having a long-term plan to stay on"; (2) social assimilation, which is shown by questions like "who are your close friends" and "who can you and your children marry"; and (3) attitudinal identity, which is imagined membership in a social group and especially the claim of an inclusive or exclusive Taiwanese identity.

The data for the study came from a project called "Lives and Attitudes of the Taiwanese in Mainland China," which was done by the University of Hong Kong and National Chengchi University between the summer of 2009 and the winter of 2012. In that poll, the twelve researchers, or six research teams, spent a total of six weeks talking to Taiwanese people who were moving to the cities near Dongguan and the area around Shanghai. We started the interview by asking the people we were talking to the questions on our semi-structured form. Then we asked more questions about the questions we had already asked and started talking more casually about things that were connected. The conversations were taped and turned into transcripts so the researcher could keep track of how the Taiwanese sojourners felt and what they thought.

Since we don't know much about the Taiwanese groups in China, which are the people in our sample, it was hard to come up with a way to pick people at random based on what we already knew. Instead, we used the snowball method for interviews and the "maximum variation" rule to get information from a variety of sources. So, our interviewees include both Taiwanese businessmen and their families and Taiwanese students; both first- and second-generation Taiwanese; employees from both labor-intensive and high-tech manufacturers; employees of Taiwanese firms, joint ventures, foreign firms, and Chinese firms; Taiwanese sojourners with different levels of education, from primary school to PhD; Taiwanese affiliated with different political factions; and Taiwanese of different ethnic backgrounds. In the end, 452 Taiwanese living in China were interviewed and their opinions were written down as part of a project that turned out to be the biggest systematic survey of Taiwanese living in China. This helps us learn more about who the Taiwanese are in China.

Based on the summary of results in Table 10.1, it's easy to see a pattern in how Taiwanese in mainland China see themselves: they are mostly settled and can easily blend in, but they don't call themselves "Chinese."

First of all, we found that more than half of the Taiwanese people we talked to (52.3%) had already moved to the mainland with their families or had plans to do so. This often has to do with long-term plans for work and family, as well as a feeling of "home" in the area. One Taiwanese person who moved to Shanghai said, "I don't mind calling myself a new Shanghainese." This sets the stage for the next step, which is called "assimilation."

Two different ways can be used to measure how well Taiwanese people fit in with society. The first is based on behavior and is measured by a question about close friends. Even when things like arrival time and chances to talk to people were taken into account, 26.3% of Taiwanese already thought of mainland Chinese as their best friends. The second is based on their attitudes and is tested by asking them who they would marry. Only about 5% say they wouldn't marry a mainland Chinese person, but 58.9% say they would be very happy to do so. In other words, Taiwanese people have no trouble making friends and building trust across racial lines. One Shanghainese person said, "Compared to the people who moved here from Jiangsu and Anhui, Taiwanese aren't anything special to me, and I would never avoid them."

Even though Taiwanese want to settle down and don't have any trouble fitting in, they don't want to give up their original identity or change to one that is less strict and includes fewer people. As shown in Table 10.1, at least 62% of Taiwanese people believe in the "exclusive Taiwan identity." One young Taiwanese person said, "I am from Shanghai, but if someone thinks I am Chinese by mistake, I will correct them right away." I would never accept that the neighborhood Chinese were Chinese. This trend can be seen more clearly when the identities of Taiwanese in Taiwan are compared to those of Taiwanese in mainland China, as shown in Table 10.2.

From Table 10.2, we can see that the Taiwanese who live in Taiwan and those who have moved to China have very different political views, especially when it comes to which party they belong to. The number of people in the pan-Blue camp (KMT, People First Party [PFP], New Party [CNP], or Minkuotang [MKT]) almost doubles from 26.4 percent to 45.1 percent, while the number of people in the pan-Green camp (Democratic Progressive Party [DPP], Taiwan Solidarity Union [TSU], Taiwan Independence Party [TAIP], or Taiwan Constitution Association [TCA]) drops from 28.6 percent to 15.7 percent. When it comes to a more in-depth opinion on independence or unification, there are even bigger differences between the Taiwanese in Taiwan and China. The number of people who back independence goes down from 25.8% to 5.5%, while the number of people who back reunification goes up from 9.9% to 21.4%. If this is true, how have people's ideas about their own identities changed, since these are often tied to the two views above? Table 10.2 shows that there is almost no difference between Taiwanese in Taiwan and Taiwanese in China. When it comes to "exclusive Taiwan identity," the proportion of Taiwanese in Taiwan is 62.7% and the proportion of Taiwanese in China is 60.2%. In other words, the Taiwanese who live in China are very different from the Taiwanese who stay in Taiwan when it comes to their political views and where they stand on the issue of unification vs. freedom. This is partly due to self-selection and partly due to environmental factors. But there isn't a big difference between the two groups in terms of personality. What does this strange fact mean? Why are Taiwanese people willing to live in China and fit in, but not willing to change how they feel about who they are?

Table 10.1 Aspects of Taiwanese identity

Settling and staying			**Close friends**			**Someone to marry**			**Personal identity**		
	Counts (#)	Ratios (%)		Counts (#)	Ratios (%)		Counts (#)	Ratios (%)		Counts (#)	Ratios (%)
Very unwilling	31	5.7	Largely as Taiwanese	247	45.6	Taiwanese only	27	5.2	Inclusive Taiwan ID	200	38
Unwilling	136	25.1	More as Taiwanese	152	28	Preferably Taiwanese	187	36	Exclusive Taiwan ID	327	62
No opinion	91	16.8	Roughly equal	101	18.6	Both are acceptable	300	57.7			
Willing	203	37.5	More as Chinese	31	5.7	Preferably Chinese	6	1.2			
Very willing	80	14.8	Largely as Chinese	11	2						
Total	541	100	Total	542	100	Total	520	100	Total	527	100

Source: Joint Research Project on the Lives and Attitudes of the Taiwanese in Mainland China (National Chengchi University and Hong Kong University, 2009-12).

Table 10.2 Political attitudes of Taiwanese in Taiwan compared to Taiwanese on the mainland (%)

Party identification			**Unification-independence position**			**Personal identity**		
	Taiwanese in Taiwan	Taiwanese in China		Taiwanese in Taiwan	Taiwanese in China		Taiwanese in Taiwan	Taiwanese in China
Pan-Blue	26.4	45.1	Pro-independence	25.8	5.5	Taiwanese	62.7	60.2

Neutral	45	39.2	Pro-status quo	64.3	73.1	Chinese	3.6	6
Pan-Green	28.6	15.7	Pro-unification	9.9	21.4	Both	33.7	30.8
Total	100	100	Total	100	100	Total	100	100

Source: Information about Taiwanese in Taiwan draws from Taiwan's Election and Democratization Study (TEDS; 2012). Information about Taiwanese on the mainland draws from the Joint Research Project on the Lives and Attitudes of the Taiwanese in Mainland China (National Chengchi University and Hong Kong University 2009-12).

Movement, Integration, and Identity: Exploring the Persistence of Taiwanese Identity

What's wrong with the earlier ideas that said Taiwanese culture would slowly fade away? How do Taiwanese people keep their unique Taiwanese character when they move to a new place? The key is a tug-of-war between "environmental pressures" and "personal will." In the traditional model of immigration, migration is forced and one-way, and it is hard for migrants to keep links with the country or hometown from which they came. So, "environmental pressures" are very strong, and most migrants can't fight back, especially those who don't have the support of their own ethnic groups. In the end, they have to slowly give up their old identities and take on the new ones. This is similar to how the "melting pot" model of social acceptance sees people changing over time.

This could have happened to people who moved to New York in the early 1900s or to people who moved there in earlier waves of immigration. But even in the past, it hasn't always been true, and in the global age, it's even less true. Borders can often be crossed and recrossed, and thanks to improvements in transportation and communication, it's easy for travelers to stay in touch with their home country. We think that this makes it easier for them to fight outside pressures and stay true to who they want to be.

Changes in global production networks have put Taiwanese people in mainland China in a worse economic and social situation. Their decision to go there or stay there is partly up to them. Taiwanese can come and go as they please. Also, changes in transportation and communication technology have made it easier and more convenient to journey and talk to people across borders. So, the urge to integrate isn't as strong and hard to resist. Also, it's not hard for Taiwanese people to keep up social and emotional ties with their home places. Most Taiwanese we talked to went back and forth across the Taiwan Strait four to six times a year, but not for work. One business owner from Dongguan, Taiwan, said, "Many of us still do business in Taiwan. At least we have friends, family, and relatives in Taiwan. We have to go see them from time to time, of course." And another Taiwanese person who lives in Shanghai says, "Most Taiwanese here have satellite TV so they can watch Taiwanese shows, especially Taiwanese news. Some people, of course, do not agree. But they don't know this because they don't watch TV. I've never heard that Taiwanese people spend all day watching Chinese shows."

Also, in order to support economic and cultural exchanges around the world, most nation-states make it easy and quick to move people from one country to another. Given the unique political position between China and Taiwan, this is also true for travel across the Taiwan Strait. Both governments accept some alternatives to passports and allow some "flexible citizenship" when it comes to permanent residence, owning land, and getting help from government programs. Tomas Hammar has called this arrangement "denizenship." It is a status of permanent residency without citizenship that lets people work and live in a country forever without having political rights. So, as one Taiwanese business owner from Kunshan says, "I've never heard of a Taiwanese giving up their health insurance, let alone their identity card." You would never give up those things, no matter how long you stay in China."

In other words, the Taiwanese can easily resist pressures to become more like the people on the mainland because it is easy for them to move, talk to people every day, and live there. But movement doesn't just "make it possible" for them to keep their Taiwanese identity; it also "makes it impossible" for them not to. Many of these Taiwanese don't know if they will live in China, Taiwan, or maybe even somewhere else. China is just a place to stay in this way. One Taiwanese person uses jet lag as a metaphor for the way people think: "If you know you're leaving in a week, you probably don't have much reason to change your body clock."" In a way, the mobile lifestyle that has grown up in an age of globalization has made it much harder and less appealing to become more local or even to change who you are.

From this point of view, the Taiwanese reluctance to change their character has a lot to do with how globalization has changed the world. So, this trend isn't just about Taiwanese people living in mainland China. It works for most skilled workers and business owners who go all over the world. The Taiwanese are different from other groups because they went to a place where their culture came from. In the end, the fact that Taiwanese people don't want to become part of Chinese culture shows how much globalization has changed the country and its people.

The Unyielding Taiwanese Sense of Self

Taiwanese can hold on to their old identities, but they don't have to. Most Taiwanese will end up living on the mainland, where they don't have much trouble fitting in. So why don't they change their Taiwanese identity to make it more open and welcoming?

Identity is a proof of how different you are from other people (the difference between "us" and "them"). Most of the time, the feeling of being different comes from meeting people from other groups. If the experiences are bad, and people form a bad (hostile or derogatory) picture of the other person as a result, the group boundary will get stronger, and it will be harder to break the boundary or relax it. This is likely true of Taiwanese people in mainland China. It is very common for Taiwanese people who have a good view of China (da zhongguo zhuyi) while they live in Taiwan to change their minds when they visit or move to China. But if that's the case, another theory, called the "contact hypothesis," says that constant and regular contact may still cause them to change their minds about who they are and how they fit into Chinese society. And if this is true, is it possible that Taiwanese living on the mainland are in the middle of a process that will lead to a new Chinese identity taking the place of the old Taiwan identity? In other words, is it possible that the process of assimilation isn't done yet and that we jumped to a conclusion too soon?

Based on what we saw in the field, we don't think this theory is true. Intergroup contact does have an effect on refugees and can change a person's identity in the long run, but it also has its limits. Migrants don't have to talk to everyone; they only talk to the people they want to talk to. So, a person's personality, which is shaped by their past, also affects who they talk to and keeps some people out. Once people have a bias or a stereotype, they avoid certain people. This means they never have experiences that could help them change their bias or stereotype, and in the end, their identity. One member of our study team says, "Once these Taiwanese people believe the stereotype, they don't talk to local Chinese people very much." And those brief encounters can't change the way people think. Most of the time, their'selected' contacts support and reaffirm the stereotypes. So, the stereotypes keep going and going because they are true." This is especially true for migrants who are in a higher or better place than others: they can choose to meet with whoever they want. And Taiwanese people on the mainland usually hold these better jobs. So, unless something really strange happens, it's likely that most Taiwanese won't change who they are, no matter how long they stay. Settling down, even for good, has little effect on personality change because of this.

What kinds of events, then, play a big part in how Taiwanese who live on the mainland see the Chinese and Chinese society? According to our field study, the most important experiences are those that show the differences between Taiwanese and Chinese cultures. These differences are rooted in the economic and political differences between the two countries. Such events made it clearer to responders that there was a difference between the Chinese and the Taiwanese. In private life, these differences have to do with how Chinese people show their "class" or "civilization" (shenghuo shuiz-hun). If you ask a Taiwanese person what they think of local Chinese people, they will usually say that they spit, throw trash away, talk loudly, and never follow traffic rules. All of these things lead to the belief that Chinese people "have no class" (mei shuizhun) and make most Taiwanese on the mainland "feel ashamed if they are mistakenly identified as Chinese." One young guy who was going to China for a few months said, "I didn't know about this until I got there. When I get here, I feel very strongly, "Why should I be Chinese?" In the public space, these differences affect how civilized the Chinese government is seen to be. Respondents say that it is "so backward, so uncivilized, falling behind the government of Taiwan by almost a century." In a nutshell, Taiwanese residents' interactions with local Chinese and the local government form a "ladder of class between ethnic groups," and most Taiwanese feel that "we" are better and "they" are worse. So, even though they have already moved to China and haven't had much trouble getting along with Chinese people, these Taiwanese don't want to "become Chinese." And when they hang out with Taiwanese people, they often make fun of Chinese people in their own country.

There are differences. For example, Taiwanese who move to big cities like Shanghai or Beijing tend not to make fun of local Chinese. On the other hand, Taiwanese who live in isolated rural factory towns where most local Chinese are peasants or migrant workers tend to think poorly of local Chinese and have a "exclusive Taiwanese identity." In general, younger Taiwanese are more aware of the oppression and corruption of local Chinese governments. This makes them more likely to have a "exclusive Taiwanese identity." People who have run a business in Taiwan, where the government is very strict, are much less likely to say bad things about the Chinese government. From these notes, we can confirm what we learned on the ground: The "class" or "civilization" that Taiwanese think the Chinese people and government have is a big part of why they have different bad ideas about "China" and why they want to be different from the Chinese. We used the data to test the hypotheses we came up with from our field study. In Table 10.3, the findings are summed up.

Table 10.3 Explaining the Establishment, Integration, and Identification of Taiwanese in Mainland China

	Settling and staying		**Close friends**		**Someone to marry**		**Personal identity**		
	Coeff.	S.D.	Coeff.	S.D.	Coeff.	S.D.	Coeff.	S.D.	Exp(B)
Education ("above college" as base group)									
Below college	-0.166	0.115	-0.19	0.097	-0.034	0.058	0.081	0.22	1.084
Gender (female as base group)									
Male	0.054	0.129	0.288**	0.109	0.226**	0.066	-0.879**	0.264	0.415
Ethnic origin (Hakka as base group)									
Mainlanders	0.274	0.204	-0.063	0.17	0.135	0.103	-0.704	0.381	0.494
Minnan	0.057	0.173	-0.113	0.145	0.099	0.089	0.278	0.326	1.321
Generation ("born between 1970 and 1978" as base group)									
Before 1969	0.021	0.134	0.161	0.113	0.04	0.068	-0.621	0.259*	0.537
After 1979	-0.094	0.156	0.094	0.131	-0.309***	0.08	0.072	0.313	1.075
Arriving time	-0.012	0.011	-0.012	0.009	-0.003	0.006	-0.004	0.021	0.996
Living environment	0.122	0.058*	0.001	0.048	0.003	0.029	0.105	0.112	1.111
Location ("settling at Zhu River Delta" as base group)									
Yangtze Riv. Delta	0.281	0.111*	-0.089	0.093	0.024	0.057	-0.091	0.214	0.913
Sector (manufacturing sector as base group)									
Service	0.016	0.115	0.226*	0.097	0.073	0.059	-0.156	0.224	0.855
Hometown in Taiwan ('coming from Central Taiwan" as base group)									
Northern TW	-0.045	0.142	-0.052	0.119	0.02	0.072	-0.133	0.275	0.875
Southern TW	0.131	0.196	0.013	0.165	-0.011	0.1	-0.317	0.378	0.728
Political positions (neutral as base group)									
Pan-Blue	0.039	0.119	0.094	0.1	-0.064	0.06	-0.416	0.221	0.66
Pan-Green	-0.305	0.158	-0.125	0.133	-0.285***	0.081	1.123**	0.371	3.074
Constant	27.373	22.488	25.794	18.842	7.732	11.403	9.79	41.974	17858

N	541	542	520	N	527
Adj. R2	0.029	0.027	0.078	Nagelk-erke R2	0.182
S.E.E.	1.163	0.979	0.579	G2	35.155
d.f.	14	14	14	d.f.	14
P	< .05	< .05	< .001	p	< .001

Source: Joint Research Project on the Lives and Attitudes of the Taiwanese in Mainland China (National Chengchi University and Hong Kong University, 2009-12).

First, let's talk about where the people being interviewed came from. Table 10.3 shows that schooling doesn't have a big effect on identity status, which is very different from what surveys done in Taiwan found. Also, gender plays a big role in how social and sure of themselves Taiwanese who live on the mainland are. Men, who make up most businesses, make friends with mainlanders more easily and are more sure of who they are. But our study didn't find any proof that men and women are different in who they are. Whether Taiwanese are "natives" (benshengren) or came from the mainland after the Chinese Civil War (waishengren) doesn't seem to have much of an effect on who they are as a people. This means that the difference between Taiwanese who moved to Taiwan from the mainland and Taiwanese who were born there no longer serves as a social dividing line once Taiwanese move to China. Lastly, the "generation" factor doesn't seem to have a big impact on Taiwanese identity, even though we did find differences between the generations. In general, individuals who were younger were more likely to say that they were only Taiwanese.In the "contacts and experiences" group, the only thing that had a big impact on Taiwanese identity was working in the service industry, which helped them make friends with Chinese people in the area. None of the factors, such as (1) the time of arrival, (2) the neighborhood, (2) the location, and (4) the person's past life events, had a big impact. This suggests that earlier beliefs about how quickly Taiwanese people would blend into Chinese society, which were based on immigration theories that said migrants would quickly blend in if they stayed in the host country longer, lived in places where they were more likely to meet people from other groups, and had more positive experiences with people from other groups, are not supported by facts.

Last but not least, the person's political stance had a big impact and led to a more open and inclusive view of Taiwanese identity. This may have something to do with how the person feels about the Chinese government, which was already stated.

Migration and Identity in the Global Era: Readiness, Opposition, and a Diverse Tapestry of National Identity

The goal of the study is to figure out why Taiwanese people who have moved to the mainland and could easily fit in keep insisting on being Taiwanese. We think that this kind of study can add to and shed light on the idea of migration. First, we have to decide if Taiwanese people who live on the mainland are immigrants or just people who live there temporarily. Many or even most of the Taiwanese in our study who moved to China and made it their home would never go back to Taiwan. Based on this, they are not expats. Even though they went to China without planning to stay, they did end up settling there, and they have had few problems getting along with Chinese people there.

But there's another reason why many Taiwanese experts don't think of these people as migrants: they still hold on to their Taiwanese identity. And that goes against the usual ideas about how immigrants become part of the culture. But, from our point of view, this may have something to do with the fact that the usual ideas don't go far enough. In the most popular versions of these theories, most people who move to migrate are going from places that are worse to places that are better. In the age of globalization, though, migrants also travel around the world and may not plan to stay there forever. Also, a large number of them move to places where the standard of living is lower. Because of this, many migrants have little reason to integrate into the local culture, and they also have the freedom to keep moving or stay in touch with their home country. So, these people are not travelers in the usual sense. Some academics call these groups "transnational communities."

Our study shows that the Taiwanese in mainland China do not fit the traditional definition of "immigrants." Instead, they are an example of "immigration in the global era." Because Taiwanese share many cultural traits with mainland Chinese and can blend in with them, but don't want to change who they are, they are the best example of how globalization has changed the way people move. So, they can help us understand ideas like "borderlessness," "transnationalism," and "national identity that looks like a mosaic." They can also help us learn more about how cultural differences and the ability to move change and keep identities the same in a globalized world.

The different cultures on both sides of the Taiwan Strait also have a big effect on the question of identity for Taiwanese living in mainland China. Over the past 60 years of being apart, these have slowly grown, to the point where people on either side of the Strait don't share many events, thoughts, or feelings. It will take time to close this gap between cultures. Before China and Taiwan do that, there will never be a bottom-up unity of China. These results help explain why the status quo across the Taiwan Strait is more important to Taiwanese than either unification or independence. From this point of view, and given that most Taiwanese people have similar views, it doesn't matter that much whether President Ma of the KMT or President Tsai of the DPP is in charge. Their China policies would be pretty similar.

Chapter 11
Pivot, Hedge, or Ally
Approaches of Minor Powers Navigating Hegemonic Powers

Taiwan is in a good place because it is between the U.S. and the People's Republic of China (PRC). You can't understand relations across the Taiwan Strait without looking at this global strategic backdrop. Even if you don't agree with the pessimistic prediction of the power transition theory, which says that the closing gap between the United States and China will lead to a titanic clash between the world's hegemon and its challenger, you can't deny that the two strongest countries in the world today are in a fierce strategic competition. China wants to get back to the center of the world, where it used to be. The United States, which is the hegemon right now, is naturally against this. This is not to say that Washington and Beijing don't work together on things like fighting foreign terrorism and dealing with climate change. But as the two giants' powers get closer and closer together, their relationship is getting tense. China wants to have an equal say in foreign affairs, but the U.S. is hesitant to give that status to its rival. One clear example is that China was not given a vote weight in the International Monetary Fund (IMF) that matched its economic power. Another is that China and Japan were at odds over the Asian Infrastructure Investment Bank (AIIB). East Asia is where China and the United States have the most trouble with each other politically. Over Ukraine, the West and Russia are also in a big military fight with each other. Like their peers in East Asia, the smaller powers in eastern Europe are caught in the middle of a competition between two big powers.

Given how tense things are between Beijing and Washington and between Moscow and the West, it is interesting to look at how the smaller powers on both geostrategic fault lines act when they are stuck between the two giants to see if there is a pattern. Before we can do this, we need to look at what's already been written about international relations (IR). But there isn't much in the way of theory here. Traditional theories of international relations (IR) focus on how bigger powers act or treat all players as if they have the same abilities. Small states' foreign actions are, to put it mildly, not studied enough. Theorists rarely pay attention to relationships between a big power and a small power that aren't balanced, let alone the way a small power acts when it's stuck between two big powers that are in competition with each other. In the pages that follow, I will first make a framework for analyzing this situation and then use it to look at the East Asian and eastern European theaters. The main goal of the analysis is to figure out what strategic roles a smaller country can play between two big powers that are at odds with each other. This will be done through a critical case analysis of Taiwan and Ukraine, which will help figure out why a smaller power chooses a certain role and how that role may change over time. Even though East Asia is the main focus, a comparison with eastern Europe is made to add more detail to the analysis. We hope that by making this analytical framework, we will be able to learn more about cross-Strait interactions from a theoretical and comparative point of view.

Theoretical Framework

The balance-of-power (BOP) model is a good place to start. When a country faces a rising power, BOP theory suggests that it will use either an internal strategy (like building up its military) or an external strategy (like making an alliance) to keep the balance. Stephen Walt's "balance of threat" theory changes the traditional BOP theory. In this theory, the balancing behavior is based on how dangerous something is seen to be rather than how strong it is. For weaker states, "bandwagoning" is added to the toolbox. This means that the weaker state should do things that match or don't go against the core values of the growing power. But since both balancing and jumping on the bandwagon come with high costs, either in the form of a heavy budget load, the need to keep up alliances, or the loss of strategic independence, there is a third choice: hedging. Hedging is a two-part plan that a country uses to both work with and protect itself from the target country. The "hedger" doesn't just use a balancing strategy or a connection strategy, but a mix of both. The goal of the engagement is to strengthen a friendly relationship with the target country, bring about economic benefits, and hopefully change the target country's values and institutions so that it stops being a danger. The goal of balance is to make sure everyone is safe, either by building up the military or making a deal with another big power. Most of the time, balancing happens in the security realm and engagement happens in the economic world.

Unfortunately, none of the above theories are good enough to explain what happens when a weaker country is stuck between two strong countries. First of all, small countries and how they act internationally haven't been given enough attention, since most IR theories are about how big countries engage. Second, the writing on small states in world politics tends to focus on their general strategies for surviving in a realist world, not on their asymmetrical relationships with other countries. Third, most studies that look at power imbalances focus on a pair of countries, not a weaker country stuck between two strong countries. In other words, they look at the relationship between two players, not three. When a smaller country is in the middle of a competition between great powers, it can't look to standard IR theories that focus on bilateral relationships for help. We need a three-way theory.

The fact that the policies of the smaller power toward the two big powers are tied together shows that mutual IR theories aren't good enough. Assuming that G1 and G2 are the two big powers and L is the small power, we find that L's policy toward G1 is not separate from its policy toward G2. If L thinks G1 is stronger or more of a threat than G2, it may do something to keep G1 in check. Since L is much weaker than G1, it can't just build up its forces to keep the balance. Instead, it needs to find an outside ally. G2 is a natural choice to go up against G1. But since L is much weaker than G2, the partnership between L and G2 means that L is just riding on G2's coattails. So, L's joining forces with G2 and balancing against G1 happen at the same time. So, L is both managing and jumping on the bandwagon at the same time, with all the costs that come with both. If L thinks that G2 is the biggest danger, then the opposite will happen: L will fight G2 by joining forces with G1. In Figure 11.1, the rightmost and leftmost places of L show this "coupling of strategies": "Balance against G1 and Bandwagon with G2" and "Balance against G2 and Bandwagon with G1," respectively.

L can also try betting as a way to win. Again, if we believe that G1 is stronger or more dangerous, L may try to protect against it. In the part of the plan called "engagement," it says to build economic ties between L and G1. The balancing part involves building up the force or making an alliance with another country. As L is much smaller than G1, internal balance is not enough, so an alliance with G2 is necessary. Figure 11.1: This is the second one from the right. If G2 is the main target, L will take the second place from the left. Now, L doesn't have to decide between balancing and leaning toward G1; it can just jump on the trend. But since G1 and G2 are in a fierce battle with each other, joining G1 is the same as going against G2. This makes L go to the far left in Figure 11.1. If G2 is the main threat and L chooses to join, it will take the right position and balance against G1. In short, no matter what strategy L takes toward G1 (balancing, hedging, or bandwagoning), there is a related strategy for L toward G2. So, the relationships between G1, G2, and L are all tied together. This shows that a trilateral analysis framework needs to be made right away.

Figure 11.1. Choices of a lesser power placed between two great powers (Gi and G2).

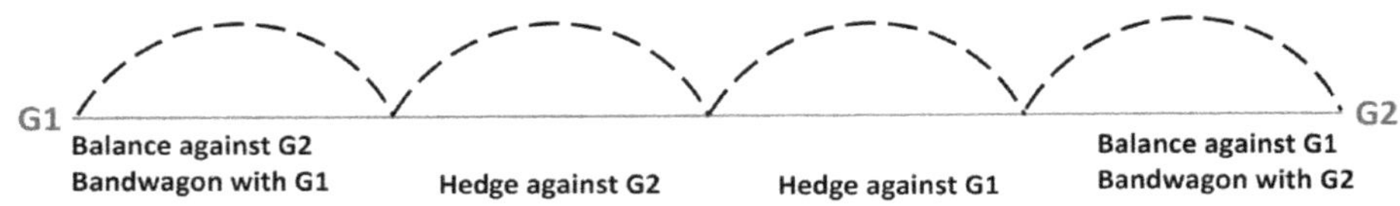

The goal of the strategic triangle theory is to look at relationships between three groups. There are four good types of strategic triangles: menage a trois (three friends), marriage (two enemies and one friend), love triangle (two friends and one enemy), and unit veto (three enemies). All three people who play menage a trois are "friends." In a marriage, two "partners" work together to help a "outcast." In a love triangle, there are two "wings" and one "pivot." In a unit veto, all of the players are "foes" of each other. With the four ideal types of strategic triangles (menage a trois, marriage, romantic triangle, and unit veto) and six roles (friend, partner, outcast, wing, pivot, and enemy), we can start to analyze any triangular situation by using the strategic triangle types and roles to describe objectively the structure of the triangular game (see Figure 11.2).

In a strategic triangle, a player thinks that being friends with the other players is always better than being enemies with them. But the player thinks that the other two players' shared dislike is better than their friendship. So, the best role is to be a "pivot," or a player who gets along well with two other players even though they are at odds with each other. Figure 11.1 doesn't show what the shift does, which is interesting.

We can now combine the points of view from figures 7 and 8, bringing together the ideas of tactics and triangular roles. Figure 11.3 shows how we again put L's decisions on a continuum. L can move toward Gi by jumping on its train and balancing against G2, which is the far left end of the continuum. If this happened, L would be Gi's "partner" in a marriage triangle. Or, L can move toward G2 by jumping on its train and balancing against Gi, which is on the far right of the continuum. This makes L a partner of G2. L can also change its position by moving a little closer to its threat while still keeping its main link with its ally. Then, L would "hedge against Gi" or "hedge against G2." In either case, L becomes a "hedging partner." If we move L to the middle of the line, but not so far that it tips over to the other side, L becomes the "pivot." A pivot doesn't really lean toward either of the two big forces, but it moves back and forth between them. So, we can say that a smaller power can play three parts between two big powers that are at odds with each other: partner, hedging partner, and pivot. Figure shows the three different roles.

In strategic triangular analysis, the best position is the center, because it lets L keep good relationships with the other two players and keeps them from working together against it. The center can be moved in different ways to get both "wings" to give in. But it's not easy for a smaller power to act as a link between two strategic giants. Tilting by pivoting naturally makes the wings worried, which can lead to reactions that aren't always good. So, if L is on the fence between Gi and G2, one or both of the giants may try to force L to take their side instead of trying to win it over. A skilled L might be able to get good concessions, but it always runs the risk of making the giants angry and putting itself in a dangerous situation.9 Theoretically, the role of partner is worse than the role of pivot, especially for the younger partner, who could be tricked by the senior partner. So, it makes sense for a smaller power stuck between two giants to choose to be a "hedging partner." This gives the smaller power some security through an alliance with one of the giants, but also gives it some room to move so that the other giant can court it and its ally can't take the hedging partner for granted.

Figure 11.2. Types of strategic triangles.

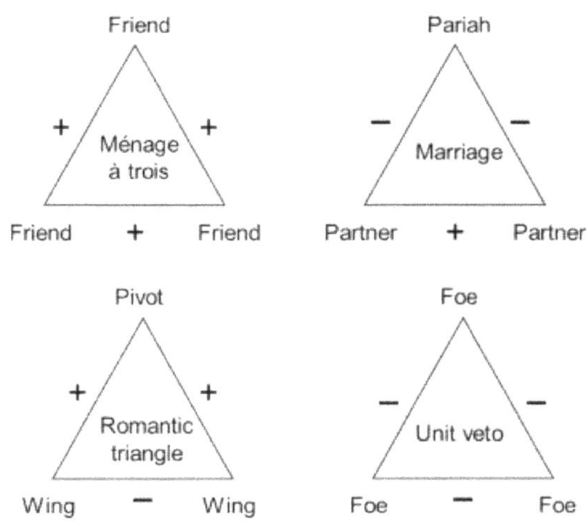

Figure 11.3. Choices and roles of a lesser power placed between two great powers (Gi and G2).

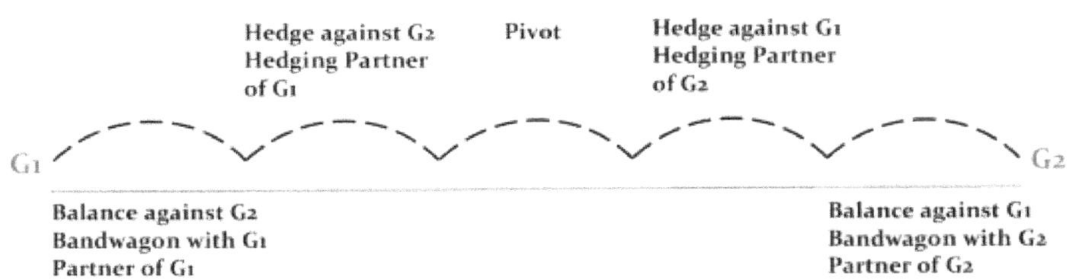

In the next section, I'll use the framework to look at how China's rise affects its relationships with its East Asian neighbors, with the strategic battle between Beijing and Washington as a backdrop. Then I'll do the same thing for the European show. I will also put the different ways that East European countries deal with Russia on a spectrum and compare them to how Asian countries deal with Russia. The strategic battle between the US-led West and Russia is in the background. Then, using the above framework, I'll look at cross-Strait relations and the situation in Ukraine as two important cases to compare.

Revival of Contradictory Alliances and Stances along the Fault Line

During the Cold War, two partnership systems with different levels of power faced off in East Asia. The continental system, which was made up of the Soviet Union, the People's Republic of China, North Korea, and North Vietnam (the communist league), and the hub-and-spoke marine system, which was led by the United States. The shift in power in the continental system broke up the Sino-Soviet pact, as the PRC rose to question Moscow's dominance, while the stability of the US-led alliance in the maritime system was a result of hegemony. The split in the continental system gave Washington chances to get along with Beijing, and it also pushed Washington's friends to do the same. The strain from competitive rapprochement was taken care of by the way the maritime system is set up. With the exception of Taiwan, the Republic of China (ROC), this led to joint hedging (balancing with engagement) against the PRC. Taiwan stood out because it and mainland China were the only ones who both claimed to be the boss of the other. The basic goals of the two sides of the Taiwan Strait didn't match up, so cross-Strait relations didn't move in the same way as the rest of the region, which was collective hedging against the PRC. Taiwan didn't join the chant, but that didn't mean it wasn't affected by systemic forces. Instead, it was because of things in Taiwan that worked against systemic forces. In the long run, though, those things weren't able to win.

In the time after the Cold War, when the US was in charge, the Beijing-Moscow nexus was brought back, but this time as an equal relationship. Even though China and Russia have changed a lot, the West doesn't think they have fully adopted Western ideals and institutions, so they are suspicious of them. The two continental powers are seen as foreign and dangerous by the maritime allies, so they need to be kept an eye on. For Beijing and Moscow, the constant eastward expansion of NATO and the EU is a danger to Russia, while the strengthening of security ties between Washington and its allies in East Asia puts a lot of pressure on the PRC. Beijing and Moscow know that the

West doesn't want anything less than a total change of heart, in the form of a peaceful regime change. With China's astronomical rise and Russia's recovery from its post-Soviet depression, the two continental powers have stuck together to form a semialliance, bringing back a strategic tie that existed in the 1950s. Again, the continental and maritime systems are at odds with each other, just like they were during the Cold War. The only change is that the U.S.'s main target is now the PRC instead of the Soviet Union.

Cross-system hedging is unavoidable because it makes smart players more money. As China grows quickly, US allies like Japan, South Korea, and Australia feel both the need to balance against it and the need to work with it in the maritime system. This causes stress in their own politics and in their relationship with the US. The US domination, on the other hand, keeps the maritime system strong. Taiwan's late decision to join the chorus is especially interesting because the same systemic forces that got rid of its previous allies in the maritime system also got rid of Taiwan. Due to the problem of shared sovereignty, Taiwan was the last country to use the hedging strategy and make peace with Beijing. This didn't happen until 2008, when the Kuomintang (KMT) took power again and the political situation in Taiwan was ready.

From the Cold War to the time after the Cold War, the mainland and maritime alliances have been at odds with each other on and off. It has been going up since the turn of the century. In the first decade of the 21st century, there was less tension between the maritime and continental alliances than in the 1990s. This was because the threat of international terrorism grew and became a top worry for both alliances. Jiang Zemin and Vladimir Putin's promise to help the U.S. in its war on terror after September 11 was not just a way to improve ties with Washington and ease pressure from the West. It was also a sign that the two countries had similar goals. But the constant expansion of NATO and the EU into former Soviet bloc countries and even post-Soviet republics, the color revolutions, the Russo-Georgian War (2008), the fact that it was easy to get political support by stirring up nationalism, and Russia's growing confidence as a result of steady economic growth led Putin to be more assertive toward the West. For China, territorial disputes with East Asian neighbors that are allies of the United States, frustration with the way major international organizations make decisions that don't take into account China's astronomical rise, and a rapid shift in the balance of power in China's favor since the start of the global financial crisis in 2008 all contribute to Beijing's more assertive foreign policy. The responses of the West, lead by the U.S., like shifting diplomatic focus "back to Asia" and punishing Russia for being aggressive, pushed the continental powers closer together and made the two alliances stronger. When the West put pressure on one continental power, the other would never join in, but would instead show "understanding" for what its continental ally was doing. For example, Russia didn't criticize China on Tibet or human rights when Beijing hosted the 2008 Olympics. China did the same when Russia hosted the 2014 Winter Olympics in Sochi, which the West heavily criticized. China also helped Russia during and after the Russo-Georgian War by not joining the West in criticizing Russia and by supporting "the active role of Russia in promoting peace and cooperation in the region" along with other Shanghai Cooperation Organization members in the August 2008 Dushanbe Declaration. On Syria, neither country would support sanctions against the Assad government, and Sergey Lavrov, the Russian foreign minister, worked out a deal to stop a Western invasion of the country that was about to happen. In answer to Tehran's nuclear program, both countries pushed for talks with Iran and opposed sanctions. Russia and China both didn't like how the West used armed force against Qaddafi's forces, which led to the dictator's death. This move was justified by a liberal reading of Security Council Resolution 1973, which only said that civilians needed to be protected. Putin thanked China very much for "taking into account the full historical and political context" when it came to Russia's taking over of Crimea. Under pressure from the West, Russia and China put aside their disagreements, solved border problems, made deals on cutting-edge weapons, and worked together more on energy issues. The US-led West put pressure on the two countries, so they came together to make a core of Eurasian land.

So, there were now two global fault lines. They were made by the pressure that builds up when "political plates" hit each other. East Asia and eastern Europe are both cut by the two fault lines. The United States and Europe vs. Russia in eastern Europe, and the United States vs. China in East Asia, are two big forces that compete with each other. The smaller forces don't have many options. They can choose from five options, from top to bottom: partner of the continental alliance (bandwagon with continental, balance against maritime), hedging partner of the continental alliance (bandwagon with continental, hedge against maritime), pivot (noncommittal and leaning in between), hedging partner of the maritime alliance (bandwagon with maritime, hedge against continental), and partner of the maritime alliance (bandwagon with maritime, balance against continental). A partner is fully on the side of one of the big powers and stays away from the other. A partner who is "hedging" is loyal to one camp but also works well with the other camp. A pivot stays the same distance from both sides and often tilts between them to get the best of both.

In Figure 11.4, we show both the East Asian fault lines and the Eastern European fault lines, as well as the options for the smaller states along each line. A smaller power in East Asia can choose between being a partner of the PRC, a hedge partner of the PRC, a pivot, a hedging partner of the US, or a partner of the US. A smaller power in eastern Europe can choose to be a partner of Russia, a hedge partner of Russia, a pivot, a hedging partner of the US and Europe, or a partner of the US and Europe.

Figure 11.4. Strategic fault lines in eastern Europe and East Asia and the available choices of lesser powers.

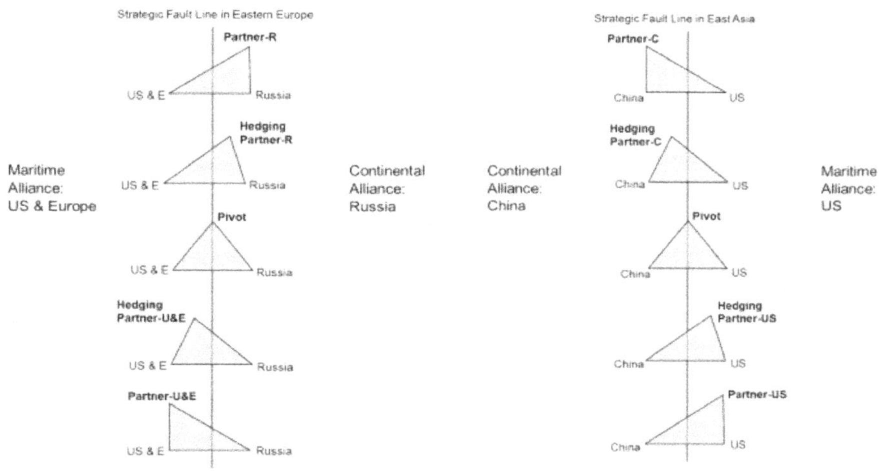

We can also find the two fault lines by finding the US Air Force sites in Eurasia that are on the front lines. The bases are in Asia and Europe so that the PRC and Russia, or the Eurasian continental heart, can't get too far away. In East Asia, the US has offices in Japan, South Korea, the Philippines, Singapore, Thailand, and Malaysia. They live in Germany, Poland, Hungary, Romania, Bulgaria, Turkey, and the Arab Peninsula in eastern Europe. Countries near the American military base have to decide between their strategic relationship with the United States and the maritime alliance and their relationship with the continental core. This is especially important when relations between the maritime alliance and the continental core are tense.

When there isn't much conflict between the Eurasian core and the US-led maritime alliance, like in the early 2000s when international terrorism was the common enemy and the main concern for both, the frontline countries are in a menage a trois triangle with the two camps and don't have to choose a side. So, the two fault lines seem less clear and important. When tensions rise, as they have since the late 2000s, though, countries on the front lines have to choose sides because of the pressure from the two big powers. Different things cause each border country to take either a pro-maritime, pro-continental, or neutral stance. On the East Asian fault line, Myanmar has mostly been a partner of the PRC, but its recent reforms and opening to the West make it more like a balancing partner. Cambodia is mostly in favor of Beijing. But Phnom Penh asks the foreign community (i.e., the West) for aid and subsidies to help the country get over what happened when Pol Pot was in power. It is a way for Beijing to protect itself. South Korea has slowly become a key player in the strategy game in East Asia. Even though it still has military ties with the U.S., its political ties with China have become much stronger. China's dislike of North Korea makes Pyongyang less of a problem for ties between the PRC and South Korea. Beijing and Seoul both remember how Japan treated them badly before and during World War II. Also, South Korea is a major power that Beijing has to take into account in its battle with the United States. Seoul has slowly come to understand that it is in a pivotal situation and how that can help it. Since 2010, relations between Japan and China have gotten a lot worse, mostly because of a territorial conflict over the Diaoyu Islands. But the very close business ties help both sides and keep the relationship from getting worse. Japan is still one of the US's hedging partners, but the balancing part of its plan has become much more important. The Philippines and China also had a disagreement about the islands in the South China Sea. That gave Manila enough reason to be glad to have American troops back in the country. The United States works with the Philippines.

On the East European fault line, the countries on the front lines each play a different part in the strategic triangles they are in. Belarus is a strong partner of Russia, in part because the West doesn't like the way Belarus is run. Bulgaria has always been close to Moscow and valued the special bond they have. Unlike some of its neighbors, Sophia's most important relationship is with Moscow, and its EU/NATO position is its safety net. This means that Russia can use Bulgaria as a hedge. Before the Maidan Revolution, Ukraine shifted between the EU and the Russia-led Eurasian Economic Union to get a better deal to join. This is the most well-known case of shifting on the East European front. After 2014, of course, the country was almost split in half because of what Kyiv did. Romania is a strong member of NATO and the EU, and it also wants to keep good ties with Russia. Bucharest has been a "hedging partner" for the United States and the European Union. The Baltic states are the West's most reliable friends. Estonia, for instance, is worried about a possible Russian invasion, especially after Moscow took over Crimea, so it sticks close to NATO and the EU. Tallinn is a partner of the West in every way.

In the next section, we'll talk about two important cases: Taiwan and Ukraine. They were chosen because they are countries on the front lines that are under a lot of pressure because of where they are in East Asia and eastern Europe. Over time, they made different strategy choices between the competing big powers (the US and the PRC, the US/EU and Russia), and the results were different. Ethnic factors make the situation more complicated and make it harder for the smaller power to decide what to do. When ethnic factors are involved, China and Russia are more ready to pay costs to protect their core interests than when ethnic factors are not involved. Lastly, both cases had dramatic events happen on the ground at the same time in the spring of 2014: the Sunflower Movement in Taiwan and a separatist civil war in Ukraine. These events happened in the same international setting, so they are very similar.

Taiwan's Move from Being a Half-Partner of the US

Taiwan's move from being a half-partner of the US to a hedging partner is a big change in its fighting position. Taiwan had been a semipartner of the US since the end of the 1970s, when the US stopped recognizing the ROC but promised to defend Taiwan if it was attacked by the mainland. For almost three decades, Taiwan was stuck in a stalemate with the mainland and no longer an ally of the US, but it was still protected by the hegemon. After President Ma Ying-jeou took office in 2008, relations across the Taiwan Strait improved, and business ties between China and Taiwan grew stronger. As Ma worked hard to reassure Washington that Taiwan would be firmly on the US side in the strategic game and that cross-Strait rapprochement did not mean political integration or a strategic alliance with the mainland, Taiwan became a hedging partner, doing a lot of what other US allies in East Asia had been doing for decades. This change, on the other hand, was caused by the way that a number of important forces came together at the same time. It's also not as solid as it seems because Taiwan didn't change its basic position toward the US and mainland China. To figure out why Taiwan's policy toward the mainland changed in 2008 and how long it will last, it's important to look at the basic structure.

The bond between the two sides of the Strait is affected by forces that pull them apart and pull them together. For Taiwan, the first situation led to a "stay" strategy, while the second situation led to a "exit" strategy. These forces come from four structural factors: the fact that Taiwan is a divided country, the uneven distribution of power, economic integration, and Taiwanese identity. They happen in Taiwan's competitive democracy and are limited by rules set by the outside world, mostly by the US but also in part by Beijing.

Between Taiwan and mainland China, the divided-nation situation and the integration of the economies are the most important structural factors. Divided-nation status gives a constitutional framework for "one-China" and brings together what's left of Chinese nationalism and ROC loyalty to protect the status quo. The economies of the two countries are so intertwined that any real change to the status quo would cost Taiwan more than it could ever imagine, making it less likely that Taiwan would want "independence." Legal and business ties between China and Taiwan also make it possible to think about "ultimate unification" when the time is right.

A lack of balance in power and a growing sense of Taiwanese identity are two things that push for Taiwan to leave the "one-China" status quo on its own. The growing power gap between Taiwan and the mainland is bad news for Taiwan, which is the weaker side. Taiwan's foreign space is being cut down by the much stronger opponent, so Taiwan has a reason to leave the game. Taiwanese identity has strong historical roots, but its rise has more to do with the PRC's monopoly on Chinese identity in international society and China's increasing pressure on Taiwan. So, the difference in power and the rise of Taiwanese culture go hand in hand. Taiwan moves away from mainland China, which is seen as an aggressive foreign country, when it says it is only Taiwanese. Without a shared national identity, it is harder to bring people together.

In Taiwan's competitive democracy, the two sets of forces are shown by the two main political groups, "Blue" (which wants more integration with the mainland) and "Green" (which wants more independence). Since the two camps want different things for the mainland, when power changes hands at elections, policies change, which could hurt ties across the Strait. This is where things on a global scale come in. The US's desire to keep things the same is a strong force that keeps Taiwan's election-driven political leaders from doing too much. It also makes it harder for the country to force the island to give up its independence. With this setup, it's possible to think of cross-Strait relations as moving along a spectrum, with unification, the status quo, and independence as the key points. At any given time, Taiwan's place on the spectrum is set by the result of the last presidential election, which is usually a reflection of the underlying forces of being a divided country, having unequal power, being part of the global economy, and having a strong sense of Taiwanese identity. The United States is a hegemon that tilts the balance to keep the status quo that best serves its interests. This means that the range of possible changes in Taiwan's situation over time is set by what it wants. Under these rules, Taiwan's political leaders can fine-tune the island's policy toward the mainland and change its place on the strategic fault line in East Asia.

During the 2008 presidential election, Ma was able to end the ideological debate about the nation's identity, which was a losing battle for the KMT. Instead, he focused on Taiwan's economy, which had slowed down a lot since the DPP took power in 2000. From 2001 to 2008, Taiwan's economy grew by an average of 3.8%. In the previous decade, when the KMT was in power, it grew by an average of 6.2%. From 2001 to 2008, the average jobless rate went from 2.1% in the 1990s to 4.4%. This is more than double what it was in the 1990s. With the identity issue and the pursuit of de jure Taiwan independence "delegitimized" in public debate and economic issues taking the lead, Ma was able to win the 2008 and 2012 presidential elections by showing the people that only the KMT could handle cross-Strait relations, which were necessary for Taiwan's economy to grow and develop. Even though Taiwanese identity kept growing under Ma's watch and the differences in power across the Taiwan Strait grew quickly, Ma was able to win reelection by playing the economic card well, keeping the party's "stay" policy in place. But the status quo was shaken up a lot in 2014.

Given what we've talked about so far about cross-Strait ties, we can expect things to change if the main pillars of the status quo start to shake. After Ma changed his focus to the economy, the DPP stopped talking about independence and started questioning Ma's main point, which was that economic integration with the mainland was good for Taiwan. From 2008 to 2014, Taiwan's economy grew slowly at an average rate of 3.8%, while unemployment rose to 4.7%. Distribution has become a very important problem, especially for young people. The Oshima Index, which measures the difference between the incomes of the top and bottom 20% of families, went up from 6.03 in 2000-2007 to 6.16 in 2008-2014. Part of the bad economy was caused by the international financial crisis, and part was because the government wasn't doing its job well. Even though the Economic Cooperation Framework Agreement (ECFA) with the mainland might have helped, the economy as a whole was in bad shape. Now, Ma can't say that integrating across the Strait will help Taiwan's economy. Instead, his critics have said that close business ties with mainland China are bad.

Under these conditions, students and young protesters broke into the Legislative Yuan in March and April 2014 and stayed there for three weeks. People were angry about a bill that would have made it easier to trade services across the Taiwan Strait as part of the ECFA deal. This anger led to the event. The DPP blocked the bill for a few months in the legislature, and the KMT forced it through the committee stage. The Sunflower Movement wanted to sink the bill and stop future deals that would have made it easier for people from both sides of the Strait to live together. The movement seemed to be about righting procedural wrongs, but the real reason was that the most economically vulnerable and publicly vocal people were against China. The edge Ma had in the economy was turned on its head. Since he had done such a good job of calming down ideological discussion and turning the country's attention to the economy, his administration was not ready to fight political opponents who had sharp arguments about the economy. Ma's plan to improve ties across the Strait failed because Chinese identification and even dual Chinese-Taiwanese identification fell sharply under his watch, and the economy didn't do what he said it would. Things started to change in the political world. Both the local elections in 2014 and the presidential and house elections in 2016 were very bad for the KMT. In 2016, the DPP's choice for president, Tsai Ing-wen, won by a huge margin, and the DPP won a majority in parliament for the first time. Taiwan's relationship with the mainland changed quickly when Tsai was in charge. By not accepting the "1992 Consensus" that Taiwan and the mainland are part of the same China, but willing to disagree on which government is the rightful one, Tsai took away the foundation of cross-Strait reconciliation. Beijing started to fight back, and Taiwan moved closer to the naval alliance.

In terms of Taiwan's role as a strategic fault line in East Asia, the major question is whether Taiwan is able or willing to keep getting closer to mainland China. With this protection in place, Taiwan is a United States hedging partner. Without it, it will just act as a partner, even if it is more of a half-mate. The KMT and the DPP represent these two roles based on where they stand on the 1992 Consensus and whether or not they are ready to say they support the "one-China" principle, which Beijing uses as a litmus test to decide whether they are friends or enemies. Whether the KMT or the DPP is in power, a basic stance will be taken on the 1992 Consensus and the "one-China" principle. This will then determine whether the "rapprochement hedge" is kept in place. This makes Taiwan either a "hedging partner" or a "half-partner" of the US on the strategic fault line in East Asia.

Ukraine: A Pivotal Tragedy

In the same way that Taiwan is on a critical fault line, so are many East European countries. In both cases, a powerful neighbor (mainland China and Russia, respectively) poses a danger to smaller countries. However, there are strong economic ties between the smaller countries and the big country (through trade, investment, and energy dependence). Both want a security guarantee from the U.S., but their success rates range. In both cases, there have been times when the leaders took rebellious steps against the strong power. After these actions, people often tried to make peace with each other.

Ukraine is the most like Taiwan out of all the East European countries. Both countries have well-developed political divides based on region (North vs. South in Taiwan, North and West vs. South and East in Ukraine). These divisions come from (sub)ethnic, linguistic, and historical differences in the populations. Taiwan has been torn apart by the difference in how Chinese and Chinese-Taiwanese people see themselves and how Taiwanese people see themselves. On one side of the divide in Ukraine are Ukrainian nationalists, and on the other are ethnic

Russians and people who know Russian. Different groups in Ukraine have very different ideas about Russia and think that relations with Russia will go in very different ways. Chinese people and people with two identities in Taiwan are open to the idea of union with the mainland if the time is right. People who are only from Taiwan think that mainland Chinese are from another country and that China is a foreign country. The same can be said about East and West Ukrainians in terms of how much they like or dislike Russia. In both cases, some businesses and areas are more connected to the strong neighbor than others. This makes the economies of those areas more or less vulnerable. Language is a sensitive topic, starting with whether Taiwanese can be called a southern Fukien accent and whether Ukrainian and Russian are basically the same language. The most important thing the two countries have in common is that different political parties took turns winning elections and running the country. This led to big changes in how they dealt with their strong neighbor and the West.

In Ukraine, as in Taiwan, different groups want to treat their neighboring superpower in completely different ways. Ukraine was one of the founding members of the Commonwealth of Independent States, and after the Soviet Union broke up, it kept close institutional links with Russia. For hundreds of years, it was a part of the Russian Empire and then the Soviet Union. Ukraine and its eastern neighbor have strong cultural, ethnic, and political ties, especially in the south and east of the country. Its modern economy was set up and made official as a part of and to help the Russian Federation's economy. The Soviet Union's economic plans connected Ukraine and Russia, which had the most people, in a way that didn't happen between Russia and other parts of the Soviet Union. Ukraine is so dependent on Russia for its market and oil that any break in these economic ties would be too much to bear. On the other hand, since Ukraine became independent, Kyiv has been building a new country by promoting Ukrainian nationalism and making Russia the main "other." In this new democracy, where political competition was high, ethnic organizing had to get stronger. Russia's rise and growing confidence under Putin gave a big boost to a Ukrainian nationalist movement that sees Russia as a threat to Ukraine's identity and independence. In short, legal and cultural ties to Russia and deep economic union bring Ukraine closer to its eastern neighbor, while rising Ukrainian nationalism and growing power differences push the two Slavic countries apart.

Since Taiwan became a democracy, power has changed hands between the Blue and Green camps. One Blue president, Lee Teng-hui, changed his political views while he was in office and after he left office. The same thing happened in Ukraine: the first president, a fierce Ukrainian nationalist named Leonid Kravchuk, was replaced by the pro-Russian Leonid Kuchma in 1994; Kuchma was replaced by the pro-Western Orange Revolution leader Viktor Yushchenko in 2004; Yushchenko was defeated by Viktor Yanukovych from the East in 2010, when Yanukovych made a political comeback; and Yanukovych fled the country and was replaced by the The country's policy toward its huge neighbor to the east changed a lot every time a new leader took over.

During the height of the Orange Revolution, Yanukovych lost his job as president because he was accused of fixing the votes. After he won the election for president in 2010, Ukraine changed its policies to move toward the east. But even though he was pro-Moscow, Yanukovych started shifting between Russia and the EU in 2013 to get the best deal for Ukraine, which was on the verge of an economic crisis. As a first step toward joining the EU, he showed that he was willing to sign an association deal with them. Putin was very worried about this sudden turn, so he used both carrots (promising to buy $15 billion of Ukraine's government bonds and lowering the price of Russian gas by a third) and sticks (stopping Ukraine's exports to Russia) to get Ukraine to change its mind. Russia and the EU ended up in a bidding war for Ukraine because of this. Yanukovych finally gave up on signing the deal with the EU on November 21 and took Putin up on his offer. In a way, Yanukovych was able to turn Ukraine from a country that worked with Russia into a true pivot and use that position to his benefit.

But Yanukovych's blatant manipulation on the international stage was not liked by the Ukrainian people, especially those in the west of the country, whose dreams of joining the EU were dashed by the president's success. So, there was the Maidan Revolution, where long fights between protesters and cops turned into a sort of civil war in the center of the capital city, Kyiv. After about 100 protesters were shot and killed in February 2014, the situation quickly got out of hand. As pressure from the West grew, Maidan protesters got ready for a fight, and Yanukovych ran for his life. Moscow quickly said that this was a coup backed by the West and moved to take over Crimea, where the majority of people are ethnic Russians. Then, the separatists took over most of the cities and towns in Luhansk and Donetsk, which are the two easternmost provinces of Ukraine that border Russia and have the biggest number of ethnic Russians and Russian-speakers. From Russia's point of view, the West and pro-Western Ukrainians had changed the rules of the game. Instead of fighting with the pro-Russian East in elections, they now kicked out "Moscow's" president and took power in a fake "revolution." So, Russia didn't have to follow the rules that had been broken. So, Crimea was taken over and people's republics were set up in Luhansk and Donetsk. Crimea seems to be lost for good, and the two people's republics are becoming places of "frozen conflict," just like Transdniestria, Nagorno-Karabakh, South Ossetia, and Abkhazia. In the past, power changed hands from one person to another. Now, the country is almost split in two.

Tragically, Ukraine played a key role. Yanukovych's big swings between Russia and the West were too much for his people and for the two big powers. The effect was that the country was almost split in two, and there was a constant economic crisis. During the process, Russia and some other European countries paid a high price. This was at a time when the European economy was in a bad place. But the Russian people have shown that they are ready to stand by their leader in a showdown with the West over Russia's core interests: strategic areas in Luhansk and Donetsk, control of Sevastopol, and protection of ethnic Russians and Russian-speaking people in East Ukraine.

At the same time that the situation in Ukraine was getting worse, Taiwan was going through its Sunflower Movement. The two crises had nothing to do with each other directly, but they were both caused by the same strategic conditions: a small country's controversial policy in the middle of a battle between two big powers on a strategic fault line. A big part of the population didn't agree with the way the government treated the big neighbor, so they rebelled in different ways and to different degrees. Yanukovych's change of heart caused more trouble because it was about something important to Ukraine's future and identity: whether to join the EU or the Russian-led EEU. In contrast, the service trade reform agreement was just one part of a larger economic deal between Taiwan and the mainland. The Maidan revolutionaries and Yanukovych's government were much more violent than the Sunflower students and the Taipei cops. The People's Liberation Army also did not do anything like what the Russian force did. Still, the root cause of both problems is the same: the tension that comes from being a smaller power stuck between two bigger powers. The fact that Taiwan and Ukraine have different national identities made things even worse. From Taiwan's point of view, it's very important to not end up like Ukraine. There are many things to learn from this.

Conclusion

This part starts with a list: the strategic choices of a smaller country caught in a competition between great powers. There are three choices: partner, hedge partner, and pivot. The list is based on standard theories of international relations, the idea of power asymmetry, and the strategic triangle type. In the time after the Cold War, a later geopolitical study says that the conflict between the maritime alliance and the continental alliance has come back. Because of their fight, there are now two major fault lines, one in East Asia and one in eastern Europe. Taiwan sits on a fault line in East Asia, and its relationship with the rest of the China is an example of a small country that is stuck between two big forces and has to choose from a short list of policies. Under Ma Ying-jeou, there was a big change in policy toward getting along with the Chinese mainland. This was made possible by the president's plan to stop talking about the identity dispute and focus on the economy. After that, Taiwan's bad economic performance made Ma's biggest strength into his biggest weakness. Taiwan's place on the strategic fault line in East Asia is determined by its policy toward the mainland: hedging partner (with rapprochement) or semipartner (without rapprochement). In contrast, Ukraine's policy toward Russia and the EU is shown to show how Yanukovych changed the country's role from being a "hedging partner" of Russia to being a "pivot," which had tragic results. The moves that Yanukovych and his successor made were way too risky for the Ukrainians and the big powers to accept. The tilting of Ukraine led the country to almost split in two. This suggests that pivot is a less safe position than hedging partner or partner for a smaller country stuck between two competing giants, and that decisions on fundamental issues (like joining the core organization of either camp) could lead to a lot of unrest at home and international intervention. Once a country is forced to choose between two great powers, there is no longer any doubt about which side it supports. This makes the losing side angry. This could lead to the collapse of democracy, a domestic revolution, a military intervention, the division of territory, and a long-lasting economic disaster. For a center player, it seems like a must that they don't make such important decisions.

Putting cross-Strait ties in the category of smaller powers' interactions with two competing giants on strategic fault lines in East Asia and East Europe serves a few purposes. First, it makes IR theories better in areas they don't cover, like small countries, unequal relationships, triangular interactions, and geostrategic analysis. The above analytical approach gives us a theoretical view of cross-Strait relations, which helps us understand them better. Third, it lets us compare the structures of Taiwan and other smaller powers along the East Asian fault line as well as the border countries in eastern Europe. This helps us learn more about all of the cases we compare. This makes it possible to talk about and compare cross-Strait relations and the situation in Ukraine. In future research, the factors and mechanisms that affect these smaller powers' decisions when dealing with two giants can be fully identified and tested in multiple case studies with a comparative perspective. This will help us learn more about how smaller countries make strategic decisions when competing with great powers in general.

Chapter 12
Diverse Forms of State Capitalism across the Taiwan Strait

In both the real world and the scholarly world, interest in state capitalism has grown over the past few years. State capitalism is not a new idea, but the global financial crisis of 2008, which hit a big part of the liberal capitalist system, made it seem like a good alternative way to grow the economy. Developing economies like Brazil, China, India, and Russia, which have big government sectors, did better than their more liberal developed counterparts. These economies were heavily controlled by the government and counted on their state-owned enterprises (SOEs) to stand up to the crisis and soften its effects. But if we look more closely at these countries, we can see that the SOE sector is not the only player. In contrast to the old form of state capitalism from the 1970s, new types of state capitalist economies grew and thrived in the late 1990s and 2000s. The SOE and non-SOE sectors of these new types have worked together more strategically.

Most experts, policymakers, and journalists only pay attention to how this new type of state capitalism challenges Western capitalist systems through strategic cooperation. There hasn't been much research into how different state capitalist regimes set up their internal markets, as if they were all the same. But as the examples of China's state capitalism after the 1990s and Taiwan's state capitalism from the 1960s to the 2000s show, the ownership structures of these two systems are very different. In China's state-capitalist system, SOEs are at the top of the political pecking order, while private companies are usually small, many, and weak. On the other hand, Taiwan's state capitalist regime is made up of small and medium-sized private companies that are treated the same way by the government when it comes to industrial policy. Why is there this difference? In particular, since state capitalism is a political-economic system meant to help a country grow, it makes sense to think that the domestic ownership structures of economies with state capitalism will be similar, with a focus on the SOE sector. While this is true of China's state capitalism, it is not true of Taiwan's state capitalism. These differences in how people own their homes are strange. This chapter tries to figure out why domestic market structures are different on both sides of the Taiwan Strait and what that means for understanding how the two economies interact.

The work of Aldo Musacchio and Sergio G. Lazzarini is used in this part to explain what state capitalism is. State capitalism, according to Musacchio and Lazzarini, is when the government has a large impact on the economy, either by having a majority or minority stake in a company or by giving private companies subsidized credit and/or other special rights. Based on this description, there are three types of state capitalism: "leviathan as an entrepreneur," "leviathan as a majority investor," and "leviathan as a minority investor." The first model is the old model of state capitalism that was mostly in place in the 1970s. The second and third models are the new wave of state capitalism that is happening now. Musacchio and Lazzarini put China's state capitalism in the category of "leviathan as a majority investor" and Taiwan's state capitalism in the category of "leviathan as a minority investor." To be more specific, Taiwan's state capitalism went from "leviathan as entrepreneur" before 1989 to "leviathan as a minority investor" in the late 1980s, when democracy was a goal.

One reason makes the forms of state capitalism in China and Taiwan similar. That is, both China and Taiwan have used a Leninist form of control in their industries. During the time before reform, the Chinese Communist Party (CCP) had control over every work unit in China. During the reform period, the Chinese party-state has loosened its grip on industry through different SOE reform agendas. Industrial policy still supports the SOE sector over other types of ownership, and China is still a "commanding-heights economy," which means that the CCP's Leninist model of control still has a place in the Chinese political economic system. Leninism was also an important part of how the Kuomintang (KMT) ran Taiwan's political and economic system for almost four decades, when it was in charge. Even though Taiwan became a democracy 10 years ago, the KMT's Leninist control plan is still a big part of how decisions are made. In short, both China's state capitalism and Taiwan's state capitalism can be traced back to Leninism.

Three parts make up my main point about why China's and Taiwan's state-owned capitalist economies have different internal market structures and what that means. First, the similar institutional roots of the Leninist legacy don't always predict how state capitalism will change in China and Taiwan, which are both run by dictators. Second, the way that state capitalism changes in both authoritarian regimes depends on the means that the leaders can use to help their countries grow. When the state capitalist system was being built in Taiwan, the authoritarian KMT government had just been defeated in the civil war and could only build its economy with help from the United States. The US aid was based on the idea of market liberalism, which favored private ownership over public ownership. So, Taiwan's state capitalism did not discriminate against private holding in the first place. When China's leaders were building up their state-capitalist system in the years after the 1990s, on the other hand, China's relationships with other big powers in the world were tense. With help from a huge state-owned banking system and a variety of state firms, bureaucratic agencies, and research centres, the state capitalist system was built up in a reliable and effective way. State capitalism in China was built on the idea of public control. Third, China's preference for state ownership over private ownership has raised concerns in Taiwan about unfair competition and security problems, making it harder and less stable for businesses in the area to work together.

This part is put together like this. I start by looking at how Taiwan's state capitalism changed from the 1960s to the 2000s. Then I look in depth at how China's state capitalism has changed since 2003. I end by talking about what it means for understanding cross-Strait relations that the internal market structures in Taiwan and China are different.

State-Driven Capitalism in Taiwan

Before I look at the case of Taiwan, I need to make it clear that Taiwan had a state capitalist government from the 1960s until the early 2000s, which is almost 40 years. Before the privatization plan was started in 1989, Taiwan's state capitalism was a "leviathan as an entrepreneur," which Musacchio and Lazzarini call the most basic type of state capitalism. As democratization and its consolidation continued through the second half of the 1980s and the 1990s, the Taiwanese government changed its own role in the market and began to privatize state firms. This led to what Musacchio and Lazzarini call a "leviathan as a minority investor."

The push for democracy kept growing, and the state's involvement in society and the market ended with the first party switch from the KMT to the Democratic Progressive Party (DPP) in 2000. This was the beginning of the end of Taiwan's state-capitalist system. Because the Taiwanese government kept working on its privatization plan, state ownership in Taiwan's home market became less important. Even though the Taiwanese state capitalist system changed from "leviathan as an entrepreneur" to "leviathan as a minority investor" over the course of four decades, it is important to note that the private sector has always been important (see Table 12.1). In the next section, I talk about why the private sector was the most important part of Taiwan's state capitalism. I do this by looking at the foreign and domestic environments in which Taiwan's authoritarian KMT leaders worked and where they could get resources to build up the economy.

As soon as Chiang Kai-shek and his KMT government fled to Taiwan in 1949, the United States became Taiwan's most important friend. China's possible attack has always been the biggest threat to the survival of Taiwan's authoritarian KMT government, especially since China has never given up on its goal to free the island. But ties with the United States have made these demands less severe. During the first half of the Cold War, one of the most important goals of American grand strategy was to stop the communists from taking over Taiwan. Even though American politics at home downplayed Taiwan's strategic importance after the US and China got along better in the 1970s, the US still gave Taiwan formal security guarantees. American development aid, security guarantees, and access to the US market gave Taiwan's authoritarian government more tools to build up its economy in the 1950s and 1960s, when the Taiwanese state capitalist system started to take hold. To put it another way, during Taiwan's early stages of state capitalism, the authoritarian Taiwanese government was brought into the American security circle and wasn't forced to rely on its own security. So, putting together a team of national winners to catch up was a good idea, but it wasn't necessary.

The United States also had an effect on Taiwan's business plan for the country. As we've talked about, Taiwan's authoritarian government relied greatly on economic and military help from the United States. This gave the US power to change Taiwan's political and economic system by imposing its liberal market ideology. During most of the aid time, from 1950 to 1965, the US kept putting pressure on the SOE sector as part of the KMT regime to reduce the amount of state shares in public companies. In the meantime, the US government also pushed the KMT government to do land reform, which turned a lot of landowners into private entrepreneurs who were then helped by the KMT government to do export-led growth. In particular, because the authoritarian KMT government was not from China, it had to build up local networks to keep its power. In this way, private businesspeople, most of whom were born and raised in Taiwan, were good candidates for KMT's patron-client system. With help from the United States, the authoritarian KMT government gave business owners a lot of special rights in exchange for their political backing.

Also, the KMT leaders' view of the market changed because of how they did during the Civil War. Before the KMT government fled to Taiwan, it had to deal with high inflation in the second half of the 1940s. After the financial crisis, Taiwan's KMT government learned from it and used market processes to run the country's economy. So, even though Taiwan's authoritarian government took a Leninist approach to running its economy, it was not ideologically committed to state ownership and never used bureaucratic coordination to replace market mechanisms like communist regimes did. So, the KMT's development plans did not favor public ownership over private ownership, which is one of the most important parts of a free market economy.

Table 12.1 The Privatization Initiative in Taiwan

Firm	Time of privatization	Revenue (NT$100 million)
China Petrochemical Development Corporation	6/20/1994	170.95
BES Engineering Corporation	6/22/1994	113.69
China Steel Corporation	4/12/1995	1195.08
Taiwan Machinery Manufacturing Corporation (Steel Production Plant)	5/20/1996	48.24
Taiwan Machinery Manufacturing Corporation (Shipbuilding Plant)	1/10/1997	22.75
Taiwan Machinery Manufacturing Corporation (Alloy Steel Production Plant)	6/30/1997	3.54
Taiwan Fertilizer Co., Ltd.	9/1/1999	170.29
Taiwan Hsing Chung Paper Co., Ltd.	10/16/2001	0.05
Taiwan Machinery Manufacturing Corporation (Head Office & Manufacturing Plant)	11/19/2001	35.09
Tang Eng Iron Works Co., Ltd. (Transportation division)	8/1/2002	0.2
Tang Eng Iron Works Co., Ltd. (Steel Plan, Machinery Plant)	9/1/2002	0.198
Taiwan Agricultural and Industrial Development Corporation (Chiayi Machinery Plant)	12/31/2002	0.078
Taiwan Salt Industrial Corporation	11/14/2003	28.36

Source: State-Owned Enterprise Commission, Ministry of Economic Affairs, ROC, Jingjibu suoshu shiye minyin-ghua [Privatization of state-owned enterprises in Taiwan] (Taipei: Ministry of Economic Affairs, ROC, 1996), 179.

Compared to other newly industrialized economies in East Asia, like South Korea, the relationship between the KMT regime and private capitalists was not as strong. This was because the mainlanders who ran the KMT regime didn't trust the Taiwanese capitalists. But the distrust was made worse by two things:

the US pressure described above and the fact that local elites were split up after the February 28 incident of 1947, which was an uprising in Taiwan that the KMT-led ROC government put down violently. In this situation, Taiwan's authoritarian KMT government chose the private sector to play a key role in changing Taiwan's development pattern from one of import substitution to one of export-led economic growth.

Lastly, it's important to remember that the private sector's action would not be possible in Taiwan without a meritocratic and Weberian bureaucracy. Peter Evans has shown that Taiwan's bureaucracy had "embedded autonomy." This meant that it could make and carry out policy goals without being influenced by special interests, but it could still stay linked to those interests through social ties. The authoritarian KMT regime couldn't protect its SOEs too much at the cost of the private sector because of the way its bureaucracy worked. One good example is the high-tech business world. In the 1970s, the Taiwanese government started to work on industrial improvement. They did this by giving tax breaks and helping with money and infrastructure, among other things. Then, in 1980, it set up the Hsinchu Science Park to help high-tech companies with mostly private cash run their businesses. During the whole process, a lot of business experts like Kwoh-ting Li were very important. Taiwan's industrial policy gives private companies the same weight as government firms, which is not the case in China.

State led Capitalism in China

China is a different story when it comes to state capitalism. Since China is an economy in change, it is important to know when state capitalism became the most important part of China's political and economic system. Since the beginning of economic reform, Chinese reformers have tried many times to separate SOEs from the state. However, it wasn't until the second half of the 1990s that the "grasping the large, releasing the small" reform program made it possible for the remaining state firms to become corporations. Instead of running the corporatized SOEs itself, the Chinese government gave that job to leaders at the ministerial level who were chosen by the CCP's central organization department. At the same time, Chinese reformers made these companies even more diverse by putting them on the public market and turning them into stock companies. Along with the plan to turn SOEs into corporations, the Chinese government set up the State-Owned Assets Supervision and Administration Commission (SASAC) in 2003 to keep an eye on how the SOEs were doing. It is safe to say that China's state capitalist system was put together starting in the late 1990s and ending with the creation of the SASAC in 2003. Since 2003,

China's political economy has been a good example of state capitalism with "leviathan as a majority investor."

Like Taiwan, China's government set up the state capitalist system to help the country grow. But instead of depending on a lot of private companies, China decided to turn its failing state companies into national champions. This choice was made because Chinese leaders figured out how much help they could get from both the foreign and domestic environments. During the reform period, China got help with its development from international organizations like the World Bank. However, the Chinese government didn't trust the aid systems because they were run by major Western powers like the United States and other countries that had bad relations with China. For example, the Tiananmen Square protests in 1989 and the penalties that followed from the West made it a top priority for Chinese leaders to build a strong SOE sector. In the ten years after the incident, China's relationship with the United States, which at the time was the only superpower, was tangled up with American domestic problems like the debate over giving China most-favored-nation trade status.

Table 12.3

Year	State-owned and state-holding enterprises	Collective enterprises	Private enterprises	Others
1957	53.77	19.03	0.83	26.37
1963	89.33	10.67		
1964	89.54	10.46		
1965	90.07	9.93		
1966	90.18	9.82		
1967	88.46	11.54		
1968	88.42	11.58		
1969	88.71	11.29		
1970	87.61	12.39		
1971	85.91	14.09		
1972	84.88	15.12		
1973	84.02	15.98		
1974	82.41	17.59		
1975	81.09	18.91		
1976	78.33	21.67		

1977	77.03	22.97		
1978	77.63	22.37		
1979	78.47	21.53		
1980	75.97	23.54	0.02	0.47
1981	74.76	24.62	0.04	0.58
1982	74.44	24.82	0.06	0.68
1983	73.36	25.47	0.12	0.78
1984	69.09	29.71	0.19	1.01
1985	64.86	32.08	1.85	1.21
1986	62.27	33.51	2.76	1.46
1987	59.73	34.62	3.64	2.02
1988	56.80	36.15	4.34	2.72
1989	54.06	35.69	4.80	3.44
1990	54.60	35.62	5.39	4.38
1991	56.16	33.00	4.83	6.01
1992	51.52	35.07	5.80	7.61
1993	46.95	34.02	7.98	11.05
1994	37.34	37.72	10.09	14.85
1995	33.97	36.59	12.86	16.58
1996	36.32	39.39	15.48	16.65
1997	31.62	38.11	17.92	18.45
1998	28.24	38.41	17.11	22.91
1999	28.21	35.37	18.18	26.14
2000	47.33	13.90		64.07
2001	44.41	10.53		71.46
2002	40.78	8.68		75.73
2003	37.54	6.65		80.36
2004	34.81	3.90		84.49
2005	33.28	3.42		85.67
2006	31.24	2.90	87.40	
2007	29.54	2.51	88.51	
2008	28.34	1.77	89.03	

2009	26.74	1.75	89.93	
2010	26.61	1.49	90.35	
2011	26.81	1.31	90.79	

Source: National Bureau of Statistics of China, China Industry Economy Statistical Yearbook. (Beijing: China Statistics Press, 2012), 19.

Note: The total percentage figures for several years exceeded 100 percent, which challenges the accuracy of the data. Yet the data provided by the National Bureau of Statistics of China can still convey useful information on the general trend of changes in the SOE sector.

When China joined the World Trade Organization at the start of the 21st century, it put Chinese companies in direct competition with companies that had grown up in developed countries. All of these pressures were made worse by the fact that the international community didn't trust China's economic rise. This was shown by the fight over whether the PRC was a revisionist or status quo state. Unlike Taiwan's state capitalism, which grew when the United States offered a stable alliance, China's state capitalism was built in the middle of a security crisis, when the only reliable and effective support for national development came from SOEs that the Chinese government owned.

Since state ownership is the only source of legitimacy for the CCP government, its distrust of the growing number of private business owners also affects how leaders decide to build the state capitalist system. In the early years of China's economic reform, ideological fights against workers being exploited led Chinese leaders to limit the nonstate sector to privately owned businesses with no more than eight employees. In the meantime, uncertain property rights led to a common practice called "wearing a red hat," in which private capitalists registered their businesses as collective ones to hide what they were really doing. Deng's 1992 Southern Tour of China, which was meant to show how important his economic reforms were, gave private capitalists a new sense of confidence in running businesses. However, they didn't get legal protection until 2002, when Jiang Zemin said that the PRC stood for "three represents": advanced economic production, cultural development, and political consensus.

Even though private businesses and their property rights are now legal in China, they are still treated differently by the government. As a government that bases its authority on socialist ideas, China's party-state continues to favor state ownership over other kinds of property rights. As an example, China's $586 billion stimulus plan after the global financial crisis in 2008 is a good example. Most of the money from the investment plan went to infrastructure projects that were mostly run by state companies. Private companies, on the other hand, had trouble getting steady sources of funding like bank loans and government subsidies. Because of this, the saying "the state advances, the private sector retreats" (guo jin min tui) came true. Even now, the government still has a monopoly on a number of businesses that are important to the growth of the country but are closed to private firms. Since private capitalists are the main force behind democratization in a number of countries, it is not surprising that the CCP's leaders keep a close eye on the private sector and use the ownership discrimination tactic. Based on what has been said about China's international and domestic issues, it is clear that Beijing's leaders, who are worried about the political effects of the private sector, can only depend on SOEs to help the economy catch up.

In conclusion, both Taiwan's and China's state capitalist systems are strong and have similar industrial policies. However, state involvement in the two political-economic systems has very different effects. Under Taiwan's state capitalism, industrial policies have put an emphasis on social success indicators like social equality, while China's industrial policies have put an emphasis on how well the authoritarian political system can hold up. The two types of state capitalism have different ownership structures in their home markets because they care about different things.

Reconsidering Economic Integration Across the Taiwan Strait

As a response to the changes in the economy caused by the 2008 financial crisis, more and more study is being done on how state capitalism has grown in different parts of the world. The scholarship has done a great job of showing how states that use a system called "state capitalism" use flexible tactics to interfere with markets and still grow. Even though there are different kinds of state capitalist governments, the literature hasn't yet explained why they are different. This chapter looks at state capitalism in Taiwan and China to show that the resources available to leaders when they try to build state capitalist governments affect the main driver of economic growth and, by extension, the ownership structures in the domestic markets. Small and medium-sized private firms are more common in Taiwan's model of state capitalism because of help from the US and a commitment to a liberal market. In China's model of state capitalism, the SOE sector is more common because of tensions with major powers and the CCP's reliance on state ownership as one of its sources of legitimacy.

This finding fits with the most recent change in historical institutionalism, in which researchers are giving more attention to what people can do in order to avoid the determinism that comes from the analytical concept of path dependence. In other words, even though both Taiwan and China have used Leninist control models in their markets in the past, this does not mean that their internal market structures have changed in the same way over time. But the positive effects of growing returns that come with the path dependence process can't explain why they are different. Instead, as Taiwan and China show, the way a state-capitalist system changes depends on the choices of its leaders.

As a good way to end my argument, I should talk about how the results of my study would affect the growth of cross-Strait relations. As of this writing in the second half of 2016, ties between the two sides of the Taiwan Strait have been getting worse since Tsai Ing-wen of the DPP became president of Taiwan in May 2016. Tsai's rejection of the so-called 1992 Consensus, which said that there is only one Chinese nation but that the PRC and the ROC can disagree about which of them is its legitimate representative, was seen as a defiant statement of Taiwan's separateness and independence. It remains to be seen how both sides will deal with this new situation, but it is safe to say that Tsai's attitude toward China has made the Chinese and Taiwanese less likely to trust each other. I will only talk about what these research results mean for cross-Strait relations from 2008 to 2016.

Tsai's predecessor, Ma Ying-jeou of the KMT, had a strategy of engagement with China and built up a lot of economic ties with the Chinese market. Chen Shui-bian, who was president of the DPP from 2000 to 2008, had a strategy that was very hostile to China. Even though Ma has been accused of giving Taiwan to China, his work has been successful. In 2010, China and Taiwan signed the Economic Cooperation Framework Agreement. Since then, trade between the two sides of the Taiwan Strait has grown by more than 50%, hitting US$198 billion in 2014. At the same time, the Ma government slowly made it easier for Chinese companies to invest abroad. This growing economic union happened at the same time that people from Taiwan and China got to know each other better. During Mas's first term, Chinese students were able to sign up for and graduate from Taiwanese colleges for the first time. In the meantime, it is said that the opening of Taiwan to Chinese tourists, with a daily limit of 5,000 visitor groups and 4,000 individual travelers, is good for Taiwan's economy. All of the previous talks laid the groundwork for peaceful growth on both sides of the Taiwan Strait. This made it possible for Taiwan and China to start talking to each other again.

Without a doubt, the case for detente across the Taiwan Strait is based on a theory, which is the commercial peace research agenda. Based on the democratic peace research program, which says that democratic countries can promote peace among themselves, the commercial peace literature says that the economic institutions that are part of these democracies and the frequent commercial exchanges between them make it possible for these countries' governments to become more stable. If we apply the logic of commercial peace studies to cross-Strait ties under Ma's presidency, there are reasons to be hopeful. As was said above, trade, cash, and people-to-people exchanges across the Strait have reached a level that has never been seen before. At the same time, China's economic system has changed into a capitalist one, and the market has become the most important way to organize economic activities within the country. Together, these two changes have brought the economies of both sides of the Taiwan Strait closer together to the point where neither side would do anything to make things worse politically between the two sides. Yet, the results of this chapter show that it's best to be careful when trying to figure out how economic integration affected peaceful growth across the Taiwan Strait during Ma's presidency.

People say that international trade is good for the country as a whole, but the effects on different people in the country rely on whether they work in sectors with comparative advantages or not. In other words, foreign trade makes it so that some people in a country get more money than others. Because of this, political competition over the trade problem gets worse when both sides try to lobby and sway decision makers. In this way, Taiwan's trade politics are no different, especially since the Chinese political-economic system is dominated by a strong SOE sector, as we talked about in the last part. Ma's presidency was characterized by closer economic links with China. However, his party, the KMT, had a hard time during the Sunflower Movement protests and lost by a huge margin in 2014 and again in January 2016. This study tells us three important things that help us understand why people didn't like Ma's business deals with China.

First, the clear hand of the Chinese government makes people worry about fair competition on the market in Taiwan. As was already said, China's state capitalism system gives more power to the SOE sector than to the private sector. State meddling and state subsidies have helped Chinese state firms grow not just in their own country but also around the world. A discriminatory industrial policy is shown by the two trends in China's internal market that are described by the saying "The state advances and the private sector retreats" and by China's "going out policy" on the global market, where SOEs have been the main players. Under state capitalism, the Taiwanese government has also used its power in the market and created an industrial strategy to help the country grow. But, as we've already seen, the Taiwanese government did get involved in the market without hurting private property rights. Instead, private ownership was a key part of how Taiwan's economy grew and changed over time. So, whenever the Ma administration took steps to further open Taiwan's domestic market to Chinese capital, there were worries that Chinese firms backed by state subsidies would drive out Taiwanese local private companies.

Second, and this is linked to the first point, as economic integration across the Taiwan Strait has moved forward, the distributional problem in Taiwan caused by trade with China has become worse. Even though Ma's policy of engagement is said to help Taiwan's economy, the gains of economic exchanges do not benefit everyone in Taiwan equally. Since Ma's second term began in 2012, the difference in income and wealth has been one of the most talked-about topics. Even though there is no proof that growing economic integration across the Taiwan Strait is making income inequality in the U.S. worse, the public's feelings about the lack of transparency in China's political and economic system are becoming even more complicated. This is mostly because the new pattern of economic growth is different from what Taiwanese people ever saw under Taiwan's state capitalism, which stressed both high economic growth and low income inequality.

That is, even though the state capitalist systems on both sides of the Taiwan Strait look identical, they have grown in different ways. As Patrick McDonald's argument about "the domestic version of commercial liberalism" shows, international trade by itself does not necessarily lead to peace between countries. Only international trade between economies where private ownership plays a major role can stop potential wars. When you look at it this way, the Chinese government has been working on economic liberalization for decades, and internationalist economic interests in China's domestic politics have had a calming effect on its foreign policy goals. However, the fact that the Chinese government owns most of its economy still makes economic actors in Taiwan skeptical about China's political goals in promoting economic exchanges across the Taiwan Strait. So, let's move on to the next point.

Last but not least, the strong economic ties between Taiwan and China make people more aware of Taiwan's independence. International trade makes countries dependent on each other and brings up the question of security externality. Several studies show that trade between allies has a good effect on security, while trade between allies and non-allies has a negative effect on security. A new national security law that China passed in July 2015 says that China claims authority over Taiwan. This means that political rivalry between China and Taiwan is as strong as ever. So, even when Lee Teng-hui and Chen Shui-bian were in charge, Taiwan's trade politics never got rid of security worries about growing economic dependence on China. Ma's "engagement policy" and China's increasingly active and aggressive behavior on the world stage have made Taiwanese people more worried about further union. A certain amount of Chinese investment in Taiwan comes from the state sector, which makes people in Taiwan think that their operations might have goals other than getting money.

Chapter 13
Cross-Strait Economic Connections and China's Ascendancy

Since 2008, cross-Taiwan Strait economic ties have been through a lot. Early on in Ma Ying-jeou's presidency, people had high hopes, but problems at home and doubt lowered those hopes. Taiwan's efforts to join the global economy through China were hampered by the complicated situation at home. In 2014, the Cross-Strait Service Trade Agreement and other economic deals were put on hold because of the Sunflower Movement. This movement was led by students and was a protest against the agreement. At the same time, China has changed its big plans by making more business deals all over the world. China's top leader, Xi Jinping, has also shown his strong will by gaining more control over politics and focusing his power. The rise of China's all-around power and Taiwan's reluctance to make the cross-Strait business relationship official are both interesting cases for academics to study.

In this chapter, we'll talk about how the rise of China's economic power affects cross-Strait economic relations and whether Taiwan can still keep its current situation. First, I'll talk about the current development models of Taiwan's information technology sectors in the context of the division of labor across the Taiwan Strait. Then, I'll talk about how China's place in the global political and economic arenas has changed. In the third part, we'll look at how well Taiwan's IT sector handles pressure from the other side of the Taiwan Strait that comes from the government. Lastly, I'll talk about some policy thoughts on how Taiwan can deal with the rise of China.

Fluctuations in Cross-Strait Economic Relations

Taiwan's ability to be fluid and make changes in how it manages the global supply chain is the key to its economic globalization. In the post-developmental state age, Taiwanese companies are known for making things on time and with high quality among global brand owners. This original equipment manufacturing/original design manufacturing (OEM/ODM) model of growth was built on mutual trust with upstream designers, close interaction with major high-tech hubs, and access to the major manufacturing bases of mainland China. In other words, Taiwanese companies are the main bridges between American technologies, Taiwanese know-how, and Chinese processing skills.

The IT and electronics business is becoming more and more important to Taiwan's economy. Because of this, too much of Taiwan's exports are now made up of IT and electronics goods. Based on export figures collected by Taiwan's Directorate General of Budget, Accounting, and Statistics, information and communications technology (ICT) products always make up more than 30 percent of Taiwan's total exports. IT and electronics goods have a high level of income elasticity, so people often wait to buy them until they have more money. But changes in the global economy can hurt Taiwan's trade and economic growth rate in a big way. Taiwan's ability to make changes in reaction to changes in the world economy is also hurt.

The way things have always been done says that Taiwan benefits a lot from the global division of labor because of how big IT design centers like Silicon Valley handle outsourcing. Returnees from overseas are a big part of how talent moves across the Pacific. But new studies show that there are different ways to look at this unique trend of IT globalization. For example, Martin Kenney, Dan Breznitz, and Michael Murphree doubt that overseas returnees are important for Taiwan's IT growth and globalization. They say that only three of the top ten firms in Taiwan for integrated circuit (IC) design were started by people who had lived or worked abroad. Only one of the owners of these three firms has worked in Silicon Valley, while the other two were started by people who went to school in Silicon Valley. Kenney and his colleagues say that the returnee-centered view of Taiwan's development doesn't take into account the important roles of multinational corporations, indigenous entrepreneurship, and the spin-off policy of the Industrial Technology Research Institute (ITRI) in making an environment that would be appealing to returnees. In other words, experts haven't given the ecosystem enough credit for what it did before the returnee entrepreneurs came back, mostly in the 1990s. Such an environment set up the conditions for returnees to use the education and skills they had gained abroad to fill the structural niche in Taiwan that they would later grow.

The overseas connection may not have had a big effect on the amount of IT made in Taiwan, but it did improve the level of IT made there. In the IT field, people who went abroad and came back planted the seeds of cultural change. Instead of focusing on how overseas returnees affect the globalization of Taiwan's IT industry, Taiwanese businesses have been raising the learning curve to gain technological know-how in the IT and electronics sectors. The business ties between Taiwan and Japan show how this kind of model for learning is getting better. The growth of the transnational division of labor and the long-term economic downturn in Japan, which was caused by global capitalism, gave the Taiwanese thin-film-transistor liquid-crystal-display (TFT-LCD) industry a key strategic chance for dependency management. The Taiwanese basically brought in Japanese workers because they learned how to make things straight from Japanese engineers. After that, Taiwanese TFT-LCD makers came up with their own next-generation technology without counting on Japanese engineers or buying Japanese technologies over and over again.

After May 20, 2016, the new government, which was led by the Democratic Progressive Party (DPP), put in place new policies to encourage innovation and IT growth. One of President Tsai's five main goals for industrial growth is the "Asian Silicon Valley" project. The goal of this project is to give entrepreneurs and new businesses a better place to work so that Taiwan can get a bigger piece of the global IT market. It also wants to improve Taiwan's IT research and design capabilities by encouraging creative people, making it easier for capital markets to grow, and changing rules in this area. Also, the Taiwanese government is going to set up a one-stop center to help integrate its research and development (R&D) skills with those of Silicon Valley in California and other innovation hubs around the world.

In contrast to IT development policies of the past 20 years, the Asian Silicon Valley plan aims to get Taiwan more involved in setting international standards and certifying IT-related products. The policy's goals include putting Taiwan's hardware strengths to use in software applications and making use of what universities and research institutes find in their study. The IT and other high-tech equipment is also a big part of this plan. For example, it wants to set up a good Internet setting, build a variety of smart test beds, and make apps for smart logistics, smart transportation, and smart medicine.

The Hon Hai Model

People have said for a long time that the best way to stop Taiwan from being too economically dependent on China is for Taiwan to do business in different places around the world. Taiwan has been economically dependent on Japan in terms of industrial know-how, upstream technology innovation, and improving the service sector. This is in addition to having technological links with the United States. Taiwan's main way of doing business with China has always been through purchases of the OEM and ODM type. The Taiwan Semiconductor Manufacturing Company (TSMC), one of the largest IT companies in Taiwan, focuses on making the manufacturing process as good as possible rather than on the creation of the product itself. Taiwanese firms don't want to control base core technologies because of how they are set up. Even though these OEM/ ODM firms combine US and Japanese technologies, Taiwanese know-how, and production capabilities on the Chinese mainland, their profit margins have been getting smaller. Companies like Foxconn have had to cut costs in order to stay in business. This has led to problems like factories that look like sweatshops and labor issues. As a result, Foxconn and other OEM manufacturers have tried to make their businesses more global and find new ways to sell their products in foreign markets. But well-known Taiwanese brands like Acer, Asus, and HTC are still rare in the global market.

Even though there have been problems with labor disputes and questions about sweatshop factories in China, Hon Hai/Foxconn is still one of the most popular OEM/ODM companies from Taiwan in the world. Foxconn's rise in the world of IT production is mostly due to how well it fits into Apple's global supply chain. Foxconn is able to form relationships with other manufacturers and set up large networks of cooperation thanks to Apple's complex supply chain. For example, Apple's famous iPhone is made by several growing global production networks. One of these networks is made up of one of the world's best-known brands, Apple, and the world's largest provider of electronics manufacturing services, Hon Hai, which is based in Taiwan. Another uses three different types of suppliers: the world's best integrated semiconductor maker (Samsung of South Korea), the best fabless smartphone chip design company (Qualcomm of the US), and the best semiconductor foundry (TSMC of Taiwan). At these points where various production networks from different parts of the ICT sector meet, the interfirm partnerships that make a big consumer product successful on the market happen.

The Foxconn/Hon Hai model of globalization is interesting because it doesn't involve a lot of help and backing from the government. Instead, it shows how innovative forces and self-reinforcing forces work at the company level. Henry Yeung says that Hon Hai did not directly get help from the government. The state's industrial strategy is not to blame for its success. Hon Hai is not a "national champion" by the terms of the developmental state. Instead, its rise to prominence is mostly due to its strategic partnerships with some of the biggest companies in the world in the electronics business. Hon Hai's competitive advantages come from its ability to blend privacy, a good track record of quality control, and low prices. Yeung says that the fact that Hon Hai became Taiwan's biggest industrial company has nothing to do with state-led industrialization or the "brain circulation" of global technologist elites. Instead, he says, Hon Hai became Taiwan's biggest industrial company because of its own industrial skills. Instead, its success as the world's top electronics manufacturing service provider can be explained by the changing industrial dynamics of global production networks, which give it important chances to be a strategic manufacturing partner of leading global companies.

Hon Hai has become an even more important part of Apple's supply chain, and it has also expanded into high-tech service areas and made a number of strategic partnerships with other ICT vendors and service providers. Hon Hai put out a plan for building an intelligent society with gadgets and services that work together by combining hardware and software. To meet customer needs, the company plans to change into a technology services company and has no plans to start selling its own goods.

In the future 5G era, the company will focus on developing automation and artificial intelligence, combining hardware and software skills, using technology to make people's lives better, and making more money for its shareholders. Because of this, Hon Hai/Foxconn is working with Google to make robots that can be used in the making process. It needs Google's help to automate its factories more because, despite having a big workforce, it has the lowest sales per employee among contract manufacturers. Also, the company wants to cut down on labor costs and expand its business in order to find new ways to grow as income from contract manufacturing slows down. Hon Hai has built many ties with its customers, including one with the American PC maker Hewlett-Packard, which was signed at the end of April 2013.

Hon Hai has done things to make itself less dependent on Apple. In 2014, 25 to 30 percent of Hong Hai's total income came from Apple. Since then, Hon Hai has bought shares that give it control of Taiwan's Asia Pacific Telecom and is planning to move into the car business. At the end of December 2014, it told the public that it had bought a 10.5% stake in China Harmony, a big dealer of luxury cars in China. It recently revealed that it is working with Tencent, the company that runs the Chinese social network WeChat, to make electric cars that can connect to the Internet. It says it can make electric cars for less than US$15,000, which is a lot less than what big automakers charge for their current models.

In 2016, Foxconn bought the Japanese IT giant Sharp. This shows that Gou wants to grow in the global market. Gou says that Sharp has a lot of technology but can't sell it. Foxconn plans to speed up the commercialization of Sharp's patents by turning them into technology and then into goods that will help the business make money. Foxconn is now facing tough market conditions, like a growing trend of protectionism in many countries, so it needs to make new strategy moves to stay alive and grow.

The $3.5 billion deal for a 66 percent share in Sharp is meant to make Foxconn a more attractive partner for Apple. The American tech company uses

Sharp screens, which could give Foxconn more power in negotiations with the American company. In recent years, Apple has been expanding its supply chain by giving some production contracts to other assemblers and component makers. Meanwhile, Foxconn is dealing with rising labor costs in China and a slowdown in the global smartphone market. Analysts are worried about greater competition from China-based suppliers, which has helped boost Foxconn's sales thanks to a surge in orders for less expensive smartphones made by Chinese companies. Also, as part of its attempts to diversify its supply chain, Apple has given orders for iPhone assembly to Pega-tron, a Taiwanese contract manufacturer with a big factory near Shanghai.

Efforts to Establish the IT Brand

The change from an original equipment manufacturer (OEM) to an own-brand manufacturing (OBM) style of production is another thing to think about in terms of Taiwan's global ties in the IT industry. As profit margins get smaller, some Taiwanese OEM makers have started to change course and take on more risks. HTC, a well-known maker of smartphones, is a good example. HTC was started in 1997 and made laptop computers at first. It made hand-held devices for other companies for many years and was the first to make phones with touch-screen controls. In 2006, it started making goods under its own name. A year later, Google released Android, which became HTC's preferred operating system. By 2011, the market price of the company was bigger than that of Nokia, which used to be the industry giant. HTC sold more smartphones in the US than any other company in 2011. Since then, the value of HTC's shares has dropped by almost 90%, going from $33 billion to $4 billion.

But the HTC case also shows how weak Taiwanese IT companies are in the market when it comes to their own names. Even if you have world-class manufacturing knowledge, that doesn't mean you can easily make it in the global marketplace. For example, the HTC One, which came out in 2013, was named "Smartphone of the Year" in February at the Mobile World Congress in Barcelona. It was only the third phone to get a five-star review. But HTC's biggest problem is not that its design is not too fancy. Samsung, HTC's biggest competitor, spent $14 billion on ads last year, which is about the same as Iceland's GDP. In the third quarter of 2013, HTC had its first operating loss ever. ABI Research, a consulting business, said that once a handset company stops making money, only 10 percent are likely to be around in two years.

In China, which is the biggest market for consumer electronics in the world, global names and cheap local producers are putting more pressure on HTC. As a well-known brand, HTC has trouble figuring out where its brand stands in the Chinese market. Most people in the Mainland don't know much about the Taiwanese brand whose letters used to stand for "High Tech Computer." They go to Apple and Samsung as well as their own smartphone names, like Coolpad, Huawei, Lenovo, Xiaomi, and ZTE. Local names sell phones that are the same as HTC's for the same price, or sometimes even less, while HTC is held back by higher production costs.

HTC's decline and losses show that second-tier smartphone makers are having trouble in a market that is getting older. HTC's shares in Taipei hit an all-time low of NT$71 on June 30, 2015. In April 2011, they reached an all-time high of NT$1,300. Ahead of the company's statement, the price of the shares stayed the same at NT$73.80. Cher Wang, who is in charge of HTC, says that the company just put out a fitness band and a virtual reality gadget.

In August 2015, HTC's market value went below the amount of cash it had on hand. This caused headlines to say that the brand was worthless. This design-focused company seemed to have lost a piece of its heart. If the company doesn't want to keep going down, it will need to make better hardware, change the way software works, and make its marketing pitch less defensive and negative. In 2016, HTC changed its plans and became the OEM maker of the Google Pixel Android phone. There are different reactions from the market. Experts say that because Google keeps saying that the new phone is "made by Google," HTC has been demoted to the role of OEM manufacturer instead of working with Google to design the device. This method is the same as Apple's deal with Foxconn to make the iPhone. It's a step back for HTC from being an OBM to becoming an OEM. On the other hand, critics say that since HTC's own goods don't do well in the market, it makes sense for the company to choose safer ways to make money for the next stage of changes. Virtual reality products could be a possible target for HTC's niche.

The strengths and flaws of Taiwanese IT companies in cross-Strait business are shown by both the Hon Hai and HTC models. Taiwan has put economic ties across the Taiwan Strait on the world stage. But China is no longer a developing country with low pay and little technology. "The rise of China" has become a key phrase in both academic and political arguments around the world. In other words, China is not just a place where cheap goods that require a lot of work are made. China has shown that, with its newfound power and standing on the international stage, it wants to be the new global economic powerhouse.

In the next part, we'll talk about how China's new global position has changed its political and economic big plans. In terms of economic ties across the Taiwan Strait, Taiwan is dealing with a partner that is very different from the one it was dealing with before 2000. These political and economic plans help explain whether China will be a rival, a dominant player, or a partner in economic interactions.

Obstacles in Cross-Strait Economic Relations

The Rise of China's New Global Political Endeavors

A lot of both foreign and domestic political calculations go into the term "grand strategy." The Chinese government has put a lot of emphasis on how internal and international politics are linked. China's recent proactive foreign policy moves are an attempt to deal with the "two major situations" (at home and abroad) at the same time. In January 2013, at the Third Politburo Studying Meeting, Xi went into detail about a way to combine the two big situations. Under Xi's leadership, this kind of integration has become a big part of China's foreign strategy. This policy directive can be seen in the framework of integrating domestic development with foreign relations, Chinese development with global development, and the interests of the Chinese people with the interests of other countries. Xi says that based on the principle of integration, the Chinese government should be more positive and proactive in foreign affairs and look for ways to help the world grow.

The strategy of "handling the two major situations" shows that China is becoming more confident in its ability to handle international issues. Also, keeping both domestic and international stability will help China continue to grow and progress over the next few decades.

In foreign affairs, however, the policy still runs into problems. Wu Xinbo says that in foreign affairs, contradictions are common. As Chinese society improves, the Chinese tend to use peaceful methods instead of military ones to solve problems in the world. They want to find "natural ways" to deal with the differences. If the time isn't right, the best thing to do is to put aside disagreements and look for a middle ground where both sides' goals meet. Wu Xinbo also says that the present relationships between political groups in the Asia-Pacific region are based on a mix of worries about hegemonic stability, power balance, and group security. The connection between China and the United States is one of controlled competition and limited cooperation. In the end, the most important thing is to avoid direct disputes. From Wu's point of view, the Asia-Pacific area is a "unharmonious world" for China, full of conflicts, contradictions, and opportunities. In high politics, the balance of power and big-power politics will win out. But when it comes to human security, countries in the area tend to work together toward goals that are good for everyone.

Chinese academics have also looked at how China's views on world order and governance have changed. For example, Wang Jisi says that since 2005, the State Council white paper hasn't talked about a strategy of "establishing international political and economic order." Instead, the white paper from 2011 focused on making an effort to be involved in foreign affairs and take on responsibilities. Wang thinks that these changes show that China accepts the current political and economic order in the world and is working to support more change. In other words, China has changed into a "central nation" that acts as a link between the North and the South.

A center nation's new sense of who it is is facing new problems. First, the biggest threats to security come from countries that depend on each other economically the most, like the United States and Japan. China's business ties with the U.S. and Japan show how work is divided around the world, which goes way beyond bilateral relations. Second, China needs to broaden its view of the world and play a more positive role in the Middle East, Africa, and Indian Ocean if it wants to make sure the security of its neighbors. Getting involved in a wide range of security problems will have a big effect on China's home security. The only way to improve the national security of neighboring countries is to make a security strategy that covers the whole world and takes into account both Chinese and global interests. Third, with a new global policy like this, China needs to make sure its relationships with big countries like Russia, India, Japan, and the United States are stable. It needs to take on more global duties, but it also needs to be humble and smart.

The Chinese know that China's recent rise is because of its growing wealth, not because of its culture. The Chinese need to make their voices heard on the international stage and upgrade their culture to "Chinese culture 2.0." This will help them deal with more complicated problems at home, such as ethnic autonomy and "one country, two systems" arrangements, in which different parts of China keep their own economic, political, and legal systems. This improved culture will be able to work with different religious, national, political, and even local subsystems all over China. But a study from Peking University's Institute of National Development shows that cultural pluralism has to work within the socialist system of the Chinese party state. It is a part of China's history that is necessary for its future growth.

As the analysis above shows, Chinese leaders and experts are looking for a new "grand strategy" to guide how their country acts in the world. Barry Buzan says that we can think of a grand plan as having the following roles:

1. To establish criteria for foreign and security policy formulation and evaluation.

2. To create coherence in foreign and security policy by providing a stable overarching framework for policy choices.
3. To embed and legitimize foreign and security policy politically by explaining it to the citizenry in broad terms, and especially to explain difficult choices.
4. To project an image of the country to the rest of the world.

Buzan says that the "peaceful development" policy of China is a grand strategy because it meets these four conditions. It has a theory about how the world works and how China should connect to it, given that development is its most important goal. It takes into account military, political, and economic factors and is aware of how China should look to the rest of the world. So, it gives a framework for figuring out what China's national interests are and a simple rule for how to connect means and ends.

Under the general principle of peaceful development, Chinese leaders and academics are looking for new ways to balance their traditional low-key foreign policy with more proactive diplomatic efforts. Wang Jisi, for example, says that China needs a more complex grand plan to serve its domestic goals. He talks about four changes that China's strategic thought is going through: (r) China's new concept of security, which goes beyond power politics to include things like preventing disasters and protecting the environment; (2) a shift from a country-focused to a more multilateral and issue-focused policy; (3) more focus on economic efficiency, product quality, environmental protection, the creation of a social safety net, and technological innovation; (4) an increase in China's cultural soft power and a push for good governance; and (5) a shift from a country-focused to an issue-focused

Recent Chinese foreign policy directives show that China wants to adjust to its role as a major power in the international field. This is in contrast to a more cautious and low-key approach to the outside world. Yan Xuetong says that Xi's grand plan is more proactive because he is "striving for achievement." Yan says that if China wants a good international setting that will help it get back on its feet, it needs to make changes to the outside world instead of just reacting to what happens there. This method aims for cooperation in areas like politics, security, and culture, as well as the economy. It also encourages China to take on foreign responsibilities that match China's goals, abilities, and status as the second-largest power in the world.

Yan Xuetong says that the most interesting thing about Xi Jinping's grand strategy is that it puts more stress on China's relationships with its neighbors than in the past. China has put Sino-American ties at the top of its list for a long time. After Xi's adjustment, diplomacy with neighboring countries has become more important, especially the building of cross-regional economic corridors. These corridors include not only a Silk Road Economic Belt that connects China to Europe through western and central Asia and a 21st Century Maritime Silk Road that connects China to Southeast Asia, Africa, and Europe through the South China Sea, the Indian Ocean, and the Red Sea, but also a China-India-Myanmar-Bangladesh ec

China's plans to "regionalize" its power show how it wants to change its place in the Asia-Pacific region and pay attention to more than just politics between the world's biggest countries. Foreign Minister Wang Yi talked about China's foreign policy goals in a very important speech. He stressed the "Asia-Pacific Dream" that Xi Jinping first talked about at the 2014 Asia-Pacific Economic Cooperation (APEC) meeting. Wang said that China would try to get everyone to agree on how to improve cooperation in the Asia-Pacific area as a whole. He also said that it was important to work for common, all-around, cooperative, and long-term security in Asia and to build a community of people with the same values and goals.

As the pages before this one show, Chinese leaders want a better foreign situation so they can keep their country stable and growing. As China's overall power grows, the Chinese are using their economic power to change the country's place in the world. This new strategy needs to help the country's own interests and calm fears of a "China threat." Also, the Chinese are looking for new ways to change international economic, political, and security systems to make China a stronger leader on the world stage.

In 2013, Chinese President Xi Jinping announced the "One Belt, One Road" (OBOR) strategy. The plan says that China will set up a $40 billion "Silk Road" building aid fund to help countries along the Silk Road Economic Belt. It would be like the trade network that ran through central and western Asia during the Han era and linked China to Europe. As part of OBOR, the 21st Century Maritime Silk Road was also revealed.

Wang Yi, China's foreign minister, explained that OBOR is made up of projects that are meant to help China and Eurasian countries work together in a way that is good for both sides. This is in the spirit of learning from each other and living together peacefully, like on the old Silk Road. The people in charge of China think that OBOR will be a way for China to work with other countries in the modern world. Also, it will help national interests both inside and outside the country. As Wang points out:

> *Internally, this initiative dovetails with Chinas development strategy of developing our central and western regions while addressing regional*

> *imbalances and fits well with our "go global" strategy aimed at building all-directional cooperation with the outside world.*
>
> *Internationally this initiative aims to secure common development and shared prosperity in all countries along the routes, as it upholds the vision for a community of shared destiny and highlights a win-win approach featuring consultation, joint development and sharing. The initiative is bound to bring new life and vigor to the ancient land of Eurasia and give this vast continent two strong wings on its journey toward prosperity.*

OBOR shows that China wants to move away from its previous low-key foreign policy plan, called taoguan yanghui. Some people have seen OBOR as China's Marshall Plan, with the long-term goal of becoming the most powerful country on the Eurasian region in terms of geopolitics. In this situation, OBOR is also seen as an economic countermeasure to the United States' efforts to rebalance in the Asia-Pacific region. The assumption is that China will use OBOR as a chance to invest more in its large western region and try to keep its growth rate, which is going down. China could use this plan to prepare for possible problems if its sea lines were to become threatened. China could also have more political power if the economy of the area becomes more dependent on Beijing. Promoting the connections between Eurasian countries would require more money than any one country has, so there needs to be a way for everyone to pay and share.

OBOR also helps China's own economy by giving Chinese capital a way to "step out." In 2014, China was the biggest trade country in the world. It had US$39 trillion in foreign exchange reserves. Such stocks can set the stage for China to take a more active role in international affairs. At the same time, there needs to be a way for domestic capital to flow into the foreign market. Since 2008, when the world economy slowed down and a stimulus plan was put in place, China's building industries have become economic leaders under the state capitalist system. China's iron triangle of train lines, roads, and airports was made possible by large-scale infrastructure projects. With China's experience and technology in building infrastructure, the OBOR policy gives these state-owned businesses the chance to work on new projects for foreign markets. New institutions, such as the Asian Infrastructure Investment Bank (AIIB), will also back up these kinds of moves.

Details are still coming out about how Taiwan will take part in OBOR and the AIIB. But Taiwanese companies have made a number of smart partnerships as part of this new investment plan. For example, in 2011, Taiwan's Asia Vital Components Co., which makes thermal solutions, bought a 45 percent share in a company that China South Locomotive & Rolling Stock Corp. had set up as a partner. Local institutional investors think that the company will benefit from the expected growth in demand for high-margin railway heat dissipation and electrical goods like power resisters, water-cooled transformers, and rackable connectors. Power Mate Technology Co., a business that makes power supplies, got a spot in the supply chain for China's railroad equipment in 2010 when the EN 50155 standard approved its electronic equipment for use on trains. Since the company started, Power Mate's goods have been used in a wide range of industries, such as medicine, weapons, solar power, and cars. The company makes goods with their own designs and sells them under the brand name P-Duke.

The largest investment banking and research company in China, China International Capital Corp., said it expects Beijing to put more than US$1.65 trillion into its OBOR strategy over the next ten years. Most of this money will go to Asian countries that are close to China. At the same time, investors are more optimistic about Taiwanese companies like Asia Vital Components Co. and Power Mate Technology Co. because they are seen as companies that will do well as the efforts led by Beijing take shape.

Change in China's IT Policy

As with its more active foreign policy, the Chinese government has shown its strong desire to rebuild the high-tech and IT industries through direct state involvement. These kinds of actions are typical of how a developing state uses financial tools and industrial strategy to pick winners and help technological breakthroughs. The Chinese government is now spending a lot of money and time on new policies that will help the semiconductor business grow. Officials in China have put together a special task group whose job is to come up with an aggressive plan for growth. This group helped make a policy plan that aims for the industry to grow at a rate of 20% per year between now and 2020, with up to RMB 1 trillion (US$170 billion) in financial support from the government over the next five to ten years. The investments will be made by the National Industry Investment Fund and by organizations at the regional level. These organizations will invest in many different areas, such as project financing, domestic and international acquisitions, and standard research and development subsidies and tax credits.

To avoid the problems caused by fragmentation in the past, the Chinese government is focusing on making national champions—a small number of leaders in each important part of the semiconductor market, such as design, manufacturing, tools, assembly and testing, and a few provinces that have the potential to develop industry clusters. This time, however, the task force is made up of the top ten to fifteen leaders in China's semiconductor industry. This includes executives from fabless designers, foundries, and equipment manufacturers. Vice-Premier Ma Kai, one of the government's highest-ranking officials, is in charge of the project as a whole. This group had a direct effect on how the State Council wrote the Guidelines for Promoting the Development of the National IC Industry, a high-level policy framework that was made public in June 2014.

The "National Guidelines for the Development and Promotion of the IC Industry" were released by the State Council of China in June 2014 to help the local semiconductor industry. The document talks about goals, approaches, and measures for growth. It has made waves in the semiconductor industry and gotten attention from around the world because it has high goals for growth and a lot of money to support a national IC industry investment fund.

At the same time, Beijing, Shanghai, Wuhan, and Hefei have all set up local investment funds for the IC business. Of these, Beijing took the lead in setting up an RMB 30 billion (US$4.8 billion) fund in June 2014. It is set up as a "fund of funds" with two smaller funds inside it. The "fund of funds" is also handled by CGP Investment. Hua Capital manages the other subfund, which helps with IC design and packaging. In November 2014, the Shanghai Summitview Capital IC Information Industry Merger Fund, which is the city's IC industry fund, was set up with a total of RMB 10 billion (US$1.6 billion). With local industry funds in place, it is thought that all government funds will add up to $100 billion.

Since most Taiwanese IT companies have set up their manufacturing centers in the Yangtze River Delta region, new policy initiatives from the central government to the local governments bring both challenges and chances for the Taiwanese. In the late 1990s, Shanghai became the most important place in China for IT growth, even though there were other important places. Director of the Shanghai Academy of Social Sciences Wang Zhan says that the service sector is just one of the most important parts of an economic center. Shanghai's economic growth shouldn't depend only on the service industry. In making Shanghai an economic center, the main goal is still to create a high-end, globalized, innovative industrial industry. The problem in Shanghai right now is that scientific study, technological innovation, and industrial development are not working well together. Most private businesses, like those in trade and real estate, are in the service industry. Foreign companies focus on low-end products and the Chinese market rather than their R&D capabilities. There are many structural limits on state-owned businesses. Wang thinks that the best policy for Shanghai is a mix of market forces and government direction. Small and medium-sized businesses in the private sector will be the ones to drive growth. The government's job is to make a place where new ideas can thrive, and the private sector doesn't need any more help from the government. But under these kinds of policies, the private sector will have to deal with uncertainty and risks when it has to compete in the world market.

Taiwanese companies are looking for new ways to work with local governments as part of new policy efforts led by the local government. The city government of Shanghai revealed a plan to spend 50 billion (US$8 billion) on new infrastructure in the IC industry, such as two production lines for twelve-inch wafers. Before the funding program, the city had just set up the Shanghai SummitView IC Information Industry Fund, an RMB 10 billion ($1.6 billion) fund in which Taiwanese chip designer MediaTek is a partner. MediaTek Inc. , which makes the most handset chips in the country, signed an agreement in November 2014 to spend RMB 300 million (US$48.9 million) in a Chinese government fund in order to take advantage of China's fast-growing semiconductor industry. MediaTek is the biggest chip maker in Taiwan right now, and it has the biggest share of the market for smartphone processors in China. Ming-kai Tsai, the chair of MediaTek, says that by investing in the fund, MediaTek hopes to gain a better place in the global semiconductor industry and help China and Taiwan's high-tech industries work together better. The fund was started by the city government of Shanghai and the Chinese venture capital company SummitView Capital. At first, the fund will have 3 billion in funding, and over time, that amount will grow to 10 billion. In addition to MediaTek, partners in the fund include the Shanghai Jiading Venture Capital Fund, Semiconductor Manufacturing International Corp. (SMIC), Tsinghua University's Tsinghua Holdings Co., and Knight Capital from the US.

The pages before this one show the new political and economic steps China is taking to make its economy stronger and more independent. The rise of China's overall power poses clear problems for the way the two sides of the Taiwan Strait divide up economic work. In the next part, we'll look at how Taiwan's efforts to stay at the top of cross-Strait economic interactions are affected by a mix of state-led efforts and firm-specific incentives.

Red Supple Chain

Novel Policy

The fact that a mainland Chinese supply chain could take the place of Taiwanese firms shows that the government is very supportive of local businesses. Made in China 2025 is a 10-year national plan that was released by China's State

Council in 2015. Its goal is to turn China from a manufacturing giant into a world manufacturing power. Priorities have been set for nine tasks: improving manufacturing innovation, integrating technology and industry, strengthening the industrial base, fostering Chinese brands, enforcing green manufacturing, promoting breakthroughs in ten key sectors, advancing restructuring of the manufacturing sector, promoting service-oriented manufacturing and manufacturing-related service industries, and internationalizing manufacturing. The ten key sectors are information technology, numerical control tools and robotics, aerospace equipment, ocean engineering equipment and high-tech ships, railway equipment, energy-saving and new energy vehicles, power equipment, new materials, medicine and medical devices, and agricultural machinery.

The "Outline to Promote National Integrated Circuit Development" scheme was started by the Chinese government in 2014. To help the semiconductor business grow, the central government is going to set up an investment fund worth $20 billion. By setting up holding companies to help Chinese companies make more semiconductors, the Chinese government will become a direct player. China's semiconductor business had to depend on imports for 80% of its domestic needs until 2014.

Also, the Chinese government is pushing for state-owned semiconductor companies to join or be bought out. The Chinese government has been pushing companies more and more to buy breakthrough innovation skills rather than rent or steal them. This can be done by buying both technology and talent. In the last two years, for example, the Qinghua UNIS group's flagship company bought the Chinese IC company RDA for $1 billion. UNIS also bought Spreadtrum, a big IC designer, for $1.78 billion. CEO of UNIS Zhao Weiguo says that Taiwan's No. 2 semiconductor company MediaTek is the clear goal. Zhao says that his company will spend $50 billion to beat MediaTek in the next five years.

In 2015, Apple added two more Taiwanese companies to its list of businesses that make parts for the iPhone and iPad. Wistron Corporation was chosen to put together iPhones, and Compal Electronics was chosen to put together iPads. Apple has also added BYD, a company in China, as a final assembler for its goods. They are now part of a group of companies, along with Hong Hai and Pegatron of Taiwan, that put together Apple goods from China to Brazil. In other words, Taiwanese companies still control Apple's factory lines because Quanta makes Macs and iPods and Inventec supplies iPods. The biggest non-Taiwanese players were BYD, which used to be on Apple's list of border suppliers, and Flextronics, which makes Macs in Austin, Texas.

But the growth of China's local manufacturers also puts Taiwanese suppliers in Apple's iPhone supply chain in danger. Taiwanese manufacturers say that Apple's long-term plan is to help China's local manufacturers and grow its share of the Chinese market. Sun-Wonda, a Chinese company that makes Li-on batteries, is now a part of the iPhone 6 supply line. Taiwanese company Merry has been replaced in the iPhone supply chain by Chinese companies like GoerTek and AAC Technologies, which make electroacoustic parts.

In a study from 2014, Barclays Capital Inc. said that the rise of the Chinese supply chain could be disruptive for some second-tier players in the Taiwan supply chain who don't have differentiating technology, scale, or relationships with Chinese domestic brands. Chinese supply chain businesses should move up the chain as a result of their growing size and investments in research and development. They should also be able to make parts for top-tier brands that are competitive on the international market. In the IT supply chain, Taiwanese companies are becoming less important and Chinese companies are becoming more important. The Barclay study points out two key aspects of this change. First, the Taiwanese IT hardware business is having trouble because of problems with succession and an aging corporate culture. Only a small number of Taiwanese tech companies have had their founders hand over control to the second generation of leaders or to new professional management teams. Some Taiwanese companies, like Acer, Asustek, and Compal, are still being run by the founders and professional managers at the same time while the companies are in change. Second, China's high-tech companies have an advantage over their competitors outside of China because the government helps them. Help from the government comes in the form of lower taxes, grants from local governments, and money. Also, the parts markets where Chinese companies are making progress have always been dominated by Taiwanese companies. This is especially true for batteries, cases, camera lenses and modules, handset antennas, and LEDs. The Barclays report says that Chinese component makers are taking market shares from their Taiwanese rivals not only because of price, but also because of service intensity and aggressive investments in R&D and capital spending. The Chinese government is also helping by giving subsidies and tax breaks.

Change in Marketing Strategies

As was said above, the case of Taiwan's HTC shows the limits of a medium-sized Taiwanese company that wants to sell products around the world. China is no longer a world workplace; it is now a world market. It makes sense for business leaders to put the Chinese market first. Because of this change, mainland Chinese IT companies now have an advantage over companies from other countries.

Five years ago, when HTC was at the top of its game, Xiaomi was a newcomer to the Chinese market, which was controlled at the time by well-known brands like Apple and Samsung. Xiaomi may not be one of the most innovative companies in the world right now, but its slick marketing campaigns, fast growth, and online sales efforts give it points. It has been talked about as a Chinese high-tech company on the rise that could follow in the steps of Alibaba. Xiaomi is also working hard to fix one of its weaknesses in innovation—its small number of patents—by trying to double the number of patent applications it files each year.

One of Xiaomi's marketing plans is to "gain strength at home first." The company has put most of its focus on China, and 97 percent of its sales go there. People have said that in the future, Xiaomi will focus on Southeast Asia as well as Brazil, Russia, and India. Hugo Barra, who used to work for Google and is from Brazil, has become the foreign face of new Xiaomi. The company is not in a hurry to get into more developed markets where Apple and Samsung are already strong. Instead, it would rather stay focused on its own base, where the market is still growing.

Lei Jun, the CEO of Xiaomi, says that the company sells smartphones for close to what it costs to make them, or at cost, and will make money through services. They are offering more of a way of life than phones. MiUI and Mi.com are the services Lei Jun is talking about. They sell the goods and link them all together, but in the end, they are all Xiaomi products. The company doesn't just want to be the best at smartphones; it wants to be the best at everything. This plan was made especially for the Chinese market and is aimed at young professionals who want to set up a new home. It could also be used in places like Brazil, Russia, and India that are still growing. For the developed world, the house is already full of brand-name items.

Advancement in Research and Development

Since the 1990s, multinational high-tech companies, such as Taiwanese IT companies, have had a technological edge over Chinese businesses. In order to move up the supply chain and become technologically independent, the Chinese developmental state has worked in different ways to help companies consolidate their R&D capabilities. Foreign entrepreneurs say that China needs "capable" companies much more than "innovative" companies, and that the government should back both. Once Chinese companies have learned how to put together relatively simple products for foreign multinationals, they need to learn how to develop and make more complicated goods on their own. They need to get much better at higher-order planning skills like coming up with strategies, managing multiple brands, building relationships with customers, integrating systems, and managing performance.

China has close to $4 trillion in foreign exchange reserves, which means it can buy the foreign industry capacity it thinks it needs. New purchases back up the idea that a change is happening that can be seen. Lenovo recently bought Motorola Mobility, Donfeng Motors made a bid for Peugeot-Citroen, and Zhejiang Geely, a car company with big goals but not a strong brand or design experience, bought Volvo from Ford. Two-thirds of China's overseas investments in 2014 were in services, which is an area where Chinese companies still have a lot to learn. Through direct investments and acquisitions, many Chinese companies have set up their R&D centers in the United States and Europe. Their goal is to integrate their businesses into the innovation communities of the developed world so they can learn about and use foreign technologies, brands, and marketing techniques.

Attracting High-Caliber Talent in the IT Sectors

The Chinese government knows that if it wants to take off or jump ahead in the IT field, it needs to attract the best and brightest tech people from around the world. The National Medium- and Long-Term ability Development Plan, which was put out by China in 2010, was an ambitious plan to grow ability. In addition to spending in hardware, the plan shows how China can use money from international financial institutions and loans from foreign governments to build programs that train people to do jobs that require specific skills. The plan says that the total number of talented people will go from 114 million in 2010 to 180 million in 2020. The plan also names six major types of talent that the government will help develop: political leaders and officials, business entrepreneurs, technical professionals, highly skilled workers in different industries, people with practical skills for rural areas and agriculture, and professional social workers. Also, to put more pressure on state-owned enterprises (SOEs) to change, the plan wants to train around 100 business leaders and CEOs who can lead Chinese companies to join the Fortune 500 by 2020. It also wants 40,000 talented foreign business people to work for SOEs by 2020, with 50% of them being hired through market competition. In the past, almost all of the top managers of SOEs were either promoted from within the system or hired from outside.

Also, Chinese companies are more than happy to take short cuts by hiring the best people from their Taiwanese competitors in order to improve their technology and market presence. Epistar Corp, which makes the most LED chips in Taiwan, said early in 2015 that it might ask the government to cancel an investment deal that Chinese LED chip maker Sanan Optoelectronics Co. had proposed in 2013 to buy a 19 percent stake in local LED chip maker Formosa Epitaxy Inc. for $7.38 million if it kept poaching its employees. Also, Chinese local governments are setting up public R&D centers that look like Taiwan's ITRI. China pays ITRI's middle and high-level employees more than four times as much as Taiwanese companies do. To stop the flow of smart people to China, ITRI has made it easier for its best people to start businesses in the United States. ITRI wants to help people start their own businesses instead of giving them high pay.

But there is a lot of disagreement about whether China's system of authoritarian control can encourage creativity and bring in top elites. As the main way that Chinese people learn about politics, the higher education system has seen big changes in how ideas are taught. At the beginning of 2015, China's Ministry of Education put out a document with rules about how schools should handle propaganda work. According to the document, the government will push for four major tasks in colleges: 1) putting socialist materials with Chinese characteristics into "classrooms and students' minds"; 2) improving the ideological purity of college teachers; 3) strengthening mainstream thought in colleges; and 4) improving the management of college ideological work. In making these rules, Minister of Education Yuan Guiren said that China would make it harder for schools to use Western textbooks. China will never let materials in college classrooms that teach Western ideals. Also, statements on college campuses that attack party leadership, socialism, the Chinese constitution, or the legal systems will not be allowed.

Conclusion

With the rise of China, business ties across the Taiwan Strait have moved into a new era. In the beginning of their relationship, Taiwan relied on its unique place in the global supply chain and gained from the growth of mainland China's ability to make things. Most of the time, Taiwan's close technological ties with American and Japanese high-tech companies helped create an economic niche built on mutual trust and benefits with upstream brand holders. Part of the reason for this cross-border division of labor was that Chinese vendors and producers were not very good at what they did and didn't know much about technology. China was seen as a workshop, not a market, by people who owned global brands.

Today, US high-tech companies still have the best technology, but the way work is done on both sides of the Taiwan Strait is changing. As the pages above show, Taiwan's OEM model of manufacturing is now being threatened by both shrinking profit margins and the rise of Chinese domestic makers. The OBM approach for making IT is limited by the fact that it can't do marketing or global logistics. Also, Taiwan's internal politics make it hard for people with high skills to move between Taiwan and China. The "made in China, by Taiwan" approach for making IT products is losing some of its advantages over time.

Taiwan's cross-Pacific strategy for IT growth is tied closely to its security and political dependence on the United States. The Xi administration's grand plan shows that it wants to learn more about what "the West" means beyond the rivalry between China and the United States. By putting the Asia-Pacific area at the top of their list of priorities, the Chinese have built up the confidence to change the rules of the international game by combining economic plans for the sea and the land into a grand strategy. From China's point of view, its recent "assertiveness" in foreign policy is just a reflection of its new role as a big power. OBOR and AIIB are also examples of how China is trying to get out of its tangle with the United States and take advantage of new possibilities brought about by new types of geopolitics.

China is working on a new grand plan, but that doesn't mean they are trying to break away from US-led high-tech development. The United States still has some benefits when it comes to innovation and starting new businesses. But the growing ties between China and the countries of mainland Europe are making it possible for China to join a more inclusive global system for working together. Taiwan needs to change its economic plans so that Southeast Asia and Europe are included in its global transportation plans. One choice for policy is to work together with Chinese companies to explore these growing markets. The Chinese market will not be replaced by this kind of strategic alliance. The real goal is to work together with the new sources of global growth and ensure economic security at the same time.

But political changes in Taiwan could make it harder for Taiwan to make a "strategic move" to join the global market by working with new Chinese projects. A recent story in the Economist said that Chinese companies that make petrochemicals, steel, computers, and digital displays have moved into areas that Taiwan used to control. Taiwanese companies that do business in China are getting more supplies and equipment from Chinese suppliers. Chinese companies are now trying to get into Taiwan's last big economic stronghold, which is the semiconductor business. The economic problem could be solved by making it easier for manufacturers and service providers to work with the Chinese home market. But Taiwan's politics make it clear that this kind of policy change is not possible. Early in the spring of 2015, the Sunflower Movement organized against the Cross-Strait Service Trade Agreement. This showed that further economic union with the other side of the Taiwan Strait was not possible from a political point of view.

Still up in the air is whether Taiwanese companies can switch from making just tools to also offering IT services. Because of this weakness, it will be hard for these companies to get into China's home market. Also, it's not clear if the Taiwanese government has the power to move Taiwanese cash to the Southeast Asian market. Taiwan's "Go South" policy in the 1990s showed that state-led attempts to change business behavior didn't have much of an effect. Theories of economic statecraft could help explain why Chinese IT firms are now more competitive. As economic pressure from the other side of the Taiwan Strait grows on the Taiwanese government, it has less power to make deals to help its IT business.

Overall, China will be a key part of Taiwan's plans to grow and progress around the world. Understanding the risks and benefits of China's rise in a global rather than a bilateral way will help Taiwan grow and succeed in the future. So, the standard ideas of economic statecraft and interdependence need to be changed even more. Taiwan has to make hard decisions at home in order to deal with China's rise. Taiwan won't be able to stop its national development from turning inward unless it takes on more chances and looks at the changing world with a more realistic eye.

Chapter 14
Xi Jingping's Taiwan Policy

Cross-Strait relations are generally stable and getting better under Xi Jinping's leadership, even though there is growing anti-Beijing sentiment in Taiwan. This is shown by the Sunflower Movement, which protested the passing of the Cross-Strait Service Trade Agreement between Taiwan and the mainland, and the embarrassing failure of the ruling Kuomintang (KMT) party, which ran on a platform of strengthening Taiwan-China economic ties in the 2014 election. Both sides have been prevented from making any substantial progress in cross-Strait relations since Xi came to power in 2012 (coinciding with Ma's second term)—Taiwan by growing anti-Beijing sentiment, especially among young people, and a drop in President Ma Ying-jeou's popularity, and China by Xi Jinping's preoccupation with fighting corruption and restructuring the economy amid a substantial economic slowdown. But since 2008, when Ma Ying-jeou took power, the Taiwan Strait has been moving in a peaceful direction. Cross-Strait ties are still based on the 1992 Consensus, which says that there is only one China and that Taipei and Beijing agree to disagree about which government is the real one. Also, the two sides are better able to understand and accept each other's different ideas about what it means to say that there is only "one China" at home and abroad. At the same time, economic, social, and political exchanges between the two sides of the Taiwan Strait continue to grow.

Considering all of this, this chapter will try to answer the following questions: What is China's plan for Taiwan while Xi Jinping is in charge? Since Xi Jinping took power, have there been any changes to how China treats Taiwan? Is there a change in Hu Jintao's strategy toward Taiwan? How much will an exit change things between the two sides of the Taiwan Strait?

This part will start with a quick look at how things have changed since Ma Ying-jeou took office in 2008. Then, it will say that the status quo is still the same, even though a lot has changed. But in the long run, the status quo helps Beijing reach its policy goal of reuniting the two sides of the Taiwan Strait into the People's Republic of China (PRC). In this way, Xi Jinping's Taiwan policy still follows the basic approach taken by Hu Jintao, which is to put stopping Taiwan from becoming de jure independent ahead of promoting reunification. However, Xi has been putting more and more emphasis on strengthening the strategic framework of the "one-China principle" in cross-Strait relations. The goal is to put Taiwan in a corner so that China can be reunited, which is one of Xi's big goals for China that is spelled out in his "Chinese Dream." Even though Taiwanese people seem to be identifying less and less with mainland China on a national and political level, Taiwan has been deeply drawn into China's economic orbit, while its foreign status, in terms of both legitimacy and impact, continues to decline. So, Taiwan is finding it harder and harder to get away from the economic and political impact of mainland China. Taiwan is in a tough spot because it will either get even closer to China or be left out of foreign affairs and regional economic integration. Taiwan doesn't have many options other than to accept that it will be more dependent on the mainland. I've come to the conclusion that, while there may be a bounce or response against mainland When it comes to China's policy toward Taiwan after the 2016 presidential election, this will be a small storm that won't change the general direction of things.

In 2004, the Taiwan Affairs Office of the State Council of the PRC put out the May 17 Statement. This was the turning point in ties across the Taiwan Strait. In this speech, Beijing made it clear for the first time that the top goal of its Taiwan policy was to stop Taiwan from becoming de jure independent. As the international community became more worried and suspicious about China's rise and a possible "China threat," Beijing realized that a policy aimed at reunification was not possible in the current situation and would go against its efforts to show the world that China is a peaceful rising power. The Anti-Secession Law, which was passed by the third conference of the Tenth National People's Congress on March 14, 2005, made this strategy official. After that, Beijing and Washington worked together to make sure that Taiwan's president at the time, Chen Shui-bian, didn't push Taiwan's freedom too far. Chen's efforts reached their peak when he won his second term in 2004. The fact that Washington and Beijing work together to stop the movement for Taiwan's de jure independence has helped Beijing's strategic vision for "one China" in cross-Strait relations, even though there are some fundamental differences between the one-China policy that the United States supports (which agrees that there is only one China but allows different interpretations of which government is the legitimate representative of it) and the one-China principle. The two sides seem to have reached a temporary but fundamental agreement on the Taiwan issue, which is that the move toward Taiwan's independence is not in either China's or the US's best interests, even though the US does not support China's policy of eventual reunification. Since then, both the Bush and Obama administrations have supported Hu Jintao's policy of "peaceful development across the Taiwan Strait." However, the US policy goal has been "peaceful resolution," not necessarily reunification, while China s goal has been eventual reunification. With the US stance now more clear and China's policy change from supporting reunification to opposing independence, President Ma Ying-jeou was able to accept the 1992 Consensus as the basis for cross-Strait relations as soon as he took office.

During Ma's first term, this led to a long-overdue breakthrough in cross-Strait relations: the "three links," or the start of direct flights, ships, and mail service across the Taiwan Strait in 2008. This has led to an irreversible economic integration between the two sides of the Taiwan Strait through direct transportation, trade, and communications. Also, the Economic Cooperation Framework Agreement (ECFA) has made it official that the economies of both sides of the Taiwan Strait are interdependent. People hope that ECFA will increase trade and economic exchanges across the Taiwan Strait, leading to the "one-China market" that Ma Ying-jeou's first vice-president, Vincent Siew Wan-chang, has been pushing for. So, the two sides of the Taiwan Strait have already been moving toward unity in terms of economic growth.

Since President Xi Jinping took office in 2012, relations across the Taiwan Strait have been stable, but there haven't been many big wins. This is mostly because Taipei has been reluctant to agree to any political agreement or formal or informal steps to build trust between the PRC and ROC militaries, even though Beijing has been pushing for this. Xi Jinping told Vincent Siew in October 2013 in Bali, Indonesia, on the sidelines of the Asia-Pacific Economic Cooperation (APEC) forum that "increasing mutual political trust across the Taiwan Straits and jointly building political foundations are crucial for ensuring the peaceful development of relations." He also hinted that a cross-Strait framework for mutual military trust and confidence was important. Ma Ying-jeou's government hasn't done much to answer Xi's pleas, though. There are several reasons why the two sides haven't been able to make any political deals. Ma Ying-jeou's quickly falling popularity in Taiwan and his poor handling of fighting within the KMT have made it much harder for Taipei to handle relations across the Taiwan Strait. Given that China's leaders are changing and that the US is moving toward Asia, it is no longer possible for Beijing to push for more in cross-Strait ties.

But Xi Jinping told Lien Chan, the honorary chair of the KMT, that Beijing is patient and sure of itself. Taiwan is no longer a top priority for Beijing right now. This is because China is focused on building "a new type of great-power relations" with the U.S. and promoting the "One Belt, One Road" initiative, which would build overland and maritime economic corridors connecting China and Europe through central, west, and south Asia. Xi Jinping might not want to push things any further in cross-Strait ties. He might just want to keep the status quo stable. This is clear from Xi's speech at the Chinese People's Political Consultative Conference (CPPCC) in March 2015. In that speech, he emphasized that keeping the 1992 Consensus as a foundation for cross-Strait relations was important for peace and stability on both sides of the Strait, while reunification was a long-term goal that couldn't be reached until there was significant development on both sides of the Strait.

Xi Jinping has a lot of experience with cross-Strait issues because he was the provincial party leader in Fujian, Zhejiang, and Shanghai, where the governments have strong ties with Taiwan. Not only do these provinces work for the central government in Beijing, but they also have strong social, economic, and political ties with their peers in Taiwan. So, after Xi was named a successor at the 17th Party Congress in October 2007, he became more important in ties across the Taiwan Strait. As China's vice-president, he met former US president Jimmy Carter twice, once in December 2007 and once in January 2009. Hu Jintao's six proposals for the peaceful development of cross-Strait relations were emphasized by Xi, who also said that China was willing to work with the US against Taiwan's de jure independence. This, he said, would not only be in both countries' best interests, but would also help keep peace and development in the region. The most impressive talk he gave about Taiwan during this time was at the opening event for the Chinese Roots-Seeking Tour summer camp in Beijing on July 25, 2010. He said that the unity and solidarity of the Chinese country were the root and soul of all Chinese people, both inside and outside of China. So, he said, it was the dream of every Chinese person to bring the great Chinese country back to life.

After Xi took power, he kept Hu Jintao's Taiwan policy and put a higher priority on stopping Taiwan from becoming de jure independent than on pushing for a quick union. At the Twelfth Boao Forum in April 2013, Xi met Vincent Siew. Xi asked his fellow Chinese people on both sides of the Strait to work hard to rebuild the country. He also said that the Chinese mainland and Taiwan should work together more on business issues. In his speech, he didn't say anything about how the political situation had changed. When he met Wu Po-hsiung, the honorary chair of the KMT, two months later, he made four new suggestions to improve ties across the Strait: "First, the two sides should take the overall interests of the Chinese nation into account when evaluating the overall situation of cross-Strait ties"; "Second, the two sides should clearly recognize development trends throughout history to gain a better understanding of the future prospects for cross-Strait ties"; and "Third, the mainland and Taiwan should increase mutual trust, engage in positive interactions, seek common ground and set aside differences, and be patient"; Compared to his other talks about Taiwan, this one was more clear about how quiet economic growth can help build political trust between the two sides of the Strait. Xi said that the two sides "share the same destiny" and asked that they be encouraged to "strengthen their pride in the Chinese nation as well as their shared goal of its rejuvenation." He also said, "Even though the mainland and Taiwan are not yet united, they are both part of China and can't be separated." Xi said that "protecting national sovereignty and territorial integrity is at the heart of this goal," and he stressed that both sides should stick to the "one-China" framework.

Now, Xi Jinping has put forward some specific political requirements for dealing with Taiwan. These include building trust, encouraging good interactions, making the most of shared interests, and being practical. He says that the main point is to protect and strengthen Beijing's strategic advancement of the "one-China" policy, which both sides should agree on. When he met Vincent Siew in Bali in October 2013 before the APEC meeting, Xi said that "both sides of the Strait are of one family." As he stressed, the two sides should take advantage of this historic chance, keep the momentum of peacefully growing ties across the Taiwan Strait, and build trust in each other on the political level so that a political base can be set. He said for the first time that disputes across the Taiwan Strait could and should be fixed over time. "We can't keep passing these problems down from one generation to the next," he said. This comment shows that Xi is determined to make big steps toward reunification of China and Taiwan while he is in charge. Xi told the heads of departments in charge of cross-Strait relations to get together and talk about their ideas to build political trust between the two sides.

In February 2014, when he met a Taiwanese delegation led by Lien Chan, Xi's view on cross-Strait relations became clearer. He made it clear that reunion was an important part of the Chinese Dream. Again, he talked about four things to explain China's policy toward Taiwan, but these four things were more political than the first four. He said that both sides of the country wanted reunification, and he added that "no power can separate us." In his speech, he tied the Chinese Dream very closely to Taiwan's future and stressed again how important it is to keep a "one-China" framework. Even though he knew it might take a long time, he was hopeful that the disagreements on both sides of the Strait would be solved in the end. Xi asked "the two sides across the Strait to strengthen the grounds for adhering to the 1992 Consensus and opposing "Taiwan independence" and to promote the common understanding of "One China." He said, "Comrades from both sides have chosen the path of peaceful development of cross-Strait relations. This is the right choice because it protects cross-Strait peace, promotes common development, helps realize the rejuvenation of the Chinese nation, and brings benefits to people on both sides." Even though there is a general trend toward peaceful growth and more exchanges and communication, Xi pointed out that there are still problems like the Sunflower Movement. "We will try to do our best, as long as what we do can contribute to the well-being of our Taiwanese compatriots, to the peaceful development of cross-Strait relations, and to the overall interest of the Chinese nation."

After continuing Hu Jintao's policy on Taiwan, Xi put more of his attention on setting up and solidifying a strategic framework based on the "one China" concept. The goal is to make it hard for Taiwan to get back together with China. In September 2014, when a group of Taiwanese leaders came to China, Xi Jinping told them that "peaceful reunification; one country, two systems" is the main way to fix the Taiwan problem. He also said, "No act of separation will be allowed. There is no way for Taiwan to become independent. "One country, two systems" is not an official way for mainland China to talk about Taiwan. It hasn't been for a long time. With the Sunflower Movement putting Ma Ying-jeou's government in a bad light and unrest in Hong Kong, Xi seemed to have decided that certain ideals needed to be brought up again. This thought is shown in what Xi said in March 2015 when he was on a panel with members of the National Committee of the CPPCC. He said, "We should always work for peaceful development, always stick to the same political basis, always help the people on the other side of the Strait, and always work together to bring about national revitalization." At the same time, he told his fellow countrymen to be careful about the "Taiwan independence" groups. It's a good sign that Xi Jinping is taking a no-nonsense approach to cross-Strait ties as a result of new things happening in Taiwan that hurt mainland China.

Since Deng Xiaoping, Chinese leaders have understood that the U.S. is an important part of ties across the Taiwan Strait. Xi Jinping has come up with a new plan based on the political legacy of his predecessors. Even before he became the leader of China, he said that the Taiwan issue shouldn't get in the way of good ties between China and the U.S. Since he took office, he has been trying to keep the Taiwan problem from affecting the relationship between China and the United States. At the same time, he has been trying to build what he calls a "new type of great-power relationship." Because of this, the Taiwan problem doesn't come up much in his talks, communications, and joint statements with President Obama, at least not in public statements. This makes it clear how Xi feels about Taiwan when he talks to the U.S. Since Taiwan is important to China, it won't let it be used as a bargaining chip while it tries to build a new kind of relationship between big powers. The goal is to keep Taiwan out of the two-way connection between China and the US and to keep the US from getting involved in cross-Strait relations, or at least to make sure that the US doesn't get involved directly. So, it's not strange that Taiwan hasn't been talked about when the US talks about rebalancing in Asia.

Overall, the following is a summary of Xi's plan. First, he hasn't made any big changes to Hu Jintao's Taiwan policy, which aimed to stop Taiwan from becoming officially independent. Second, he is most worried about putting Taiwan in a corner by making the "one China" idea work better from a strategic point of view. So, he has put more focus on building a political relationship between the mainland and Taiwan built on a strong economic foundation in cross-Strait relations. Last but not least, it's clear that Xi is a tough guy when it comes to Taiwan. His answer to anyone in Taiwan who was against unity was, "If you move one step forward, I will move two steps forward." One example is that Xi Jinping brought back the phrase "One country, two systems," which had not been used since 2005, when the Anti-secession Law was passed. His tough attitude may not change because of things at home and in the world. This doesn't necessarily mean that Xi wants cross-Strait ties to look like Hong Kong. Instead, it shows that he is determined to keep things going well between the two sides of the Taiwan Strait as long as he is in charge. Xi Jinping thinks that Taiwan will finally return to the mother country as long as he can keep putting the "one-China" framework into place in cross-Strait relations.

Conclusion

In general, Xi Jinping's Taiwan policy has been similar to that of Hu Jintao in that it puts preventing Taiwan's de jure independence ahead of promoting reunification. However, it seems that Xi has tried to push forward some political agreements between Beijing and Taipei in response to the stability and improvement of relations across the Taiwan Strait since Ma Ying-jeou took office. But this effort hasn't been very successful, not only because Ma Ying-jeou's support in Taiwan is falling, but also because Xi's top priorities have been the anti-corruption campaign at home and the crises in the East and South China Seas, which are happening at the same time as the US is rebalancing its foreign policy.

Under Xi's leadership, there are some new trends that have been talked about in the previous parts. First of all, as China has gotten better at handling things on its Asian borders, Xi Jinping has tried to keep the Taiwan problem separate from US-China relations so that the US doesn't have as much power over this issue in their relationship with China. The United States has lost a lot of power in cross-Strait ties as a result of Xi's policies, to the point where the U.S. no longer has the final say.

Second, the topic of reunification is no longer a third rail in Taiwan politics. This is because the economies of both sides of the Taiwan Strait are growing quickly and both sides have accepted the 1992 Consensus as a basis for cross-Strait ties. Even though Beijing seems to care less and less about the problem, there are more and more conversations about it among scholars, in the media, and in politics. In Taiwanese politics, the question of Taiwan's freedom is getting harder and harder to talk about. Even Democratic Progressive Party (DPP; more pro-independence) leaders try not to say anything about the issue these days. This isn't because the DPP's policies or beliefs have changed, but because it will hurt their political support at home and abroad, which they need to win in Taiwan.

Third, as Xi Jinping's power is likely to grow, he will have to put more pressure on making "political progress" in relations across the Taiwan Strait. This is clear from what he said about Taiwan recently. Xi made it clear that the eventual reunification of Taiwan and mainland China was part of his "Chinese dream," which is based on the revival of a great Chinese nation. He said that the two sides would have to give up political agreements in the near future. This shows that Xi Jinping wants to leave a political legacy that includes some progress on the Taiwan question.

The KMT lost the midterm election in 2014, and President Ma Ying-jeou's popularity is falling quickly. This put the DPP in a good situation for the 2016 presidential and legislative elections, which they won easily. This can't be anything but a big challenge to Xi's rule on Taiwan. Xi's stance and public statements make it clear that Beijing is likely to put more pressure on Taiwan. From Xi's point of view, cross-Strait ties can't go back to how they were in the first eight years of the 21st century, when President Chen Shui-bian was in charge. Given that the mainland and Taiwan are becoming more economically dependent on each other and that the United States and China are deeply dependent on each other, it is inevitable that Xi Jinping's Taiwan policy will shift to focus on political problems. The goal of making political deals across the Taiwan Strait is to make it official that the two sides of the Taiwan Strait depend on each other and that the one-China principle is a strategic framework. So, if the DPP wins the 2016 presidential election, mainland China may react even more strongly to the Taiwan problem. After all, it was already part of Xi's strategy toward Taiwan to try to reach political agreements. So, there will be more problems in cross-Strait ties in the coming years. This is not only because the pro-independence DPP is back in power after losing the 2008 presidential election and being out of power for eight years, but also because Xi has put a lot of his political capital into this issue.

Index

A

B

C

D

E

F

G

H

I

J

K

L

M

www.ingramcontent.com/pod-product-compliance
Ingram Content Group UK Ltd.
Pitfield, Milton Keynes, MK11 3LW, UK
UKHW021321020826
14184UKWH00003B/21

9 789360 092382